CW00322248

Born in 1964, Ray Mears has
teaching the art of survival. H
Tracks, *Wild Britain* and *Ray*
the Royal Geographical Society honoured him with the Ness Award for the popularisation of geography. He is the author of many bestselling books including *Essential Bushcraft*, *Bushcraft Survival*, *Wild Food*, *The Real Heroes of Telemark* and *Northern Wilderness*.

www.raymears.com

RAY MEARS

My Outdoor Life

HODDER

First published in Great Britain in 2013 by Hodder & Stoughton
An Hachette UK company

First published in paperback in 2014

1

Copyright © Ray Mears 2013

The right of Ray Mears to be identified as the Author of the Work has been asserted by
him in accordance with the Copyright, Designs and Patents Act 1988.

All rights reserved. No part of this publication may be reproduced, stored in a retrieval
system, or transmitted, in any form or by any means without the prior written
permission of the publisher, nor be otherwise circulated in any form of binding or cover
other than that in which it is published and without a similar condition being imposed
on the subsequent purchaser.

A CIP catalogue record for this title is available from the British Library

ISBN 978 1 444 77821 2

Printed and bound by Clays Ltd, St Ives plc

Hodder & Stoughton policy is to use papers that are natural, renewable
and recyclable products and made from wood grown in sustainable forests.
The logging and manufacturing processes are expected to conform to the
environmental regulations of the country of origin.

Hodder & Stoughton Ltd
338 Euston Road
London NW1 3BH

www.hodder.co.uk

I dedicate this book to my mother, Dorothy, and to my late father Leslie John Mears. Without their love, support and patient encouragement, none of what follows would have taken place.

Contents

Introduction

For over thirty years now, I've been exploring the world through the eyes of bushcraft – writing books, making documentaries, giving lectures and training – all of which has literally taken me around the world several times over. My sole focus has been to tell the story, to all who want to listen, of the natural world – stories of the forest, the Arctic, the deserts, and all their inhabitants. My love and passion for bushcraft has grown and become my life, so with 2013 marking the thirtieth anniversary of Woodlore, the organisation I established to help thousands of people to a greater understanding of the world around us, I've decided that the time has come for me to tell my own story – how I started, what has inspired me, and what I've learned along the way. There have been some extraordinary, and heart-rending moments – like surviving a devastating helicopter crash, losing two people who were very dear to me, and tracking one of the most dangerous men in British criminal history. Although I've never previously talked about many of these events, I include them all here because I feel they have shaped the person I have become.

Talking about myself has never been easy so this has been a difficult book for me to write – I'm used to presenting the story, not *being* the story. It seemed to me a little self-indulgent to write a book about myself, but I slowly came round to the view that it was time for me to tell my story.

But perhaps you will bear with me as I revisit some of the most important and formative experiences in my life to date...

I
Prologue

Do you remember a time before Google, a time when computers were huge and mysterious, and encyclopaedias were the best – and one of the only – sources of reference we had? I remember that time in my life vividly – the analogue age, you might call it. And I can recall with great clarity sitting in my classroom one day when I was about six or seven and seeing a picture of some cavemen in an encyclopaedia. I thought it was *fantastic*. I was completely bowled over by it but I had a project to be getting on with, so the encyclopaedia went back on the shelf and I continued with my work.

A few months later I'd forgotten all about it, until there it was again. That encyclopaedia had reappeared and was perched on the edge of a desk next to me. I've no idea how, but the book started to slide off the desk. Instinctively I reached out to grab it, but gravity had it in its grip, and the hardback cover and spine had turned turtle. My hand found only a single page . . .

'No, no!' cried the teacher. 'Don't grab it, you'll tear it.'

But she was too late. As my fingers gripped the paper, the weight of this fountain of knowledge was more than my reflexes could handle. The book hit the classroom floor with a dull thud and I was left holding a single page from within it. And can you guess which one it was? Yep, the one with the image of the cavemen. I was both devastated and elated. I've always loved books, so the damage the fall caused upset me – but on the other hand, I was able to take this fascinating image home with me. I think it's true to say, that picture awakened something within me that has defined my whole life. I firmly believe it was the spark that ignited my passion for the natural world around me.

And so began my journey, travelling along a path that has led directly to my interest in, and knowledge of, bushcraft and everything it encompasses. It's been amazing and has taken me all over the world, learning skills and techniques that have been handed down over generations – in some instances from man's earliest days on Planet Earth. But I'm getting ahead of myself. This is where it all began . . .

2

From Little Acorns . . .

The first two years of my life were spent in Lagos, Nigeria. My father Leslie was a printer by trade, and by the time I came along he was working for De La Rue, a company that specialises in printing banknotes. He'd done quite well there, and he and my mother Dorothy worked overseas a lot – as a manager he'd worked in Japan and Pakistan in the 50s so they were very well travelled, especially for those days. Mum found work in the various British High Commissions near where they were based.

Shortly after I was born, on 7 February 1964, we moved to Lagos where my father had been appointed to manage the banknote printing works. I can still remember a few things from those early days – I can picture the car we had, and our home there. I remember the chickens, and some of the sights and scenes of Lagos. It seemed permanently chaotic and busy, but I have memories of the relative calm and serenity of the pool at the hotel my parents used as a retreat. That was lovely.

We returned to England just after my second birthday. De La Rue had moved to Peterborough and Mum and Dad had no desire to live there – they were Londoners – so Dad left the company and got the next best job in printing: working on newspapers in Fleet Street. He took a job working nights on *The Times*.

My paternal grandfather died when my father was very

young and, to put it mildly, my dad had a tough childhood. His stepfather was very hard on him and I remember Dad telling me a story about how he'd made a Spitfire out of wood during the war. His stepfather took one look at it, told him the wings weren't straight and snapped them off. He then told him he had to make them again.

Mum's lovely and has been a great influence on my life. She's always been a great cook and I have fond memories of her dinners, particularly her roasts. In fact, I think it's fair to say that there is nothing she cooks that isn't good. When she was a young girl, she had an affinity for the outdoors and used to play in the woods, so I wonder sometimes if perhaps that had an influence on the direction my life has taken. Her mum died while we were living in Lagos, and she brought me back to London with her for the funeral when I was just a year old. I was an accomplished walker by then – I took my first steps at nine months and was walking well by the time I was a year old. Even then there was no stopping me. Apparently, I kept a great many of the passengers on our return flight to Lagos entertained for most of the journey, and one of them said to Mum, 'He'll travel a lot when he's older, that one.' Prophetic words indeed!

We lived briefly in Purley, on the southern edge of London, before settling in Kenley, a suburb on the border between London and Surrey. It's right in the middle of the green belt, and it's where I think of as home. It was a great place, surrounded by loads of open space, and I look back fondly on the late 60s and early 70s as a magical time in which to grow up. They were undoubtedly tough times for adults – Britain was going through a great deal of change in those years and there were power and food shortages, unreliable cars, seemingly endless strikes, rampant inflation and the Cold War, but who cares about all of that when you're a kid? To me, it was a time of the sort of freedoms that would leave a lot of today's youngsters reeling. It was a great time to grow up because we didn't have computer games, or homes – and come to think of it, lives – dominated by technology. Everything in the world was on a slightly different scale. There was more space, more room to develop.

Today's youngsters are part of a digital generation, whereas back then everything was analogue and I like that – I feel enormously fortunate to be part of that last generation that experienced an analogue youth. We went 'out to play', unfettered by the bounds of smartphones, which today mean worried parents can track their children and delve into their Internet use. You made your own entertainment, and you made things.

It was a great time to be young. And the area that I grew up in was really lovely. There were a lot of trees and open space, and people seemed to have a lot more time to lavish on their gardens and their environment in a way that today's overworked and over-stressed commuters don't seem to have, sadly. It's true to say life has changed dramatically since those low-tech years.

My parents wanted me to have a good education so they sent me to a lovely prep school called Downside Lodge, and then later to Downside School, in the leafy suburb of Purley. It was a special place, one I recall as a 'summery' place rather than a 'wintry' one. It may have given its students an old-fashioned education, but it was good one, helped by the fact that class sizes were small and the teachers could teach you things that interested them. We were encouraged to read, and to take an interest in, and understand, all the things around us. We learned to be patriotic; we were taught to be loyal and self-sacrificing as well. It was a traditional way of teaching, almost Edwardian in its outlook, but that was all good – well, all except for Latin, which I detested.

There were some old stocks on the village green. They were a hangover from the past – a law was passed in 1405 that required every town and village to have a set, which were usually placed by the side of a public highway or village green. When I was at Downside, they were pressed into use for whoever came last when we did cross-country running, although there was one particular boy who must have enjoyed them a little too much; he always seemed to put extra effort into making sure he was last through the gate after a run.

Before we broke up for the summer holidays, we would be given four books to read and there was always a quiz when we got back. The quiz wasn't the point though – the important thing was reading the books, and the ones they chose were always very good. It didn't matter what age you were, the four novels you were given would be suitable for you – books like *The Eagle of the Ninth* and *The Silver Sword*; we were given some excellent titles to read. And so I developed a passion for reading. I still read obsessively now.

The ability to read is so very important in life although, sadly, there's not enough emphasis placed on that today. I despair sometimes at the poor grammar that I hear around me these days. Youngsters don't read anymore but the fault doesn't lie with them, it lies with their parents, with society at large and even the schools to some extent – or perhaps it's the fact that we haven't given the teachers the tools they need to be able to teach and maintain discipline in the classroom. I mean, if you have a classroom with no discipline, to me that's a form of child abuse. It's that serious – children simply *must* have the opportunity to learn. They need clearly defined and enforced rules at school so they can learn the pathway from which they can step out into the world.

The schooling I had was very formal and old-fashioned; we were taught to write nicely with a fountain pen – you got into trouble if you used a Biro. We were treated as individuals, whereas today's 'one-size-fits-all' education seems to be more about how to pass the exams rather than understanding the topics. It's a very different approach – I was taught to take an interest in life, the world and everything around it, and I feel blessed for that experience.

I didn't spend all of my childhood with my head buried in a good book though – far from it. For as much as I loved reading, bicycles also played quite a large part in my young life. I got my first bike for my third birthday and took to it really quickly. Once I left the Lodge and went up to Downside School, I used to ride the few miles to and from school. We didn't have BMXs or mountain bikes in those days, but we did have the Raleigh Chopper. I remember getting a little over-zealous with the front brake on one occasion as I rode down a very steep road; the front wheel locked up, I went head-first over the handlebars and knocked myself clean out. I ended up walking home semi-conscious. Still, it was all part of the learning curve. To me, bikes were all about fun. I used to tear around on the common with friends, chasing each other on our bikes. Once I reached my teens, it was like an American Express card – I never left home without it.

Not long after that day when I tore the page out of the encyclopaedia, I remember our teacher giving us the task of painting a scout. I think she had Baden-Powell in mind, but I knew nothing about Baden-Powell way back then – or the Scouting Movement that he established. So, I did a picture of a North-West Canadian Mounted Police Scout from the period of the Riel Rebellion, but I have no idea how on earth I knew anything about *that*.

Anyway, the teacher asked me what it was and I said, 'It's a scout from the North-West Frontier of course.' I must say, I've often wondered what the teacher thought – everyone else had drawn these boys in shorts and funny hats.

Perhaps in some strange way, fate chose me for this life. Looking back, I think I strolled into the woods one day and nature saw me and said, 'Walk this way.' I think something similar happens to most of us in life. We don't choose our path, it chooses us – like that page from the encyclopaedia.

My interests back then were never in make-believe; they were always firmly rooted in the real world. The films that captured my attention were the films about pioneers and the great frontiers. When I watched Westerns I wasn't at all interested in the cowboys – I always thought the Indians were better. To me, they were much cooler.

———◆·◆———

The most life-defining element of my schooling occurred while I was at Downside and it was all down to the simple fact that judo was an integral element of the curriculum. Judo would go on to create ripples that extend all the way through to my present. For it was through judo, at the age of eight, that I met the man who would become a great friend and mentor, and who encouraged me in the outdoor life that has become my lifelong quest. That man was Kingsley Hopkins and he was to become a very important figure in my life.

Today we think of judo in the Olympic sense – as a sport – but it's more than that; it's a way of life. We were exceptionally lucky though, in that we learned judo as a martial art and a life skill – not as a sport. The word 'judo' means 'the gentle way' but it's inaccurately named really because there's not much that's gentle about judo. However, it does teach you to think in a certain way. Judo is like chess – if you've never done judo, it may be difficult for you to understand what I mean by that, but any *judoka* would understand exactly what I'm talking about. Judo teaches you a certain way of dealing with things and it's a very healthy process because you can never get too big for your boots – there is always someone better at it, or more skillful than you . . . If you lose your temper on the judo mat you'll get turned over, so it teaches you to focus your energy in the appropriate direction and, if something's not working, to immediately abandon it and try something else. It teaches you to be perceptually aware of what's going on around you, but it also gifts you determination, strength, toughness and the knowledge that technique is more important than size. Really, it teaches a whole range of things – it's a great philosophy for life, as well as showing you how to fall over without hurting yourself.

Judo was compulsory for all pupils between the ages of eight and thirteen, and was taught on Saturdays – we had Saturday school at Downside. Kingsley taught it and I liked him from the off. There was a steeliness about him, but he also had a gentleness that emanated from his very core. He'd fought behind enemy lines in Burma during World War II and it showed in his strength of character.

He was an interesting man; the Kingsley I knew as a judo teacher at Downside was a man who'd lost his wife, who studied Sanskrit and who took a great interest in the world. As I said, he was to be a mentor and friend to me for many years.

Kingsley was a great judo teacher, one of the absolute best – probably because he learned it himself from one of the martial art's masters. He'd started judo when he was sixteen but his learning was cut short by World War II. He told me that his parents had asked him about his service upon his return and they were horrified when he'd described how he took off a Japanese soldier's head with a shovel that he'd 'liberated' from another Japanese soldier. Apparently, this shovel had been made from very good steel that you could have sharpened a pencil with, and he used to bemoan the loss of the shovel. He'd lent it to an Australian soldier to dig a trench a short while after and he'd never got it back.

When the war was over, his interest in judo was reignited. He was taught by Gunji Koizumi (known as GK) who had in turn learned from Jigoro Kano – the founder of Kodokan judo. GK was a Japanese master of judo and he introduced this martial art to the United Kingdom, so by learning from Kingsley, I was only two degrees of separation from the man who invented it.

Jigoro Kano founded judo in the 1880s by reformulating jujitsu. In jujitsu, there are many techniques for self-defence that are dangerous and potentially harmful, even in practice. Jigoro Kano reworked it, taking the dangerous techniques and putting them to one side – he didn't remove them, he just *moved* them from ordinary practice so you could practise using full power without necessarily hurting each other. His great genius lay in understanding that the most important thing was not necessarily just the technique itself but what the technique developed and required. The Japanese call it *tai sabaki* (body movement); Kano built judo so that you could develop strong *tai sabaki* and then just pick up any of the dangerous techniques as you needed them.

Judo is a wonderful thing for the human spirit because it's cerebral and physical all in the same moment. It's a very healthful practice because two people can go hell for leather, trying to smash one another to pieces, and then smile and laugh about it afterwards. Kingsley said that the ultimate goal is never to have to use it. But he was quite clear that in a crisis, if someone took the initiative, we should finish it for them.

I remember when I went up to grammar school, I was running along and one of the older children tripped me up. He starting laughing – but it was a little prematurely, because I didn't fall on my face as he expected. Instead I instinctively went into a forward roll and came up on my feet. *That* wiped the smile from his face.

Over the years, judo has helped me out of a number of tight corners. Occasionally you bump into people who want to throw their weight around; you know, the guy who uses his fists to send a message because his vocabulary doesn't allow him to articulate whatever he wants to say. Judo can be quite, er . . . disarming under the right circumstances. In judo, you don't hit somebody with your fists; you hit them with the ground. It's a very, very powerful and useful skill set to possess.

Kingsley was 'old school', and the judo I learned from him was old-fashioned. That's not to say it was out of date; far from it. It was pure, unadulterated. I really enjoyed it and I found a freedom in it that's hard to convey. The philosophy behind it was important to me. I read a lot on Shintoism, and the history of the martial arts; I read the Japanese creation myth and many other classic samurai texts, including *The Book of the Five Rings* (a text on kenjutsu or Japanese swordsmanship, and the martial arts in general, written by the swordsman Miyamoto Musashi circa 1645). I was a willing student of judo and immersed myself in it, keen to master its knowledge.

Kingsley and GK had become good friends and after GK died, he left Kingsley his black belt. At eighty, GK felt that his mind had started to go and he wasn't as sharp as he would have liked to have been. He wanted to be remembered at his best and he felt it was important not to be a burden on others. So, as is the way of the samurai, he put his affairs in order and took his own life. He succeeded in his aim because everyone who knew him remembered him at his sharpest. That black belt he left Kingsley was given to GK by Jigoro Kano, and Kingsley in turn left it to me.

When I was thirteen, Kingsley took me to the Budokwai for the first time. The Budokwai is the judo club where he'd learned the martial art and it's in Fulham, London. Actually, 'judo club' doesn't really cover it. It's a proper *dōjō* (a formal gathering place where martial arts students conduct training) and it's the oldest and most famous Japanese martial arts club in Europe.

The club is housed in what was once a Victorian school building with a wood-beamed roof and when you go through the door to the changing area you immediately see a picture of GK on the wall. He founded the club in 1918.

Going to the Budokwai took me into an old world of judo, full of masters of the art. People like Richard 'Dickie' Bowen, who is sadly no longer with us. Dickie had studied in Japan and was married to a Japanese lady. He was an exceptionally skilled exponent of judo and he followed a traditional attitude to it which dictated that he refuse higher *dan* gradings because he thought them unnecessary. In the old days, all belts were white but you never washed them so, as you became more experienced, your belt would get grubbier and grubbier until eventually it turned black. And that's the way that I was taught – belts weren't important. That was the way at the Budokwai – the colour of the belt wasn't the be all and end all in terms of achievement. It was useful in that if someone of a high grade was carrying an injury, they would wear a belt of a lower grade. Somebody might walk on to the mat there in a white belt, but he'd be competing at national level. It was a very healthy place, the Budokwai, a place where a lot of egos were remodelled.

During my time, two Japanese champions taught there: Katsuhiko Kashiwazaki, who was a master of sacrifice techniques, a real technician; and perhaps the person who most impressed me, Yasuhiro Yamashita, who's arguably the most successful judo competitor of all time. He won five international gold medals and 203 consecutive victories up until his retirement. He was unbeaten from 1977 to 1985 and nine times all-Japan champion. Yamashita's dedication to technique, his thoroughness in training and preparation, is something I have tried to learn from and build into everything that I do. I'd love to meet him again someday – his judo was just magnificent.

I was really lucky to practise with Neil Adams too – he won

Olympic silver at both the Moscow and Los Angeles games and then found a gear no one else had and went on to become world champion. When he came on to the mat, he'd get people to walk up in a handstand and I'm certain nobody could have done it if he hadn't been there; his presence on the mat had a galvanising effect. He was truly inspirational to me and a great many others. His judo was very acrobatic – he'd have you in an arm lock halfway to the ground. That said, his timekeeping was dreadful, so when it was announced that he was leaving to coach in France, they handcuffed a giant alarm clock to his wrist.

In what other sport do you get to practise with world champions? If you're learning tennis, you can't exactly rock up at your local court and play a few games with Andy Murray or Roger Federer, can you? But in judo you can do that, and it means experience and knowledge are easily accessible to anyone willing to put the time in. That's both instructive and inspirational.

The Budokwai was a very important waypoint in my life. It really gave me an extra dimension and I still miss the place. As I grew older, though, my life was taking me into the woods. However, judo meant that I carried both the lessons I'd learned and the judo philosophy with me always.

He was a very thoughtful man, Kingsley; he was very interested in the world. The time I spent with him was my university – he was very good at encouraging free thought and he was a very profound man. He encouraged me to always look for the source of information, to try to understand the root of the teaching, and test it out – always test what you're being taught and if it's true it will stand up but if it's not you will find out – and that was to prove important later on.

Kingsley was something of a paradox – he was gentle, but

he was as hard as nails too, and a little eccentric. I remember one night when he dislocated his shoulder doing judo – he just ran into the wall to relocate it. He loved motorbikes and had one that he rode everywhere, rain or shine. He was out on it one winter's day when I was much older, and his accelerator froze; unable to slow down, the bike reared up, he came off and the bike came down on his hand, crushing one of his fingers. I remember I hadn't heard from him for a few weeks, which was quite unusual, so I rang him to ask if he was all right.

'Yeah I'm fine,' he said, 'but I can't talk now, I'm heating a chisel on the stove.'

Kingsley was a craftsman; I mean this guy used to make beautiful chess sets and carve the individual pieces by hand, so the thought of heating a chisel was anathema to him – he'd feel like he was ruining it.

'Why on earth are you doing that?' I asked.

And he said this like it was the most natural thing in the world:

'Well, my finger's starting to smell a little, so I'm going to cut it off.'

And he would have. Had I not called when I did, had I not talked him into going to hospital, he would have cut his finger off. So he went to the local A&E with this finger that was crushed to a pulp and he didn't say a word, he just sat there while everyone else was being dealt with. That was him all over. When they took his glove off, his finger just disintegrated on the desk in front of the doctor. He was of that generation, I guess, when men seemed to be hewn from different material. He'd done stuff in his life and he'd seen and known true hardship; he knew himself in a way that most people today could never hope to achieve.

Kingsley was an awkward person to do judo with, as many people would discover to their cost. As he got older he wasn't able to turn people over in the way he could when he was a bit younger, but neither could anyone easily turn him over. He'd learned how not to be thrown and perhaps that was the more important skill. He had mastered this business of turning energy against you, making it feel like you were fighting a piece of wrought iron.

It was a privilege to train with him.

3

The Call of the Wild

As you might have gathered by now, judo played a huge role right through my childhood and into my early twenties. It shaped the person I've become and its philosophy – alongside the sage advice I got from Kingsley – has meant that I've been equipped to deal with a lot of what life has thrown at me.

But another strand was inextricably intertwined with the judo and my relationship with Kingsley, bound in a Gordian knot of destiny, and that was my love of the outdoors. Judo and my outdoor life ran like a train track through my formative years, each one forming a rail running parallel to the other, propelling me to where I wanted to go.

Yes, that image of the cavemen was indeed what sparked my passion for nature but it was fanned and set alight when I was about eight years old and I became fascinated by foxes. My parents gave me a book called *Animal Tracks and Signs* by Preben Bang and Preben Dahlstrøm. It was truly wonderful. In fact, my life spent as a student of bushcraft can be traced back to that one book. It's still in print and has been the model for every similar kind of book that's followed since.

I think I read it in two days, and when I was done I was determined to go out and put some of the lessons I'd learned into practice. However, an afternoon tracking foxes wasn't enough for me. I wanted to stay out at night too, but I didn't have any camping equipment and I couldn't really afford to buy any, not on the pocket money I was on.

I mentioned this to Kingsley.

'Well Raymond,' he replied, 'when I was behind enemy lines during the war, we had only the clothes we were wearing, plus our weapons and basic kit.

'A knife did everything else for us. With a sharp knife and the trees and plants around you, you can fashion whatever it is you need.

'We had nothing else; we had no tents, no camping equipment, nothing like that. We didn't need it. Neither do you.'

'Tell me more . . .'

'I managed to get hold of a spare set of mess tins so I always used one as a lid to keep the flies out of my food. That meant I never fell ill.'

'But Kingsley, where did you sleep?'

'We made our own shelters, Raymond. We utilised natural features and vegetation, but we were always comfortable. We survived quite comfortably with none of the equipment that people use today when they go camping.'

I listened in rapt attention as he went on to share with me some of the skills he'd used to survive behind enemy lines. He explained how I could find shelter, stay dry and keep warm. I was enthralled.

He told me, 'Raymond, you don't need camping equipment, you need these skills.'

Little did I know that those ten words would be the blueprint of the rest of my life.

I had the naivety of youth, I suppose – to me, what I needed to do seemed simple enough, and Kingsley had breathed life into the prospect of my staying out overnight by simplifying it still further. He had shared with me some of his own experiences behind Japanese lines and made what I wanted to do sound so . . . well . . . easy. I was lucky, too, in that I also had wonderful parents who were very supportive of me. Good parenting is a real skill and, I have to say, they were very good. I had a great childhood and I'm very proud of that fact.

One of my earliest 'proper expeditions' took place with a friend, out on that distant, desolate, exotic land that is . . . the North Downs. It wasn't particularly memorable for what we did, and I'm not even sure how far we went, but I've never forgotten that feeling of being out overnight for the first time on our own with no one to support us and nothing but the knowledge we carried with us (which really wasn't a lot at that time, if I'm being honest).

Neither of us had sleeping bags, although I'd bought one of those orange survival bags that never really worked. We didn't have Karrimats either (those wonderful, lightweight mats that insulate you from the ground) as they hadn't really been invented then – I don't recall seeing them until I was about fifteen. For all that we didn't have, though, we never felt disheartened or like we were missing out on anything. There is so much that we take for granted today. I'm amazed at the amount of kit that young people who are starting to stay outdoors take with them these days. What on earth is it all for? I wouldn't want to carry all that even now, and the fact is, it's not all necessary. We had none of that stuff and I never minded because, ultimately, you have to manage – and you can't miss what you've never had. We certainly didn't have a camping stove or cooking utensils; my first cooking pot was a simple old Jacob's biscuit tin. I did have an Army surplus poncho, however, and I felt lucky because I had that. It was an expensive purchase – probably around £14 or something, which was a lot of money in those days. My rucksack was awful, though – it was one of those ghastly dayglo orange things, made from cheap nylon fabric with a very open weave. I painted it olive green; it looked much better then and the paint even gave it a degree of waterproofing.

I do remember we didn't have enough food with us on that first expedition (a minor oversight) but I don't recall feeling any great hardship, just a wonderful sense of achievement and independence. I made a note to myself there and then though, that I needed to learn how to find food for myself from the land. I recall sitting around a fire that we'd lit and looking down on the town of Oxted from my high vantage point and thinking, 'I'd rather be here than down there indoors watching TV.'

On that trip, we used matches to light that fire but it didn't feel right to me – it felt like I was cheating. So, I soon set out to learn how to make fire in the traditional manner and read every book I could find on the subject, although I do recall that my first attempts weren't very successful . . .

Another early trip took place on a snowy winter's night – a friend and I were trying to make a fire without matches without much success. I was using sparks to ignite some clematis seed heads wrapped up in finely shredded clematis bark. I had a couple of Oxo cubes with me, so we boiled up some water and made Oxo drinks to warm us up. We'd taken a sledge out with us – not to play on, but to carry our 'kit' (comprising a couple of small, virtually empty rucksacks). It felt like we were on our own little mini Arctic expedition and we took it very seriously. Oh, the power of imagination when you're young.

I have to say, my parents were really great about it all, considering I was still at primary school. I do remember occasions when they'd go looking for me on the common, but then, as parents, I guess it was only natural for them to feel a little concerned about me, although I can't recall that they ever *really* worried about me while I was out. Mum always said that I seemed to know what I was doing and she and my dad were happy to let me forge my own path. Maybe having played in the woods herself when she was younger had a role in that, but who knows? She says I was always confident in my abilities when I was younger; perhaps that confidence was misplaced, but what I was doing never felt dangerous to me. It's said that the past is a foreign country – they do things differently there – and it's so true. Looking back, England *was* a foreign country compared to today: the population density wasn't anything like it is now, and it felt like a much safer place.

Besides, I had an old World War I bayonet that I used to tuck down my wellington boot. Eventually I'd use it to dig up edible roots and make fire with, but in those days it was just part of the childish adventure. I never thought of it as a weapon with which I could threaten anybody – I never felt scared being out, so that was the last thing on my mind. In fact, I felt that if there were any problems, I could deal with them. The woods were swiftly becoming my world, after all.

I'd started small and built up my experience and knowledge gradually and, for me, that's exactly how these things should start. It's very important that if someone wants to learn to go to remote parts of the world and travel in safety they should start small, and start young. You need to learn progressively, starting with the basics and working your way up from there. It really bothers me that there are some people today who don't go in for that sort of preparation. They have this idea to go somewhere, they have the money, but they haven't got the wherewithal, self-knowledge or experience to know what they're doing. The danger is that if something goes wrong, there's a good chance they could be overwhelmed by it.

———◆◆———

I'm sure most people feel that they were lucky to grow up when they did, and I'm no exception – the 70s were great. I loved that analogue side of life – the way that, if you couldn't find what you needed, you'd try and make it. My dad, like many of his generation, was very good with his hands and he passed that on to me.

'Come here, Raymond,' he'd say as he changed a fuse, or wired a new plug. 'Watch how I do this.'

In turn, I was forever asking him questions.

'Dad, how do I do this?' I'd say when confronted with something that vexed my young mind.

'Raymond, watch me solder this and then you can try,' he'd say whenever he had some to do.

He was a patient man and he always had time to show me something, or to explain how it worked.

He had a lathe in the shed, which he used as often as some people use the kettle; he was always making, repairing, shaping or just generally 'lathing' – he used to make all sorts of things, but then that was indicative of the time. Unless the house was falling down, or your car was destroyed by fire, people did what they could themselves and if they couldn't, they'd learn through trial and error. A leaky tap? You'd fix it. Car needs an oil change? You'd do it yourself. The first course of action for many young adults now is to call a plumber when a tap leaks. And it seems many drivers don't even know how to change a wheel. Back then, you had to develop a reliance on yourself and it taught you valuable lessons.

———— ◆ ————

When I was thirteen, the time came for me to leave Downside and move up to Reigate Grammar School. It had an excellent reputation and I remember it as a good school; it didn't matter what your interests were, it had a place for you. It was at Reigate that I met Mark Bailey and Adrian Braham. We got on well from the off and soon became firm friends.

Although I was now at a different school, those books we

were given at Downside to read over the summer holidays paid dividends for me as I got older and my passion for books grew. I became a regular visitor to the local library. I'd go straight to the reference section and read everything I could find on the outdoors. And the more I learned, the more I wanted to know. I wanted to know what things you could eat in the wild; which plants were edible and which ones weren't; which mushrooms and other fungi you could eat, and which ones would kill you. I found a book that told me everything I needed to know, packed with photographs of wild plants and captions loaded with information. The first wild plant I ever ate was wood sorrel, which tastes like apple peel, and once I tasted that, there was no looking back – I was hooked for life.

As well as the local library, I could often be found in the school library too. I loved the books they had there, and it was somewhere away from the cut and thrust of school life – well, most of the time. I remember this one day there, when I was about fourteen, the memory of which has stayed with me ever since. I was messing around in the library with some friends when a teacher walked in and suddenly – you know what it's like – everyone grabbed the nearest chair and sat down, pretending to read.

I sat there like everyone else, grabbed the book closest to me and started reading on a random page . . . and immediately stopped. I was completely blown away by what I read – so much so that I went straight to the beginning and started reading from the first page. I was so engrossed in this book that I completely missed the next two lessons. That book was *The Forest People* by Colin Turnbull, and it had a massive influence on me in the years ahead. Turnbull was an anthropologist and he'd written about the year he spent living among the BaMbuti Pygmies of the Ituri rainforest. I was utterly captivated – by Turnbull's writing, by what he'd done and, most of all, by the BaMbuti Pygmies. Having read about them, I wanted more than anything to meet them.

———— ◆·◆ ————

You can probably see a pattern developing here – as a young teenager, I was either out in the wilds of the North Downs, practising judo with Kingsley and the others at the Budokwai, or I was in the library. I spent a lot of time reading; reading and then going out and 'doing'. I think learning what I could eat outdoors was just the next step in the process. I read all the 'survival' books I could find; survival was the thing then – there was no bushcraft. Even so, the collected knowledge on survival back then was somewhat limited; its practice was developed and shared by a small group of people, and the status quo was rarely questioned. Information existed in something of a vacuum, so most of the books on the subject weren't very good. Even then, they were out of date.

These days I can put the survival studies of the time into context. Of course, the people who had the real knowledge back then were the military. There was the survival training that the Royal Air Force had responsibility for, which focused on escape and evasion for aircrew – if they were shot down, they needed to survive until they were picked up. The other type of survival training was that given to our Special Forces, who were much more likely to have to get themselves home – there was no rescue plan in place for them. The instructors were really good but, for obvious reasons, they weren't accessible to the public – even to as willing and committed a student of bushcraft as me. Back then, the relevant knowledge was kept within the military – just as it should be.

The first survival instructor of any note was Eddie McGee, and he really shook up the nascent survival industry. He'd enjoyed a long career in the Parachute Regiment and, after twenty-two years of service, he left to establish the National School of Survival, near Harrogate in North Yorkshire. He single-handedly knocked the industry into shape, and he was prolific. He wrote a number of books on the subject, and one of them – *No Need To Die* – was regarded as a bible at the time by survival enthusiasts.

Eddie had spent time living with pygmy groups in Africa, and among Australia's indigenous Aboriginal people, from whom he learned about tracking. I was about fifteen when I first met him, after attending one of his courses, and I learned some valuable skills from him. Eddie had been involved in tracking the multiple murderer Barry Prudom, who had shot and killed two police officers and a man he'd taken hostage. In the summer of 1982, McGee was brought in by police in North Yorkshire to help in the search. He picked up the trail after finding footprints in the early morning dew, and tracked Prudom to his hideout in Malton, North Yorkshire, where, surrounded by police, Prudom shot himself.

Having done the survival course that Eddie ran, I realised I was pulling away from the social groups at school that everyone else seemed to belong to. Given my interests and the pursuits I was involved in, it was perhaps inevitable that I wouldn't fit in with my peers at school.

I have always been a bit of a loner, so I looked forward to the weekends when I could head out into the woods – I had no restrictions, nothing to tether me, so I would wander off in whichever direction I fancied. Initially I'd go to the common, but over time the lure of the North Downs always caught me. It felt to me like it had its own gravity, reeling me in across the five or six miles that I'd hike to get there.

I loved the Downs' wide open space but it was its forest

that was the real allure. I'd started to really feel a part of that forest; I knew it intimately and felt a real connection to the forest environment that has remained with me to this day. I'm equally comfortable in Arctic, jungle, desert or urban environments, but it's the forest where I feel *really* at home. Sometimes I'd sit in the woods and just watch things happen; I used to love the time I spent there.

I learned tracking by following foxes and, as with any skill, I started with the easy stuff. Initially, I'd see their paw prints in the snow and follow them. When the snow melted, I found I could follow their tracks in the mud and so I just kept on going.

I started to look for other clues when the paw prints became hard to spot. When foxes carry a kill in their mouth, they have to stop for a rest periodically because it's hard on their neck. Often, when they drop a freshly killed pigeon, the bird will leave a downy feather or two. I'd notice these, and it started to colour in the picture I was seeing. Foxes like trails, so they would often run along the trails through the woods in the North Downs. There are hawthorn woods there, and in spring the hawthorn blossom would stick to the soles of their pads. As they left the area where the blossom was, there'd be traces of it on the forest floor where it had fallen off their pads. Sometimes I'd find where they'd cached the pigeon, because I'd see a pigeon's foot sticking out of the ground. It was fantastic to the young me, and a brilliant education in learning how to track.

When I started tracking there were gaps in my knowledge but I didn't worry about them. As a kid you don't worry about what you don't know. Over time, the gaps got smaller and smaller. I learned how to piece things together because I was always observing what was going on around me and becoming more 'at one' with my surroundings. It was almost like learning through osmosis, as my subconscious became more and more finely attuned to the environment and I'd start noticing signs that I wasn't able to spot before. The forest became a book and I learned to read not just what I could see but, perhaps more importantly, what I couldn't – the absence of the expected. Gradually I got better and better, until one day I just felt completely at home there. Being so in tune with my environment in the forest meant that I'd become quite an accomplished tracker.

I especially liked to go into the woods when it was raining because then I'd have them to myself – the rain kept everyone else away so there'd be absolutely nobody else around. I'd push myself into a holly bush on a rainy day, and use that for shelter or I'd seek out a yew tree. I learned early on that no matter how cold and wet it was, once I had a fire going and I had shelter I could stay warm and dry. I'd always make a fire, and I'd cook up an Oxo cube in an Army mug. I'd become quite adept at making fire without matches. By then, I used to carry cotton wool in a plastic bag with me, and I carried a piece of artificial flint that I used as a rod – scraping a knife down it created hot sparks. I kept it in a metal tube along with a piece of magnesium that I'd scrape for tinder. I made a habit of going out in the worst conditions again and again in order to hone my ability to make fire. Being able to make fire at will is an invaluable skill in the wild because it is a real game changer, particularly when it's cold and wet. A supply of hot drinks and food creates a paradigm shift in morale, and when I had all of that, I felt like I could stay in the forest forever.

Being able to feel at home somewhere is all well and good, but it's not much use if you don't know where you are, or how to get from point A to point B, so I taught myself to navigate – first via a map and compass, then by using the night sky. I learned quickly because I had a thirst for the knowledge, and the information I consumed was like ice-cold water to a parched throat.

I learned navigation indirectly from a *Warlord* annual one year. It told you how to use a Silva compass, so I asked my parents to get me one and they delivered in style by giving me a lovely Silva Polaris and an Ordnance Survey map (which I still have) covering the South and North Downs. I set myself targets with them; the first time I used them, I decided to go out and search for something so I opened the map up and found a spring marked somewhere in the Downs, and I thought, 'Right, I'm going to find the spring and fill my water bottle from it.' And that's exactly how I started. I'll never forget that spring because it was so hard to find – it was deep down through very tall, thick nettles and I got stung to blazes trying to get there – but I did it and I filled my empty water bottle from it. Every time I fill my water bottle now, wherever I am in the world, it makes me think of that spring.

I derived a tremendous sense of satisfaction from that little navigation mission. I'd set myself a task, one I had no idea whether I'd be able to do, and in the end I'd managed it. It's so important to step outside your comfort zone because that's usually when you learn best. I think it's really important that you do things like that for yourself – no adult with you, just you and your own self-belief. Sadly, I think many parents would be too afraid to let their children make a journey like that these days.

Having started to really enjoy navigating with my map and compass, I quickly moved on to learning to navigate via the night sky, which in many ways is just a map that's accessible for twelve hours out of every twenty-four (or thereabouts). I was really interested in all that – not just navigating by stars, but mastering and ramping up every skill I acquired. I got all the information from books, and honed the skills and techniques I learned by going out and putting them into practice. There's no substitute for doing things, ever – practice beats theory every time.

I also surveyed my own maps of all the little trails through the woods that I used to use by pacing out compass bearings and mapping the pathways. When I teach people how to navigate now, I don't let them have daylight for the first few days. Because they learn to navigate at night, they learn to trust their compass – that's how you become really good.

———◆◆◆———

It should come as no surprise that Reigate Grammar School's long-established Combined Cadet Force (CCF) had acted like a magnet on me ever since I'd been a wide-eyed new pupil. The prospect of learning to climb, shoot, acquire military tactics and live and sleep outdoors in all weathers – and on school time – didn't just appeal to me, it all but consumed me. This offered nirvana – everything I loved, plus the prospect of sponsorship by the armed services through sixth form college and university and, ultimately, a commission into my chosen branch as a junior officer.

Finally, after three long years of waiting, I was able to join at the beginning of the fourth form. I opted to join the Navy section instead of the Army or RAF sections because the Navy published a list of all its available courses at the beginning of the year whereas the Army and RAF published theirs piecemeal throughout the year, so you could never really plan ahead. The Navy section included a course with the Royal Marines, which was where I wanted to end up ultimately – a career as a Royal Marines officer seemed to offer everything I wanted in life at that stage.

The first course I did with the CCF was weapons handling, which included live firing on the range at Shorncliffe using the Mk 4 Lee-Enfield. I loved that, so I really got a lot out of it. The next course was run by the Navy – more shooting on the ranges at HMS *Excellent* shooting SLRs and SMGs, but we stayed on board a ship for the duration, which was great fun. The best elements for me, though, were the courses I did with the Royal Marines down at the Commando Training Centre in Lympstone. They included being dropped off a rigid raiding craft and marching across Dartmoor, killing your own chicken for dinner and abseiling down Foggin Tor. It was absolutely brilliant and everything I saw and experienced there just re-affirmed my commitment to a career as a Royal Marines officer. I ate, slept and breathed Marines. I honestly couldn't get enough.

I think it was while I was in the CCF that my love of the outdoors hit home. I was never scared of the dark and I've always loved wild places. I've been very lucky in my life to be able to know myself: I know that I get bored unless there's a real challenge. If it's difficult, that's when I find I'm at my best. If there's a crisis, I'll try to find a solution to the problem. I can focus on what needs doing; it's not that I don't feel fear, I can just push it out of my mind and I think that's something I learned from Kingsley. The wilder a place is, the more I like it. Every page of Colin Turnbull's book resonated with me every time I went out, and I was growing in confidence with each trip. I positively ached to undertake something bigger – like a jungle expedition as Turnbull had, rather than just my regular forays into the forest. And as I gained experience, the kit that I carried with me changed. I replaced the World War I bayonet with a British Army machete, known as a Golock – a much more effective tool. What I really wanted, though, was what Kingsley had: a rather large knife that he called a 'Dymtah'. He'd acquired it in Burma, and it had been made from a lorry spring. He used to carry it around his neck with the cord wrapped around its wooden sheath so that it rested on his chest at an angle of 45°.

Anyway, I was listening to the radio one day in 1981 – I'd have been about sixteen or seventeen then – when I heard the presenter talking to a guest who was organising an expedition to the Arctic and looking for volunteers. I thought this offered a real opportunity so I talked to my mates Mark and Adrian about it and they agreed to travel up to the Lake District with me to look into it. As it transpired, we were to be disappointed – the guy planning the expedition was big on ideas, but had nothing lined up in the way of backing, so I thought: *chalk that one up to experience.*

It wasn't a total write-off though – in fact, we ended up pulling victory from the jaws of defeat because off the back of the expedition-that-wasn't we got to climb Skiddaw in the company of Geoff Somers. Geoff was a big name in the British Antarctic Survey at the time, and he'd also been at the meeting with the expedition planner. He offered to take those of us who were there climbing on Skiddaw, so we leapt at the invitation.

On the way down, I asked Geoff if we could stop for a few minutes to watch a kestrel that was below us; I'd never been above a kestrel before. Well, five minutes became half an hour (that's become something of a theme for me ever since). I went on to climb the Alps when I was in my twenties, but even then I never subscribed to the 'Let's rush to the top, climb that one, and then rush on to the next one' mantra. I like to stop and take it all in; I need to know why I've been there. As far as I'm concerned, that's what is important.

For me, the challenge of the outdoors is not about whether you can cope, whether you can overcome nature, do it bigger, higher, faster or further than anyone else. I'm not interested in crossing a continent on foot, or doing it in record time, or any of that stuff; to me it's all artificial. Don't get me wrong – I'm not against people who do that. It just doesn't appeal to *me*. What interests me is becoming more attuned to the environment: understanding it, how it fits together, and what our place in it is. It's about how to work *with* an environment so that you bolster each other and don't feel threatened, and that's what I was learning.

We're all different though, and I really have no problem with people who have different motivations. Take Ranulph Fiennes; I like him as an individual, and I have huge respect for him and what he's achieved. I think, in terms of what he does, he really understands why he's doing it – I don't think there's any doubt about that. He's got it in perspective. But I think British society is very immature in its attitude to exploration. It's all about conquering this, conquering that, but the important thing to remember is that you *never* conquer nature. If you get to the top of a mountain, it's because you did all the right things and nature said yes, OK, you can get there. But twenty-four hours later, nature might well feel differently, and you could die trying. You can never beat nature; you have to learn to work with her.

If you are able to devote all of your time to focusing on tuning in to nature, you develop a sense, a feeling for when things aren't right on any given day. It's very hard to explain; sometimes you just develop an instinct – some people call it a sixth sense – but you can develop it to an extraordinary degree. Part of my education has been to learn to recognise the signs, to attune myself to the flow of nature so that I better understand what's going on. It can mean the difference between life and death.

Sometimes when I was tracking as a youngster, I would get drawn to things and I'd often find a sign *after* the event, when I was wandering home. It's as if something had been leading me there, when the reality was that I was seeing a sign but not consciously noticing it. I think the fact that I did this when I was so young played a huge part in my acquiring the skills I have, because when you're young you're unfettered by responsibilities so your mind is free to wander in a way that is all but impossible as an adult. Some people might call it daydreaming, but it's not that – you're allowing your mind the freedom to explore the world in its own way. I think it's interesting that Einstein had a lot of his thoughts in a similar way – not that I'm comparing myself to him! I just believe that letting the mind have free rein early on is absolutely key. As you get older, your responsibilities get in the way and they cloud your vision.

A Canadian Indian once told me that his goal in life was to be a person of power. By that he didn't mean power in terms of wealth or importance in his tribe, but rather in the sense of what we would call a 'medicine man'. That said, he would never want to be called a medicine man – someone of that nature in that society would never put themselves forward as such.

'I want to be a person in tune with nature so that nature will treat me and my clan well,' he said to me. Is it nature responding to him, or is it his reading of nature? Who knows, but the net effect is the same and that is that he's attuned to nature.

4

Transition

I can't overstate the remarkable effect Colin Turnbull's book had on me. It had a profound role in dictating the path I would take through life and my all-consuming interest in bushcraft and expeditions. It opened my eyes to the world like never before and my fascination for it knew no bounds; throughout my mid-teens, my curiosity and thirst for knowledge was like an itch I couldn't scratch.

The course I'd done with Eddie McGee played a pivotal role, too. As well as giving me a whole host of vital survival skills, Eddie had told me about the Royal Geographical Society (RGS). I learned soon after my first visit there that the Society was intending to run a course entitled 'How to Plan an Expedition to a Tropical Rainforest'. There was no way I was going to miss that, so I threw caution to the wind and enrolled. I raided the piggy bank and, at fifteen, I was the youngest person on the course. All the others were postgraduates, or proper adults with established credentials and hundreds of thousands of miles of global travel under their belts, and all of them planning to go off to interesting places. And then there was me – a wide-eyed fifteen-year-old with a dream and an insatiable drive to learn everything.

It could have been a disaster – I mean, what did I know? Would I be out of my depth? Would everyone else there look at me like I shouldn't be there? But it wasn't like that at all;

it was wonderful. I went with an open mind and a single objective: to learn all I could. The seminar was run by an incredible man, Major Roger Chapman, and he brought together some of the most experienced rainforest explorers of the time. We learned about rations, how to live in the jungle, how to navigate in the rainforest – all sorts of things. Chapman gave the most amazing lecture about an expedition he'd made for Operation Drake up the Strickland River in Papua New Guinea. I was sitting there, listening, watching, drinking in every word, and the hairs on the back of my neck were standing on end as if I'd been plugged into the mains. I'd heard of Operation Drake, which was named after Sir Francis Drake, who had circumnavigated the world on the *Golden Hind* some four hundred years earlier. Operation Drake ran between 1978 and 1980 and was a round-the-world voyage that was divided into nine ocean-based and one land-based phase, each lasting about three months. On each phase, a number of young volunteers aged between seventeen and twenty-four, who had been selected from countries all over the world, worked together on a series of scientific explorations, research and community projects. I had heard there was something new in the pipeline but details were scarce. All I knew for sure was that Roger Chapman would be involved and that it would be called Operation Raleigh. I also knew beyond a shadow of a doubt that I wanted to be involved.

That course at the RGS gave me so much – a much better understanding of the jungle for a start, and great reading lists. I started to hunt down and digest everything I could find on rainforests and it was all valuable knowledge – although it was to be a long while before I could put it to use. But that's the beauty of knowledge: it doesn't go off, and the best thing about it is that it doesn't weigh anything, so you can carry it with you wherever you go.

While I wasn't able to immediately put the lessons I'd learned on expedition planning to use, the course did confer other benefits on me. It had a galvanising effect and really focused my interests. It also woke me up to the fact that there were other organisations out there that I'd want to mesh with, organisations I could learn from and that could help me. The course was invaluable and well worth every penny.

I was still heavily involved with the CCF at school and keener than ever to join the Royal Marines as an officer – for the young me, at fifteen, it felt like that was my destiny. The Royal Marines felt like my ideal home, combining so much of what interests and drives me. But that dream was to come crashing down around my ears because of something so fundamental, so out of my control, I would be powerless to resolve it: my eyesight.

I wore glasses when I was a child and my visual acuity was outside of the accepted parameters laid down by the Marines. I knew all along that you didn't need perfect sight to join, so I'd always assumed that I would sail through that particular hurdle. Apparently not. There were degrees of imperfect vision that were acceptable, and mine fell on the wrong side of the line. I was told it wouldn't even be worth my while applying. These were the days before laser surgery was an option. There was nothing I could do, no right of appeal. That aspiration was over before it had even started.

At a rational level, I understood it. But it was still a crushing disappointment nonetheless and I think that the rejection – for that's what it was, when you get down to it – sapped a lot of energy from me, because for once in my life I felt completely helpless. Had it been my academic results, I could have worked harder. Had I not been fit enough, I could have trained harder. But my vision? It seems daft when viewed through the lens of hindsight – and given how things have turned out for me, it's not as if it matters now – but to the teenage me it was a big thing, and for a while I felt anchorless.

So, at fifteen, suddenly I was left with no plan. I sleepwalked through my O-levels, but my results were good enough for me to stay on and do A-levels, which only served to delay the inevitable. I quite literally didn't know what to do next. I felt frustrated because I couldn't find anything that I really wanted to study at university; neither of my parents had been so they didn't really understand how it all worked, and I didn't think there was anything there for someone with my interests.

For most people, university is a world of opportunity, but none of the usual subjects interested me and nobody ever said to me: 'Why don't you look into anthropology or ethno-botany, or any of those things?' Consequently, I didn't know it was possible to study them. There were lots of subjects I could have done – and would have loved to have studied – but I didn't know they existed.

In the seemingly endless summer holidays after my O-levels, I did another course with Eddie McGee that involved living out in the open for a week. By then I was very capable and living outdoors held no difficulties for me. The course involved feeding yourself and sleeping out with very little equipment – we ended up sleeping in a cave on the Yorkshire Moors. For warmth, we made blankets from bracken, which we wove with fibre that we got from brambles. It wouldn't be my choice now – there are other natural materials in abundance that are far more effective, comfortable and hold heat better – but that's what was taught on that particular course. Making the blankets was challenging enough for most of those on the course with me, but for me it felt as if we weren't even scratching the surface. I wanted more. I wanted to know how native people did things. Also, I had begun to feel that survival wasn't the whole story. Survival is just the shorthand of bushcraft – bushcraft is the bigger subject. It's more about how you live within an environment rather than just exist. And the great thing about bushcraft is that wherever you go, the skills go with you.

I didn't quite understand that then, but I knew that I wanted – no, *needed* – to know more. The problem I had was finding enough literature on the subject. There were lots of books out there, but not enough from trustworthy, reliable sources, so I had to sort out which books were good and which weren't. It was trial and error and I digested a hell of a lot of material in the process. It was tedious work at times, but ultimately it was time well spent because I came across some valuable information in the process. And let's be honest, nothing valuable is easy to come by. Among the rough, I found a couple of books that became my bibles – *Woodcraft and Camping* by Bernard S. Mason, and *Bushcraft* by Richard Graves; they were very good and well-written and everything in them worked.

When I wanted to learn about fungi, I contacted the best authority I could find – although my quest could have been over before it began. I'd been watching a TV series called *The Good Food Show* and they had a mushroom expert on: the late Dr Derek Reid. He ran courses on fungi, so I made a note of his name, tracked down a number for him and rang him up. I explained that I was a student of bushcraft and survival and that I wanted to take one of his courses . . . and he put the phone down on me. Then I met somebody else at one of the lectures I attended who was also an expert on fungi, so I made arrangements to go and see her. She gave me some instruction and then told me that if I wanted to go further I should really go and do Derek Reid's course. Of course I laughed when she told me that, and I explained what had happened when I called him. She said, 'Oh, don't worry about that. Just book in on his course but don't tell him what it is you're interested in.'

So I did just that. He was as amiable as can be and I arranged to go and attend one of his evening classes, which he held at Kew Gardens. He was more than just an expert though – it turned out that he was no less than the head of mycology at the Royal Botanic Gardens, and an acknowledged world authority on the classification and identification of mushrooms, toadstools and the like. As a mycologist, he had an unrivalled general knowledge of fungal habitats and taxonomy.

His courses were fourteen weeks long and he had all of Britain's top amateurs among his students. New faces would get one hour's instruction from him on the microscopic properties of fungi and afterwards we'd go into another room where all the old hands had been and they would bring out fungi which they identified and labelled and then laid on the table according to their spore colour. Derek would then go around explaining any mistakes they'd made. I attended these wonderful courses for the last four years that they ran.

His students included some very serious, semi-professional mycologists so, between them, they might have collected some three or four hundred different fungi there of an evening – an astonishing range really. Derek would go round, look at them and identify them all by eye. At the end, I would select all the edible ones and put them side by side with those that they could be confused with, and pore over them. In later years, Derek and I became very good friends, ironically enough, and we eventually ended up running some courses together because I had studied the different uses of fungi, including for food. There's a special knowledge not just in being able to identify which fungi are edible and what to do with them, but also in being able to find edible fungi in reliable quantities, and that's a skill that I developed.

The courses I did, however, were a mixed bag. Some, like those I did with Dr Derek Reid and Eddie McGee, and the one at the RGS, were invaluable. The others, however, didn't stretch me. That said, they were all good experiences because I took something away from each of them and learned more about my own abilities. But I still wanted more; I *needed* adventure.

I had learned to make fire by friction on one of the courses, although I ended up working it out for myself as the instructor who taught it knew all the theory but couldn't put it into practice. He was using the wrong sort of wood for the drill and the hearth, and the dimensions of the drill were all wrong so if he'd tried forever and a day, he'd never have made fire. For all I know, he's still trying.

Again, I learned an invaluable lesson from that because it taught me never to bullshit, and it's something I carry with me to this day – if you don't know something, *say* you don't know it. I feel very strongly about that and I've built Woodlore up on that basis. If anyone who works for me bullshits, they won't be there long. If you don't know, say so – then go and find out. Do otherwise and you lose all credibility.

———◆———

My relationship with Kingsley was stronger than ever when I started my A-levels. I was still going to the Budokwai on a regular basis, so judo still played a major role in my life, but I was seeing a lot of Kingsley outside of judo as well. He was very much a sage for me, and the time I spent with him at this stage was like a series of tutorials with an exceptionally good lecturer at a top-tier university. He was a very clever man, very bright. What I really liked, though, was that he took an interest in *my* interests. And his advice didn't conflict with my parents' influence on my life – quite the opposite really. As a parent you are bound by certain concerns; if you are an adult outside of that relationship, you can be nurturing in a different way. He filled that role perfectly, and I valued our friendship greatly.

Looking back, I'm grateful that my parents didn't worry unduly about my increasing knowledge of bushcraft and the way I would go about teaching myself new skills by 'doing' and staying out. By this point I was making bows and arrows, making flint into arrowheads. I used to make my own knives; I could make a knife out of an old saw – cut it out in the vice with a cold chisel and then grind it. I cut an old cutlass down and put a plastic handle on it from an old bow. It looked a bit Tarzan-ish, but really I was inhibited only by my own imagination and it was running wild. I made my own karabiner; I abseiled down an 8oft cliff using that thing. Looking back, I'm probably lucky to be alive.

I wanted to know how to be a native of my own country and that, for the next few years, was to be an important focus. Instead of walking across the common with a cricket bat and stump like other youngsters, I was walking across it with a spear and a spear thrower, bows and arrows and fire sticks. I must have looked like an Aborigine to anyone who saw me.

Mum and Dad were very supportive. They never got at me or criticised what I was doing, and consequently their trust reinforced my self-belief. That said, they must have been a little bit annoyed at times because the freezer may have housed the odd deer head and a dead animal or two, and the house was always full of sticks, flora and fauna. But hey, when you're interested in these things, that's what happens.

When you have a formal education, there's a structure, a framework for what you do, but I didn't have that with what I was doing. In some ways I was evolving something new, so I just followed my interests, flitting from one subject or skill to another, like a bee to a flower, gathering what I could to store and make use of later. There was never any great master plan or end point to what I was doing. Even after forty years of studying bushcraft, I'm still learning new things and new skills, so really there is no end to the subject. It expands, and you have to keep up. Anyone who thinks they've mastered it is deluding themselves – it's like running for the horizon: you're never going to reach it because the closer you get, the further away it is.

Fortunately for me, I was going from one little thing to another all those years ago, and somehow it all meshed together into a coherent narrative. It was informative and useful so I look back on it as quite a good way of doing things. Now though, if someone wanted to learn the subject I'd structure it for them, but that structure wasn't available for me so I had to find my own way through it, which is quite an eighteenth-century approach to things, really. In the Age of Enlightenment, if people wanted to know something they tried to work it out for themselves. It was a time when people saw for themselves. It's my belief that if you have an interest, you should explore it. I would encourage everyone to do that.

The exploration of my subject took me to the most wonderful museum in London: the Museum of Mankind. It's closed now, which is a crying shame because it was a dedicated museum of anthropology and they displayed the most amazing exhibits there. It was a really important and useful resource to me because of the range of materials on show: all sorts of bark, clothing artefacts made of birch bark from Norway and Scandinavia, rainforest longhouses . . . you name it, they had it. One of my favourite exhibitions there was called 'The Thunderbird and Lightning Exhibition' which was about the Woodland Indians of North-East America. There was a period of my life where I was in there all the time and I'd be poring over the exhibits, drawing them, making them, having a go – I wanted to understand everything about them.

Alongside my insatiable lust for knowledge on bushcraft and the outdoors, I had also developed quite an interest in photography. Being a printer, my dad appreciated the way that photography recorded history and that interest was passed on to me aged about ten when he gave me a complicated 35mm

SLR camera. I was far too young to fully appreciate it, and I wasn't too hot initially on how to use it, but my dad's enthusiasm was infectious and I gradually started to get to grips with it. It would be fair to say that as my interest in bushcraft grew, so too did my interest in photography. In fact, by the time I was in my early twenties I'd reach a fork in the road whereby I could have ended up as a professional photographer rather than a specialist in bushcraft and the outdoors. Photography has remained a big part of my life to this day, but I'll come on to that.

I sleepwalked through my A-levels in much the same way as I had with my O-Levels but then I really was in a quandary: the Royal Marines wasn't an option, I couldn't earn a living by being able to live in the wild and although I was good at judo, I was never at a level where I could turn pro. That said, I wouldn't have wanted to even if I could. For as much as I loved judo, my heart lay in the outdoors, but I had no idea at that time how I could possibly turn that interest into a revenue stream and make it pay. I had a clutch of exam passes but I was just another school-leaver in a crowd of people looking for something worthwhile to do with their lives. Given that I was unable to do what I wanted to, I followed the only path open to me and tried to find some work of a more conventional nature so that I could at least get some money behind me.

That's how I found myself in the most unlikely role possible: going to work in a suit and driving a desk in the City. I don't really understand what I did – and it's not age or a foggy memory affecting my recall. Truly, I don't even think I knew back then. Picture it: I worked in an office with thirty people, twenty-seven of whom smoked – and this in the days when you could smoke at your desk, inside buildings, on aeroplanes and, yes, on the London Underground. I hated it.

Although I wasn't sure what I wanted to do, I knew what

I *didn't* want to do and perversely it was exactly the job I found myself doing. I knew from early on that I wasn't destined for a conventional career. I think I've always been a fighter – I'm not one to be pushed down, and back in my earliest days at school, I almost always won when we played British Bulldog. If someone tries to stop me from doing something, then I'll find another way to do it. I'm very single-minded and certainly a loner. I don't want to be a part of a herd. The moment someone tries to put me in a pen with everybody else, that's the moment I can guarantee I won't be there. I'll slip the fence and be somewhere else doing something else. I don't want to be pigeonholed in any way. I'm my own person.

Consequently, I felt trapped from the off, and not just because I was constrained in a suit and wedged behind a desk inside four very smoky (and consequently yellowing) walls. I enjoyed the money I earned, and I loved the freedom of adult life, but whatever it was I did that earned me the money, it was terribly boring. I also seem to recall that whatever my job was, I wasn't very good at it. I felt like I was staring down the barrel of a gun and I didn't like what I saw at the end of it: a loan for a car, a mortgage for a flat, weekly shopping, trips to the cinema and living for the weekends. They were all metaphors for a set of handcuffs, chaining me to the monotony of a job I hated, in an office where I didn't belong, in a life that wasn't mine. I had to get out before the job sucked me in. So that's what I did. I stuck it for a year and then left.

Do I regret it? Not a bit. Like everything in my life, I learned something as a result of working there. I gained a respect for other people's interests. I knew then, but even more so now, that I had a very unusual interest to pursue – and I've been privileged, and very lucky, that I've made a career out of it. But when I meet people who work in the City, I have enormous respect for them. I couldn't do what they do. We all have different skills and I have tremendous respect for everyone who is a part of that, regardless of what they do to earn their money.

As things transpired, my resignation from my City job was somewhat serendipitous; just a few weeks later, I was invited by Roger Chapman to join Operation Raleigh. And with that, I took the first step along the road to where I am now. Although I couldn't have known it then, Operation Raleigh was to play a very positive part in everything that has followed. Without it, Woodlore would never have existed.

5

Raleigh Point

Operation Raleigh was established in 1982 by Colonel John Blashford-Snell as a successor to his previous project, Operation Drake. The origins of the two projects dated back to 1978 when Blashford-Snell and HRH Prince Charles had a shared vision of giving young people a chance to explore the world and, by doing so, discover their potential as leaders and members of a team working together to make a difference. In essence, the concept behind Op Drake and Op Raleigh was to give those who were selected the challenge of war in a peace-time situation.

I was almost nineteen when I started there towards the end of 1982, a year that was dominated by news of the battle for the Falkland Islands. We were based in a building that harked back to a much earlier conflict: our team occupied rooms 440, 441 and 442 of the old War Office building in Whitehall. I sometimes wonder if JK Rowling had ever been there because when I look back, our working environment bore more than a passing resemblance to her imagined world of Gringotts Wizarding Bank as realised in the Harry Potter films.

There was very little organisation initially, just a group of us with a willingness to help out, a belief in the objective and a desire to see it succeed. There were twelve of us at the start, divided into two groups of six – they wanted to call us the Young Lions but we were having none of that. In the end, we became known as the Selection Weekend and Administrative Team or 'SWAT Team' for short. It was never planned, but we weren't too disappointed with the acronym and enjoyed the play on words. Our job was to design, set up and run the selection process. Age-wise it was a repeat performance of the seminar at RGS where I'd first met Roger Chapman – I was far and away the youngest; all the others were postgrads.

Working on Operation Raleigh was a real life-shaping experience for me, a fascinating time in which we were all doing something really worthwhile, and I met some amazing people through it. Roger Chapman was the great unsung hero. He always worked away in the background – it was never *about* him. There was also the inspirational Wandy Swales, one of the great old-school explorers and Op Raleigh's chief of staff – No.2 to Colonel John Blashford-Snell. He was a truly wonderful man, a larger-than-life character with tremendous people skills. There were a great many other people who helped make it such a worthwhile project, and I think that's part of what made it really special.

A week or so after I started, I found myself abseiling down a 300ft-high block of flats in London's Shepherds Bush. It was typical of the kind of things we got involved in with Operation Raleigh, and I loved it. There was a 5ft wall around the edge of the roof which, having clipped on to the rope, we had to climb over. On the other side was a 300ft sheer drop; that focused the mind somewhat. I got a real buzz from that; it was just the sort of thing I enjoyed doing.

The first role for those of us on the selection team was designing the presentations that would be given by the county co-ordinators – a network of people across the UK who would be responsible for organising the interviews for the expedition. In the end, they interviewed in excess of 8,000 young people from which to select the candidates, each one of whom needed to raise at least £2,500 in sponsorship for a place on the expedition. I was tasked with writing the reference notes on how to interview people. That was interesting – back then, what I knew about interviewing could have been written on a postage stamp with room left over for *War and Peace*. But I wanted to contribute, so I did some research and worked it out for myself.

That was good; I liked that because it was a real challenge and it was way outside of my comfort zone. So I learned a lot of really useful things: I learned about interviewing; I learned about putting presentations together. And I was working with the operation's professional photographer – that was really interesting as well. I learned a lot about photography then, and moving images; it was really helpful stuff.

My role at Operation Raleigh came along at just the right time in my life, although some of the challenges I faced, such as organising a schedule of events and liaising with different organisations, stretched me. We were given responsibility, and that required a degree of growth on my part. Fortunately, those I was working with all had different skills to me – whereas I'd always been on my own in the outdoors, I was now in a team with two very good mountaineers, a couple of guys who'd become alpine guides, a guy who had been into sailing and another who was into canoeing, plus someone who'd been the president of the Cambridge University Exploration Society. They were a fascinating and really interesting group of people.

Eventually, due to cost constraints, our team of twelve became six and we were split into two teams of three – a Northern team and a Southern team. I was really very lucky to be in the North; we had to travel further than our counterparts in the Southern team so it meant we were away from the office for longer, and that I was getting to see parts of the country I'd never been to before.

Our role now was to set up and run the selection weekends. I was working with Arthur Collins, who is now one of the foremost mountaineers in the world. He taught me to climb, so I feel really fortunate to have learned from the best. The other member of my team was Jonathan Raper (the ex-president of the Cambridge Exploration Society); he's now a professor of geomorphology. They were two very intelligent and capable men, real doers, and it was a privilege to work with them. We're all of us an amalgam of everyone we've met, worked with, loved or lost, and here I was, nineteen years old, with the 'people' equivalent of a jackpot win. How lucky was that?

We each took responsibility for two selection sites, which we would then co-ordinate and run. And on the selection weekends, it was our job to get those candidates in our charge very wet, cold and tired so that a team of judges could attempt to discover their 'core' personalities. Each of us has a face we present to the world, but it's only under stress that the real person is seen. It was hard work, but enjoyable and interesting. And we had a lot of laughs – we worked hard and we played hard.

There was a really special expedition atmosphere within Raleigh, even at that fledgling stage, and even when we were back in the office. Given that we only had three rooms in what was essentially a building at the heart of government in Whitehall, it made for some interesting times. It was like the centre of the civil service universe outside our small enclave, with civil servants straight from Central Casting striding purposefully along dark-panelled corridors with folders under their arms, desperately trying to look important.

I remember a young guy – we'll call him 'Mike' to save him embarrassment – who'd had the enviable job of travelling the globe in a search for countries and locations suitable for Operation Raleigh to run its expeditions. He'd not long been back from an overseas reconnaissance trip and he'd written a report on his findings, but let's just say that he hadn't been very tactful when writing about some of the people that he'd met on his travels.

Someone told him, 'Mike, you really can't circulate this to everyone. Given its content, you'd best keep it confidential and be selective about who you give it to.'

However, he was very proud of what he'd written and wanted to share it. So he went out one afternoon and, unbeknown to anybody, had twenty or so copies of his report printed and bound. Just for good measure, he stopped off and bought a 'Confidential' stamp and some red ink. Then he carefully stamped the cover of each copy of the report with the word 'Confidential' and when everybody had gone home for the night, he called back in to the office and placed a copy on everybody's desk.

In his excitement, he'd obviously forgotten that we shared the building with civil servants so we had to abide by the same rules as they did. Perhaps unsurprisingly, given their role in government, those rules included a 'Clear Desk' policy. At some stage after the last person had left for the evening, the security team had gone in to do their usual nightly inspection and they must have had a collective fit at what they assumed was a major security breach because when we got to work the next morning, we found Special Branch officers crawling all over the place. It was incredibly funny. Well, *we* thought it was funny – I'm sure they saw the funny side . . . eventually.

Another day that stands out was the birthday of one of the women on our admin team. Someone had bought her one of those helium-filled balloons and, as it was a quiet day, the inevitable happened: a small hole was made and the balloon was passed round for us all to breathe in a lungful of helium. Cue all of us talking like Mickey Mouse and everybody present laughing like it was the funniest thing they'd ever seen or heard (some party tricks never get old). Just as we were in full flow, there was a knock on the door and who should walk in but the Governor of Papua New Guinea. Luckily for us, he was a really cool dude rather than some stuffed-shirt career diplomat and he immediately started laughing; he even ended up joining in. For us, though, it was just another day in the office . . .

On Operation Drake, they'd come up with a selection test that involved them using a real gorilla. They had it in a room, and candidates would have to open the door, walk in and take its chest measurement. It was as much about their reaction once they opened the door as it was anything else, but the idea was novel and also very successful. Of course, somebody on our team suggested we should also have a gorilla in one of the selection tests. We'd found one who had been taught to hug people in return for a chocolate biscuit, but in the end we couldn't afford a real one, so we went for the next best thing – a darkened room containing a member of the team in a gorilla suit. No, really! And oh, the laughs we had with that suit. There was a serious side though: the person in the gorilla suit learned a great deal about the behaviour of the candidates from how they approached the 'animal'.

The ruse was so good that word got out and, before we knew it, the national media started reporting allegations that Operation Raleigh was abusing this gorilla. The whole thing blew up out of all proportion and there was a story about it running in the *Telegraph* for ages, with campaigns to have the poor animal freed, and everybody very indignant and up in arms about it. There were the usual 'Mr Angry of Tunbridge Wells' letters to the editor, along the lines of: 'Oh, it's disgusting how this poor gorilla is being treated . . .' and of course it was all nonsense. We dined out on that for ages.

I remember we were invited out on one night to a party in

Killingworth, at that time a really depressed sink estate in Newcastle; it was razed to the ground not long after. Those were interesting times in Britain; it was a period of great social change and we saw a lot of it at first hand. Leaving London one day, we were delayed by the siege at the Libyan Embassy following the fatal shooting of WPC Yvonne Fletcher. We left London only to arrive at a different siege in the North, which pitted police officers against striking miners. The dichotomy was evident; there was a real North–South divide back then. We met lots of people from different walks of life and backgrounds: the well-off and well-heeled, the disadvantaged, people with learning difficulties, as well as people with other disabilities and those who work with them. It was very interesting, and seeing it all gave me a great faith in humanity. Although the world news is full of depressing tales of humankind and the terrible things we do, there is another side that you don't hear about very often and that's the remarkable work carried on across the board by people who want to make the world a better place. Those of us involved in Operation Raleigh really got a sense of that first-hand.

It was evident right from the off that some of those who attended the selection weekends belonged to an organisation that involved outdoor pursuits; this gave them the edge over those who hadn't. These candidates came from various organisations, like the Scouting Movement, the Boys' Brigade and the Cadet Forces, but they all held a massive advantage over those who hadn't been a part of something similar, simply because of the knowledge, skills and self-confidence those groups conferred. It really drove home how important those organisations are, and how great their contribution is to society at large. We saw a tangible difference in those who had been a part of one of those groups: they were more self-aware, more rounded and deeper individuals than others who had come straight from day-to-day life. I think that all young people today should try and find a club, society or organisation of that nature to join, even if it's only for a short while, because it will enrich them in a way that will benefit both them and society for the rest of their lives.

———◆◆———

I was very fortunate in that part of my role at Op Raleigh involved me visiting outdoor centres and undertaking some of their courses to get a feel for what their instructors were teaching. I remember one survival course I did where I'd get up each morning and pick mushrooms that I'd cook for breakfast. The instructors were horrified. They had no idea which ones were poisonous and which ones weren't, and consequently thought I didn't either. Meanwhile, I'm thinking, 'How can you run a survival course and not know how to do this?' Even though my knowledge of fungi was relatively basic at that point, I think that was the first time I realised that my skills and knowledge of the outdoors were more comprehensive and better developed than some of the people who were making a living out of teaching survival.

I also learned that if people are *sent* on a course, it's nothing special to them, but if they've *chosen* to be there and put their own money down, then they're going to be a whole lot more committed. That's when I first thought that I might stand a chance of making a living out of what I knew and loved. It was a moment of clarity. I really felt I had something that could be marketed, although I knew even then that while I might know more than those who had instructed me, I didn't know everything. I think that this is a recurring theme in the world of bushcraft and survival courses – too many people start too soon. In an ideal world, I would have taken a few more years to prepare myself, but back then that simply wasn't an option – there was nowhere I could have gone to learn the things that would plug the gap in my knowledge, whereas today there are lots of options.

On one of the first courses I ran for Operation Raleigh, I was working alongside a chap called Philip Wells. We had a similar outlook and got along famously, and I confided in him about my plans. I wanted to come up with a name that I could use to market my skills. It was 1983, the era of the Rambo films, and the word 'survival' had terrible connotations, conjuring up images of people running around in combat clothing with headbands and carrying big, ugly knives. I wanted to break away from that, but it would take time to reclaim the word, so I didn't want 'survival' to appear anywhere in my company or trading name. It was Phil and his family who came up with the name 'Woodlore'. I loved it the first time I heard it; I knew it was the right one.

The very first course I ran under the Woodlore name came off the back of a selection weekend that I'd held for Operation Raleigh in Birmingham. One of the judges on that selection, Terry Lewis, had a day job as an Army officer. He told me that the unit he commanded was responsible for despatching Special Forces via Hercules and he thought they might benefit from some survival training.

'Raymond, are there any things one might eat in the countryside?' he asked me.

'Sure,' I said, looking around. Nearby, I spotted the telltale leaves of the pignut.

'Terry, if you look over there,' I said pointing, 'you'll see some leaves that resemble those you get with carrots.'

Terry nodded, and we walked over to them together.

Pignuts were a major source of calories in mankind's distant past. It's the underground part of the plant that we're most interested in – the root, or tuber. I dug some up, cleaned them, and handed one to Terry.

'Here, try this,' I said.

'Pignuts are one of the more palatable wild foods. You can eat the tuber raw, it's really tasty. The flavour and consistency is reminiscent of celery heart crossed with raw hazelnut or sweet chestnut.'

Terry tried it. 'There's a spicy aftertaste too – similar to what you'd get from radishes or watercress?'

I smiled. That was all it took to secure Woodlore's first paid gig.

A few weeks later, I took Terry and twenty or so of his men to a very wet Elan Valley, in Mid-Wales, to teach them some survival skills over a four-day period. I really enjoyed working with them; it was my first experience of teaching the military and I learned very early on that they'd be great to work with. They have a lot of energy and professionalism, they love acquiring new skills and, crucially, they have a great sense of humour. I think I earned £200, but it meant so much more to me than that. It was what it represented – and that, to me, was priceless.

I taught the men how to snare, butcher and cook rabbit, and I then had them rubbing sticks together to make fire by friction. I taught them survival skills – basic things like shelter, fire, and finding water and food. I had a pretty good idea of how to go about doing these things, but in the time since, I've really been able to refine those skills. This is largely thanks to the success of Woodlore and to all the students who have made it successful. Students are far and away the best teachers; the questions they ask are the best guide as to what they should be learning. I had enough knowledge in terms of timber then to get a weak flame going, but the knowledge I've acquired over the years since is what's turned that flame into a fire.

I learned a great deal from that first course, but not from the things that went right; it's more from what *didn't* go so right. Even if I have a general feeling that things have gone well, I'm never happy with how I've done; I never have been. There are some things you can pat yourself on the back for, but I'm always focused on what didn't work or what I could have done better. *That's* how you learn, that's how you hone your knowledge and that's how you make something work properly. Generally, it's better to be critical about what you've done, the things that didn't work, and the things that could have gone better. That's how you improve your performance and grow.

6

Photographic Memory

I left Operation Raleigh in 1984 having completed what I'd been recruited to do; we'd run the assessment weekends and all the candidates had been selected for the first expedition and were making preparations to leave. I'd had a brilliant time, made some great connections, learned some valuable lessons and acquired new skills but I wanted to build on them, and develop and hone my knowledge still further. I wanted to see what I could do with Woodlore.

After a short period of consolidation back at home, I set off for the US. I'd made contact with some Native Americans before I left and I wanted to spend some time with them, learning about their traditional skills. I also spent time in the desert; that was great. In those days you could light fires in the back country, although recently the rules and regulations on camp fires have been tightened. It's a shame because it's a special thing to hike into the back country, collect a couple of mullein sticks which I'd rub against alligator juniper and make fire by friction in the evening – it's an experience that's not so easy to have now, unless you break the rules.

One night, not long after I arrived back, I was practising at the Budokwai when I noticed Kingsley lying down on the side of the mat. He looked very pale and unwell and somebody was standing beside him fanning him with a towel. I rushed over and I could see immediately that it was serious. I called an ambulance and he was rushed across the road to St Stephen's Hospital. It transpired that he'd had a massive heart attack and he passed away peacefully the following morning. He was seventy-three when he died and I'd known him for almost twenty years by then. I felt his loss terribly – my mentor, my friend. I miss him still.

His loss had a galvanising effect on me and it crystallised the fact that I felt I was drifting. His death was the catalyst for me to do something and take control, so I did something decisive and threw myself into writing for a magazine. It was a part-work on survival, and although it wasn't what I wanted to do, I couldn't afford to be choosy – it paid the bills. I'd realised that no matter how much I believed in myself and my abilities, it was going to be difficult to support myself solely by running courses on bushcraft when nobody knew what it was, so I needed another string to my bow. The magazine used to send a photographer out with me on assignments and I realised very quickly that his images were nothing to write home about; I thought I could do better, so I started to take my own. I enjoyed it, I was reasonably good at it (and learning all the time) and I thought, 'Well, maybe I'll try photography.' I was still seeking the right path and trying to find myself, really.

So, I joined a photographic society – I wanted to improve, so I was casting around for ways in which I could gather new techniques. The society had a newsletter and one of the first editions I received had some useful advice on how to make a living as a photographer. It was pretty simple, common-sense advice but effective nonetheless. It suggested browsing magazines, picking the ones with the best images in, and then ringing the editors up to arrange a meeting so you could show your portfolio.

I'm a practical man – I much prefer to do rather than just read theory – so I went to WH Smith and was immediately drawn to *National Geographic* which, from a photographic perspective, was my favourite magazine. I thought that might be a little bit out of my league, but I noticed a brand new publication called *World*, which appeared to have a similar remit and was essentially a glossy British version of the venerable US periodical. Being new, I thought they might be looking for photographers, so I put a call in to the editor, an Italian gentleman called Mark Ausenda. I was more than a little surprised when I was put straight through to him.

'Hi, my name is Ray Mears, I'm a photographer [yeah, right!], and I'd like to show you my portfolio.'

He said, 'Yeah, sure,' and gave me a date to meet with him. It was as simple as that.

Then I put the phone down and thought, 'Ah, maybe I'd better put a portfolio together.'

I already knew the kind of transparencies that *World* wanted so I selected my best images, put them together in a slide sheet and off I went to meet with Mark. I arrived at the magazine's offices in Kensington. Mark met me in the foyer, held my slide sheet up to the light and said, 'Really, these aren't good enough, but thank you for coming.'

I did a double take. I didn't think he'd looked at them closely enough. I was incensed, but he'd been very polite to me, so I asked him what was wrong with them. He sat down (a positive sign, I thought) and explained to me that they weren't sharp enough. He also said there wasn't enough depth of field and they weren't colourful enough.

'Thanks,' I said. 'I'll be back.'

He didn't look convinced.

It hadn't gone quite how I'd expected but I wasn't put off; I was still high on the success of actually talking to an editor, so I went into town and bought a wonderful book called *The 35mm Photographer's Handbook*. It was very concise – there were no words wasted – and what text there was in that book absolutely banged the nail on the head. It made me realise I couldn't carry on using the kit I had – a Canon AE1 programme camera and cheap telephoto zoom lens – so I sold it all and raided my piggy bank again. That gave me enough to invest in my first serious camera, a manual-only Nikon FM2 and a 35–105mm lens. Then I spent six months teaching myself to take better pictures.

I went up to see Mark again. He came out to the foyer, took the slide sheets from me, held them up to the light and looked at them again. I wasn't very happy with the time he spent on them but it didn't change what he said.

'No, they're still not good enough.'

And then he looked at me and said, 'But come back and see me again.'

That was quite encouraging, but I had no idea what to do next. So I went away and thought, *Right, back to the beginning. Start again.* I gathered up every copy of *National Geographic* I could find and looked for images that stood out to me. They were all stunning, but I couldn't see any pictures of stone tools. I'd become quite adept at making stone tools and I knew about them, so I decided to shoot my own.

I made some flint arrowheads and a few bone needles. Several things stood out about the *National Geographic* images. They were very sharp, they had strong colour in the background and they were artistically lit.

So I got some coloured paper, some glass and some bricks, plus two rolls of Kodachrome 25, the sharpest film you could buy. Then I put the stone tools on the glass so I could backlight them, hired another flash gun to front light them so I could capture the facets, and I put different coloured paper behind them. I shot images with a number of different coloured backgrounds, put them on a slide sheet and went back to see Mark.

Again, he came down to the foyer and had a look at what I'd shot.

I was half expecting to hear the same, 'Thanks, but no thanks,' but this time he said, 'Yeah, come with me.' We went into his office and he put the slide sheet on his light box and then called in Rachel Horner who was his assistant editor. He asked her what she thought.

'Wow, the sharpness, the colour. Pretty good.'

And I walked out of there with my first assignment for *World* magazine.

A week later, I was taking photos of some of Britain's most precious fossils behind the scenes at the British Museum. Of course, I didn't really know what I was doing but what a great way to learn on the job!

Using a manual SLR camera was instructive, so from a technical perspective it was one of the best things I could have done because I had to learn how to do everything the hard way rather than relying on a program or automatic function to take care of the settings for me. I was fortunate enough to be able to consult with the photographic legend that was the late Terry Donovan. Of course, to certain sections of high society and the media back then he had almost mythical status. Along with David Bailey and Brian Duffy, Donovan captured, and in many ways helped create, the Swinging London of the 1960s. To me, though, he was just 'Terence', someone I knew and had become friends with as we practised judo together on a regular basis at the Budokwai.

I also immersed myself in different photographic techniques such as flash formulas, reciprocity failure and colour correction, all of which were vital back then. With today's multi-function digital SLRs you can literally point and shoot straight from the box and get half-decent results, so I think having to do things manually would scare a lot of budding photographers now.

It's like many things – if the conditions are OK, then you don't encounter too many problems, but it's when they are at their worst that photographers really earn their money. If the camera can't cope with the conditions, you can visualise the image all you like but recording that image is a different thing entirely. That job at *World* magazine was very good training for me because I simply couldn't go back to Mark with nothing.

Mark was demanding as an editor – he was a perfectionist and he wanted the best, and I learned a lot from that. I was, yet again, outside of my comfort zone, which is where you need to be because you don't learn anything when you're inside it. It takes a lot of practice before you develop the ability to release the shutter at the right moment and, even now, that's a concept that escapes a lot of people. There's this notion now with digital cameras that if you just keep shooting you'll eventually get the shot you want. I don't shoot that way – I'm much more selective than that.

The assignments were tough, too. Some of them could take weeks to complete and I really had to be inventive sometimes to get the shot required. One of my assignments was to shoot some images for a piece on smuggling in the eighteenth century. Now, how the hell do you photograph something like that? And it was winter, so it was a real challenge.

First off, I read up on the topic, and I learned that smuggling then wasn't based out of Cornwall as I'd assumed, it was focused on a part of the coast near Deal, in Kent. The smugglers used certain techniques and equipment, and I thought that I might be able to make a good image of some of the kit they used, but I didn't know if any of it still existed.

I rang Customs and Excise and eventually I got through to someone there who was quite interested in that area of history, to the point that he was involved in re-enacting eighteenth-century smuggling. How's that for luck? I arranged to take photographs at his office, thinking it might be some grand Georgian building by the Thames.

What I was hoping for was a nice Georgian window that I

could lay things out beside, with a nice bit of natural light streaming through. But you hope for the best and prepare for the worst so I took along an old tent and some rope, just to be on the safe side. When I arrived at the location, I wasn't entirely surprised to discover it was a modern office building with no windows. But as I had come prepared with the canvas and rope, I managed to make it work.

I arranged afterwards to get some images of the re-enactment guys in a specific eighteenth-century scenario, so I started to give some thought to a venue for the shoot. I'd been running some courses for the Countryside Education Trust down at Beaulieu in Hampshire, and there's a historic maritime museum near there called Bucklers Hard on the edge of the New Forest, with lots of seventeenth- and eighteenth-century buildings. I arranged to meet the guys there, and when I got there, I found an old white rowing boat, so some ideas started to come together. I had various concepts: one was the Kipling poem, 'A Smugglers Song', and I felt that was the right one for the job. I put the guys in the boat and took them upriver, dressed in their eighteenth-century clothing, and equipped with muskets and old lanterns. It was a bit of a Heath Robinson approach but I got some great imagery from that shoot. Those were the sorts of challenges I was up against. It was never straightforward.

And that's how my career as a photographer started. Every couple of weeks or so, I went into the *World* offices and collected a big case of Kodachrome 25. That was unusual, but wonderful – before digital cameras, film was the biggest expense for all photographers, and the reason that all but a few high-end photographers had to choose their shots carefully. *World* was very demanding as a magazine – they wanted quality images with maximum depth of field, absolute clarity and sharpness, lots of colour and creativity, and they knew that meant providing the best quality film, unlike most other magazines whose photographers had to buy their own. *World* wanted the best and that forced me to up my game, by schooling myself in all of photography's different techniques.

But I loved it. I felt very lucky to be doing something I enjoyed, something that was a hobby for so many people, and I was not only being sent on some fascinating assignments, I was getting paid for it too. I ploughed all the money I made back into lenses and cameras, and kept on developing and expanding my repertoire.

Now I was working and doing something I enjoyed, the opportunities for teaching bushcraft were few and far between. Also, I had no time or energy to spend on marketing myself. That's not to say that my love for the outdoors took a back seat. I still headed out to the forest whenever I could – how I could I not? It felt like home to me, after all. Something had to give though, and it was judo that fell by the wayside. As much as I loved it, my outdoor life won every time and I simply couldn't commit to both as I got older.

Photography suited me as a way to make a living and I think it's fair to say that at that time, in terms of whether I made bushcraft my future or taking pictures, it was in the balance which way I would go.

I don't think I ever made a conscious decision about the direction my future would take. I was still young and I had my whole life in front of me, so all I was concerned about at the time was enjoying myself and earning a decent wage. I think rather than choose between bushcraft and photography, I deferred the decision at a subconscious level and maybe I thought fate would take care of it for me. And I guess it did, given how things have turned out. Even today, photography is still a big part of my life, but I see the two interests as running side by side. It's healthy to have more than one interest – if you do just that one thing in life, you can get stale.

My passion for photography has run like a thread right

through my life and it's enabled me to record all the things I've seen, the places I've been, the things I've done and the people I've met. In many respects, it's created a visual diary of my life. Some of the cultures and ways of life that I have covered no longer exist so, to me, that makes having a photographic record all the more vital.

—————◆—————

Alongside working for *World* magazine, I was enjoying life. Having climbed Skiddaw in my mid-teens, I wanted to learn more, but it was only now that I had the independence and money to do so. I'd been fortunate to do some climbing with Arthur and Nick Parks, two of the mountain guides at Op Raleigh, but I really wanted to tackle the Alps. I wanted to become a good climber. It was important to me, and if that's how I feel about something then I'll put my heart and soul into it. That's how I've always been.

So I did tackle the Alps; however, I never became an expert in climbing because first and foremost the trip reaffirmed for me my love of the forest. It showed me that forests are more exciting – you go up a mountain, reach the summit and then you come back down again, but when you enter one of the world's great forests, you go in one side and you come out somewhere different. Sometimes, you go in and come out and *you're* different. And that's what rocked my world the most.

That's not to say I didn't enjoy climbing; I did, and it's almost as if some unseen hand was guiding me because it conferred on me lots of skills and experience that translate to bushcraft, so it was a vital part of the learning curve I'd carved out for myself. Thanks to my Alpine climbs, I acquired lots of experience of working with ropes, so I'm now pretty good with them. I can do everything from splicing to advanced rope-working. If there was a caving ladder that needed to be thrown over a high branch, you can bet your bottom dollar that I'd be there. I particularly enjoyed winter climbing because of having to use the ice axe. I'd become accomplished using axes in the forest, so I felt there was a kinship between my bushcraft and mountaineering.

It was while climbing in the Alps that I first encountered the Therm-a-Rest. What a wonderful device it is. It's a sealed, self-inflating foam mattress. Like all the best inventions, it was produced by people with a skill in the right discipline, to help facilitate a passion they had. In this case, the inventors were two former Boeing engineers who were avid backpackers. The Therm-a-Rest is a must-have piece of kit because it's light, portable and effective – it insulates you from cold ground and retains warmth, so it's really useful when you're sleeping out. If you're sleeping in the wild, wherever that might be, you need to be as comfortable as possible. A lot of people, when they start out, don't have a good enough sleeping bag but it's absolutely vital to have the best possible. A good one keeps you sufficiently warm, is large enough for you to be comfortable in, and is as lightweight and compact as science allows. A good sleeping bag and a Therm-a-Rest are two small things that make a huge difference.

Working for *World* magazine did give me some time to do other things. I wasn't out doing commissions for the magazine every day, so it allowed Woodlore to tick over in the background, and for me to run the odd course now and then. The RGS course all those years earlier was really paying dividends now. I'd gone back from time to time, and eventually undertook one or two lectures there myself. I kept in touch with a number of people I'd met there – yes, we'd all gone our own separate ways, but we had common interests in a niche market so we called on one another from time to time.

It was at one of these lectures that I met a couple of guys

from a company called Survival Aids. It had started out in the early 80s when the threat of nuclear annihilation was at its peak and the phrase Mutually-Assured Destruction (MAD) was part of the everyday lexicon. As well as selling things like filters for your nuclear fall-out shelter and other assorted goodies, the company started a club and they asked me if I could organise a few courses for them. That's when Woodlore really started to gather some momentum.

My first car was a humble Peugeot 104. Having the car enabled me to travel further quicker and I'd do things on a whim. Sometimes I'd head off to the New Forest and hone my tracking ability, only instead of just tracking animals, I taught myself how to track people. The principles are the same but by following people, my tracking skills really leaped ahead.

There's only so much you can learn in terms of tracking animals; after a while, it becomes tricky. It all depends on the season, and the ground – if you're in desert areas and you're following animals, or in snowy places, you can follow them over a considerable distance because their tracks are easy to see. I loved it when it was snowy; I'd get a pair of skis on and follow fox tracks for miles. But a lot of the time when they're travelling through wood and the ground is hard, they're so light, they leave virtually no sign. It becomes too slow to be able to follow them effectively. But following people is a different story. People are much heavier on their feet, and they leave a more noticeable sign on the ground, especially if they're running. I'd look for a footprint and follow it – that's all there was to it. I found I could often follow people all day, and eventually I'd get to a point where I would see the person I'd been tracking. I would watch them and they never knew a thing about it.

I'd been so wrapped up in my interests that the opposite sex hadn't really figured too prominently in my life up to that point. I'd had girlfriends, but there was never anyone serious, and unlike a lot of my peers I wasn't going off to pubs and clubs at the weekend, so opportunities to meet girls were limited. However, I wasn't exactly a hermit – I was out all the time, and I was running lectures on what I'd learned, so I suppose it was inevitable that I'd find someone eventually.

It was a few months later, in early 1990, that I met a young lady who caught my attention. I'd been presenting a lecture on bushcraft up at the RGS in London and this blonde girl came up to me and said, 'Hi, my name's Ffyona Campbell, I'm walking around the world.'

Quite frankly, I didn't believe her. You meet people all the time who make bold claims and most don't come to anything. I realised she was serious a few months later, though, when she came to one of my courses to learn some bushcraft to help her on the African stage of her trip.

She was a charismatic young woman with a drive and determination that were readily apparent and, after talking to her at length, it wasn't difficult to see where her wanderlust originated. Her father, Colin, was a Royal Marine officer whose postings sometimes lasted as little as six months, so she grew up on the move. By the time she was fifteen, they'd moved home some twenty-four times and Ffyona and her sister had been to seventeen different schools. She walked from John o' Groats to Land's End at sixteen, raising some £25,000 for the Royal Marsden Cancer Hospital in the process.

At eighteen, she set her sights on crossing America and left New York to walk to Los Angeles, and by the time she was twenty-one, she had walked the 3,000-odd miles across Australia, beating the world-record time set by a man. She'd written a book about the journey called *Feet of Clay*, which was published a short time after we met.

There was an obvious connection between us and we quickly became an item. I'd been living at home up until that point but I was spending an increasing amount of time away and I'd outgrown the nest. Ffyona and I started looking for flats in South-West London; we were lucky because we found a one-bedroom flat in Wandsworth that was perfect for us, and we moved in together a few weeks later.

Life was good. We had fun, and while most of my work revolved around Mark and the magazine, I was running an increasing number of courses, too. I did the odd lecture up at the RGS, and whenever I was at home I'd help Ffyona while she planned her African expedition. I have to admit, I found her project intoxicating – perhaps it enhanced the attraction. Every Friday, I'd throw everything in the back of the car and Ffyona and I would head out of town somewhere – it didn't matter where, as long as it was outside of London. We'd try to beat the rush out and we'd head down the A3 out of Wandsworth and find some countryside and go camping.

Having made the jump from living at home to living in a flat, money was tight at first and we were really just scraping by. I was running courses for the Countryside Education Trust, so that brought in a bit, and the odd lecture helped. There was no business plan or strategy on my part – I just took what I could find and did what I enjoyed. I was learning so much in the process, and really loving what I was doing. And all the while I was meeting people who had skills I wanted to learn and vice versa, so we'd barter and swap. I've always tried to find the best teachers if I need to learn something. I wanted to learn how to work flint so I tracked down the foremost authority on flint working in the UK, John Lord.

We traded skills – I taught him to light fire by friction and he taught me to work flint. I'd be sat in the flat in Wandsworth breaking pieces of flint to make an axe head and our landlord would be constantly sticking his nose in to see what the noise was – looking back, I suppose it sounded a bit like breaking glass so no wonder he was a little concerned.

When I was younger and I'd first started to make tools, it was very difficult. I was looking up archaeological books and looking at drawings and they didn't explain the *how*. They'd be illustrated with conceptual drawings but they don't exactly show you how it's done.

You have to strike the flint in a certain way. Flint's an igneous rock and when it breaks it does so with a conchoidal fracture, a muscle-shell shaped fracture, which means that if you hit it straight down, the shock waves go out on the angles of the cone at 120°, so if you wanted to break a piece off you have to hit it at 120° from the direction that you want the shock waves to go and you also have to make sure the platform that you strike is strong enough to take the force that you're imparting.

Once you learn those two things you're off and away; that's it, in essence, but of course then there are other processes involved. The advances in flint-working technology from the very earliest tools to the very latest tools that were still being made during the metal era, during the Bronze Age, are massive. Those conceptual leaps represent the development of the human brain. People look down their noses at Neanderthals and I've never understood that, because actually they were incredibly skilful people – they were able to live through an Ice Age, after all. We still joke about Neanderthals even though we now know that they are among us, that we have integrated with them. They survived on this planet as a species longer than us fully modern humans have; we are not yet in a position to make that judgement. And that irritates me. I have a great respect for them because I have learned to do the things that they knew how to do, and I can tell you how difficult they are.

Woodlore was really starting to gain ground now. I met

someone through one of my courses who said that his family owned some land in Hampshire that might be suitable as a venue for me to operate from. It was on Lord Selborne's estate in Blackmoor and it was perfect – acres of empty fields near a hill with woods nearby. It was everything I'd been looking for.

With the rent on the flat and Selborne, and running the car, it felt like I was barely making a living sometimes. I was doing such an eclectic mix of things but I was happy. I was young, and none of it mattered to me because I knew I was on to something. I just knew it was all going to turn around at some point. I honestly don't know where the feeling came from – it was that old sixth sense again – but it was unshakeable. I felt like I'd reached a point of critical mass; I was consuming so much knowledge on the one hand, and on the other giving out, educating others in the skills required to live outdoors. I'd really got to grips with the technical side of photography, the commissions were coming in, Mark was happy with what I was producing and everything combined to make me feel that I could do anything. That was all down to the days I'd spent in the open, the time I'd invested in the libraries, the courses, and the way I'd listened to and learned skills from people I met.

Then I landed a commission from Haynes Publishing to write a *Survival Handbook* for them. I got a small advance for that and wrote the manuscript quickly against the backdrop of everything else that was going on. They were happy with what I produced and, soon after, I landed a commission from Random House to write another book. Life was good, the money was coming in and I was also spending an increasing amount of time helping Ffyona make her preparations for Africa, which was the penultimate leg in her round-the-world hike. It also represented by far the longest, and potentially most dangerous, sector of her project – she was facing a monumental 10,000 mile trek south–north from Cape Town to Tangiers. There was a lot to plan, sponsorship to arrange, and she was also in the middle of a book tour, undertaking interviews to promote *Feet of Clay*.

It took a Herculean effort but eventually everything was in place for her to leave for Africa. The date was set for 2 April 1991, just six months after she'd attended the course I'd run. The day she was due to leave for Cape Town clashed with the start of another bushcraft course that I was running under the aegis of Woodlore, so we said our goodbyes by spending the night before in the woods, alone. I had commissioned a carbon-steel knife for her from Wilkinson Sword and had made her a sheath and an antler-horn handle for it, so I presented that to her as her going-away present. We'd agreed to wait for one another while she undertook her walk, but it was a promise born of the optimism and naivety of our youth. We didn't know it as we said our goodbye, but it was the last time we'd do so as a couple.

7

Walking in Africa

'*I never knew of a morning in Africa when I woke up that I was not happy.*'

Ernest Hemingway said that and, having been there many times over the past ten years, I can understand why. I spent a few years as a child in Africa, when my dad was posted out there through work, I still have some memories of it, but who knows the impact something like that has on shaping you as an infant? I don't – other than that I've always felt a connection with the continent. When Ffyona flew to Cape Town to start her walk, little did I know that I'd be joining her, renewing some connections but losing others . . .

I knew instantly that things had changed between us when she phoned me a month or so into the walk. I could tell by the tone of her voice before she said as much – there was a distance there and it wasn't the 9,000 miles between us.

'Raymond, I've had a lot of time to think and my feelings for you have changed.' And that was that.

We agreed to stay in touch – what's the saying? 'Just good friends', isn't it? But I don't think either of us expected to hear from the other ever again. I can't say that it came as a huge surprise to me but it hurt all the same. Still, they say the best thing to do is pick yourself up, dust yourself off and carry on. And that's exactly what I did – I gave notice on our flat in London and I moved back home. There, I knuckled down to finish the book on survival I'd been working on for Random House.

While I was busy in London, Ffyona had been making good progress in Africa – right up to the point when she arrived in Zaire (now known as the Democratic Republic of Congo). Her timing was immaculate; in May 1990, Zaire's President Mobutu had agreed to the principle of a multi-party political system with elections and a constitution, but he delayed in setting out details of the reforms. Ffyona was about halfway through the country when its soldiers began looting Kinshasa in protest at their unpaid wages. Things unravelled very quickly after that, to the extent that over 2,000 French and Belgian troops, plus elements of the Foreign Legion, arrived to evacuate some 20,000 endangered foreign nationals. Ffyona was one of them, and she and her team were forced to abandon both their Land Rover support vehicle and the project in the city of Kisangani and head home to England.

She'd been back in London some two weeks when she called me again. It was the morning of 14 October 1991. She was, as ever, straight and to the point.

'Ray, do you want to come to Africa with me and walk unsupported? I want to get back to my walk but I don't think the support vehicle will still be there. Will you come and help and take care of me? I think you're the only person who can.'

By this point, things had settled down a little – both in Africa, and between us. I didn't hesitate. I had some clear time ahead so I could afford to devote a few months to her project. She said she'd pay me, but even before I knew that I'd already said yes. It would have made no sense for me to undertake an expedition like that for my own benefit, but to use my skills for someone else's? Absolutely. It felt like a vindication of everything I'd learned. She needed someone who knew bushcraft, someone who knew their way around a camera, someone who understood her and what she was doing and who supported it. I fitted the bill.

At that time, Zaire was still too dangerous for her to return to, so we decided to pick up her walk in the Central African Republic (CAR) which was the nearest northern border to where she'd abandoned the attempt at the end of September. The Guinness Book of Records said that was acceptable and so we went. We flew out of Heathrow a week later and after a short layover in Lagos, where we waited for our connecting flight, we arrived in Bangui, CAR's capital.

I'd known before we left London that it was going to be impossible to continue the walk with everything we had to carry. Even if everything had fitted comfortably into two over-sized rucksacks – and the medical kit alone would have taken up more than one – carrying that amount of weight in the African heat over such a long distance would have been a reach too far. I'd decided to look for solutions once we arrived and one presented itself almost straight away.

I noticed that the locals used carts – battered metal panels that were welded together to form a rectangular box. The box was then mounted on a couple of wheels and towed behind a bicycle. I bought us one of these – it comfortably swallowed all of our gear with room to spare, but instead of trailing it behind a bike, I decided to push it along. As it transpired, I didn't have to push it far – we had arranged a lift from one of Ffyona's contacts who took us as far as Bangassou on CAR's south-eastern border with Zaire.

We were both tired from the journey and our feet hadn't touched the ground so we needed a cheap hotel, somewhere to dump our stuff and get some sleep. There wasn't much to choose from so we selected the one that looked the best of a bad bunch. But best is a relative term – our room was the sort of place where you would want to pitch a tent on the bed. The mattress had so many suspect stains it probably had its own ecosystem. It was truly awful but the fan worked, so we cleared space on the floor and slept there. We were up and away first thing the following morning; I pushed the handcart and Ffyona's walk was on.

I wasn't in the best place, physically – two or so days in and I'd already picked up some sort of bug. I had a really bad case of the runs, which is bad enough when you're in the comfort of your own home and you've access to your own bathroom. In the African bush, it makes life, er . . . interesting, to say the least. Despite this, we settled down into a comfortable rhythm, and we were making good time – we covered over 300 miles in the first ten days.

There isn't much you can plan for on an expedition like this – again, it's very much about the journey rather than the destination, so we'd sleep in the bush at night and strike out again shortly after first light. I was just taking everything in, watching, listening and learning – getting acclimatised. We were reactive, rather than proactive, just taking everything in our stride.

I realised quite early on that it was going to be difficult to sleep in the bush on a regular basis, if only because the locals would descend from nowhere, telling us, 'You can't stay here, it's dangerous. Come stay in our village.' From our perspective that prospect didn't make us feel any safer, but after a few nights of repelling offers of accommodation we talked it over and agreed to give it a try – we both wanted to embrace and learn as much of the local customs and culture as we could and we were never going to do that if we disengaged and spent every night in the bush. So we established a pattern. Towards the end of a day, we'd arrive at a village and ask to stay under the chief's protection. That was really interesting because it was a really good learning curve and each morning, invariably, some of the villagers would want to help us by pushing the cart, which was just marvellous and really took some of the pressure off.

We were making good progress but there was no question that the loss of Ffyona's Land Rover left her feeling vulnerable and me a bit concerned. The whole point of me being there was to protect her, keep her safe and ensure she came to no harm. This would have been easier with a vehicle, as then I could have gone up ahead of her when I felt it was necessary or hung in behind her to keep watch. There was no telling where the Land Rover ended up, so there seemed little point in lamenting its loss, and on the plus side walking did give me a huge insight into how the locals lived. Walking through those villages, we met generous people with a great deal of humility. They had nothing really, but would invite us to share what little food they had and they'd cook for us. It was truly humbling.

We were approaching Bambari when providence shone on us in the form of an Exodus overland truck. The overland trucks are a frequent sight in Africa and represent the cheapest way for most independent travellers to cross the continent. They're like a cross between a coach and a truck – a truck with a coach-style body instead of an ISO container or other type of cargo platform. Travellers all muck in, cooking, digging the vehicle out if it gets bogged down, and accommodation is generally in tents out in the bush. It's completely informal and it puts continent crossing in reach of most of those with a dream. Although there's an ultimate destination for each truck, it's not about that; it's all about the journey. Consequently, if the drivers see other travellers walking, broken down or otherwise stuck, they'll often stop to offer assistance.

Unusually, at first the truck rumbled past us, leaving behind a pall of dust from the track, but then we saw brake lights come on and it started to back up. The driver wound down his window and said he didn't stop when he first saw us because he thought we were missionaries. And what was it about our appearance that made him think that? 'It was because you both looked so clean.' (We'd made a point of keeping clean – I run a tidy camp when I'm out and about because I think that it's bad admin to walk around all muddy and dirty.)

We really struck gold with the truck. The driver explained to us that he was heading across the border and back to Zaire and his was the first overland truck to make the attempt since the riots. Things had settled down somewhat since Ffyona had been evacuated. He told us that he'd be driving as far as Bumba on the Zaire River (now the Congo River) before heading east and on to Uganda. Ffyona wanted to get back to Kisangani – it had been eating at her since we arrived back in Africa and she was determined, if at all possible, to pick her walk up right where she'd been forced to abandon it. The truck wasn't going there, but it was going in vaguely the right direction, so we accepted the driver's offer to take us as far as the town of Bumba.

One thing struck Ffyona and I immediately as we drove back along the road we'd just spent so many days walking. We couldn't believe how different the Africans looked and acted as we passed them. They were the same individuals who had accommodated us, but gone were the helpful, dignified, proud people who'd given us charity, invited us as guests into their villages – we were on a truck now, so as far as they were concerned, we were a different tribe. It was instructive to say the least. As we passed, they slouched peasant-like and begged the truck, and in turn, all of us in it. I was shocked and dumb-struck. This was a very different Africa to the one we'd seen; it was all but unrecognisable. By virtue of the fact that we were on the bus, they saw us as wealthy and that made them, in turn, feel poor.

That said, it's an aspect of life in Africa that I'd never have seen had I not initially accompanied Ffyona on foot – it's a perspective that's denied so many, and it remains for me one of the most profound experiences of my life. There was so much that happened in those first 300 miles, but more than that, it was an acclimatisation. The trip gave me a really helpful insight into the African psyche.

By the time we arrived in Bumba, our two had become four. Among the ragtag group of paying tourists on that truck, we struck up an immediate affinity with two independent travellers: Michael Duffy, an American national and former Marine who was trying to cycle across Africa, and Johann Sundblatt, a huge, hairy young Swedish guy with a long, straggly beard. Meeting those guys was typical of Africa at that time. So many people were trying to cross it, but their journeys were fraught with difficulty on a good day, danger on a bad one; it was a volatile continent and trouble would suddenly erupt any time, any place, anywhere. Wars were commonplace in countries with unstable military governments and corrupt police and border officials were a fact of life. It all added up to myriad travellers from across the globe all in the same place, trying to find alternative routes to where they wanted to be.

Mike and Johann were both heading in similar directions to us so they both decided to come as far as Kisangani with us. We found another filthy hotel and took two rooms there but it was a bizarre place. Everywhere you looked there were Art Deco lanterns that the Belgians had brought in when they annexed the Congo as a colony – they must be worth an absolute fortune. You couldn't get them out though – they're an integral part of the great expanse of the peeling, dilapidated concrete structure that was our hotel. They were true works of art and so incongruous given where we were. As I was learning though, Africa is like that – a litany of things that you just couldn't make up.

The following morning, we said goodbye to the driver and the other passengers and the truck left to continue on its journey to Uganda, minus Ffyona and me, Mike and Johann. There was a definite air of intimidation around us in Bumba, a really tense atmosphere that you could have cut with a knife. Due to the violence and uncertainty that had led to foreign nationals being evacuated, all financial aid to Zaire had been suspended. The locals were really in a bad way financially – they were desperate. They all wanted our trade because it meant cash for them – *we* represented cash to them, and I guess we felt it so palpably because the four of us were the first 'tourists' since the trouble had ended. Travelling in Africa is nothing like travelling in a place that's 'safe', such as Australia or Europe. And this part of Africa most definitely *wasn't* safe – people were saying to us, 'Your lives are in danger – you should leave here.' That really didn't instil confidence in us.

We decided to head towards Kisangani upriver so we hired a *pirogue*, which was easier said than done, mainly due to the fact that I didn't know the first thing about African negotiations. I just bulldozed my way through and doubtless provided great entertainment for the locals. We got there eventually and ended up with two *pirogues* that we chained together. We also hired some locals to crew the boat and a captain – Joseph – to look after it all. Eventually, we loaded up and set off down the Zaire River, into the great unknown.

<hr />

When we were on the move along the river, we could get to the stuff in our rucksacks, but realised they would present a potentially lucrative target to any light-fingered locals if we went ashore, so we'd bought some big grain sacks in Bumba. They proved to be an inexpensive but wise investment; we placed our rucksacks inside them to make them appear a little less 'interesting'. It was a practical and simple solution to a potential problem, rendering our luggage invisible to prying eyes. The only time we really stopped was to cook on the shore, although on a couple of occasions we'd go to a local village and prepare food. We'd learned while we were walking to cook rice the way the locals cooked it. You take palm oil and heat it in your pot and then add to that washed and rinsed rice. You don't spill a single grain – coat them all in hot oil and then add the water. We'd mix it up sometimes, add tomato paste or pineapple to make it interesting, and it always went down well.

We had one worrying moment on the journey when, at a stop for provisions, a local guy tried to buy his way onto the boat. We'd made it perfectly clear to Joseph when we hired the *pirogue* and crew that there were to be no passengers. This was because we would easily be overwhelmed with people and there would be a good chance that the boat would sink. So when this guy realised he wasn't getting anywhere, he tried to play the crowd against us. He was getting them increasingly agitated and the crowd seemed to multiply exponentially; there was a real air of menace and things felt like they could turn ugly any minute. We were balancing on a knife edge.

Suddenly, one of the crew – a big burly guy, like an African Bill Sikes – turned to the guy who was causing all the trouble. He grabbed him and said in a tone that brooked no argument, 'Get away from the boat or I'll break your head.' That was all he said. No drama, no histrionics, no idle threat . . . and that was it. As quickly as things ramped up, they dissipated again. The guy realised he was beaten, so he turned around and walked away. With him gone, the crowd dispersed and we continued on our way. But it was just one more example of how unpredictable Africa could be.

Our trip along the river lasted four days. And then we were there: Kisangani. Being among the vanguard of outsiders returning to the town, we had no idea what to expect. As it turned out, we weren't the first – we were the twelfth, thirteenth, fourteenth and fifteenth white people to hit Kisangani after the riots. I know this because we were told by a Portuguese man we met on the riverbank as we struggled ashore.

'Is it safe here?' I asked.

'Yes, yes, it's fine now. The rage has disappeared; people only want to rebuild their lives and businesses now. The army is still here – the very same people who started the riots, only now they're policing the town.'

That really cheered us up.

Ffyona asked him about the main hotel – this had been something of a landmark, a beacon to all the travellers and overlanders who had been making their way across Zaire before the army rebelled.

'It's open but it's no longer a hotel – it's er . . . it's now a brothel.'

There were a couple of rooms that the hotel made available to us and, as it was almost luxurious compared to where we'd stayed so far, we took them. We may have been sleeping in a brothel but at least the rooms were clean. We decided to make camp there while we gathered ourselves and made plans.

Now she was back in Kisangani, Ffyona was obviously curious as to what had happened to her Land Rover. She'd left it at a Catholic Mission on the outskirts of town. We knew it was a long shot, but we had time so she and I set off to the Mission to see what we could ascertain. It didn't take much detective work on our part – as we walked into the compound, Ffyona let out a squeal.

'I don't believe it! It's still here! Oh my God, it's exactly where I left it, Raymond. It hasn't moved.'

She was visibly delighted and, if I'm honest, my spirits lifted somewhat too, although I counselled caution.

'That's brilliant news, Ffyona, but don't get your hopes up too much – let's see if it's OK first, shall we?'

I have to say, I was amazed when I inspected it; it had a flat battery (unsurprisingly, given that it had sat there under the baking hot sun for some five or six weeks). It needed a service, and its fluids needed a top up, but otherwise it was fine; oh, aside from the ants' nest in the driver's footwell. We found a mechanic locally who did all the work there and then for the princely sum of £2.50 for the lot. He was as delighted with the 50p tip we gave him as we were at having got the vehicle back and working again. It was against all the odds, but it meant Ffyona's walk was back on with a vengeance; and we could leave behind the handcart.

When we got back to the hotel, we decided to take a few days to recharge our own batteries. While we'd been gone, Mike and Johann had learned of a beer truck that would be leaving at the end of the week for Uganda. They'd managed to get themselves space on the roof of that, so we'd be saying farewell to them and going our separate ways. That was to come though; in the meantime we had time, space and freedom, so we cleaned out the Land Rover, sorted out the kit and drank beer in the evenings.

I started work on getting the Land Rover properly set up for the expedition when I got back because I was horrified at how it had been set up previously. I'd be driving it now in support of Ffyona and I had my own way of making sure everything was shipshape.

One morning, we went down river by canoe about five miles back the way we'd come. I was interested in traditional skills and while we'd been on the boat, one of the crewmen had told me about a man he knew of who made fire using a fire plough. I'd heard of this, but had never seen it done before so I drove to the village where I'd been told I might find this man, and there he was. There are very few places in the world where people still use a fire plough – a piece of wood with a groove along its length, in which the tip of a stick is rubbed up and down – so it was amazing to actually find someone who was still using that ancient method of creating fire. Afterwards, the villagers insisted we head into the forest to drink beer – it was their way of saying thank you to the forest for its gifts. I liked that.

I remember trying to buy some dammar resin from one of the locals – it's combustible, so they use it to light their fires. I'd managed to get some from a young guy in the village but as we were concluding our trade, some old crone came out of nowhere and started bashing him over the head with a piece of burning firewood before snatching the dammar resin back. It had obviously taken her months to collect, and there's her son selling it off for the price of a beer.

I had a look through Kisangani's market, which isn't exactly your average place to go shopping as it's on the river. There's a market in the main square that most travellers headed to, but the best one to go to was just past the town's brewery. You look upstream from the riverbank and there are hundreds and hundreds of dugout canoes all chained together. Each one forms both part of the walkway from one to another, and an open display of the goods on offer – from food to plastic goods, every conceivable item that you might find in any market. What really stood out for me was the massive bunches of giant land snails that were tied together through holes that had been made in their shells. They're huge – a giant land snail will fill the palm of your hand, and they're a good source of protein to many in Africa. That market was a real eye-opener, a really fascinating place to explore.

Ffyona and I decided to head out and see if we could find her last camp site, which she thought was about three days' walk away. There'd been heavy rains since she'd been forced to leave the country so the landscape had changed massively and we weren't optimistic – bamboo can grow more than 3ft in a day there, and there was a lot of bamboo in that region. But it was important to her, and I was there to support her, so we looked. We were a long way out from Kisangani when

My mum and dad on their wedding day.

My dad in typical relaxed mood.

My mum stands proudly by the car she was learning to drive in. You can see from the vegetation – and the sunlight – that it was in Karachi, not England!

With my dad in the cockpit of a Spitfire at Biggin Hill Air Show. He taught me to appreciate the people who fought in World War II – and to admire beautiful machines like the Spitfire.

This bike gave me my first bit of independence – it was my third birthday present and the stabilsers weren't on it for very long!

I was never very keen on team sports but I enjoyed rugby. I'm on the far left, with all the hair.

Judo became – and has remained – a very important part of my life. The Budokwai in London was where I learned most of my judo skills. It's a temple to judo and other martial arts.

My teacher Kingsley Hopkins being thrown by Gunji Koizumi, who introduced judo to the United Kingdom.

Dickie Bowen (standing) was an exceptionally skilled exponent of judo – he studied in Japan and was an old-school practictioner.

Kingsley Hopkins, my mentor and friend – I took this photo of him when I was about 15 years old.

Mark Asuenda, editor of *World* magazine, who gave me my first big break as a photographer. Like all Italians he had an insatiable appetite for fungi!

Another big career break was filming my first TV programme, *Wild Tracks*, in 1994.

My first wife Rachel, who died in 2006.

We set up Woodlore together and she was very much at home in the outdoors – this picture was taken in British Columbia.

With Ewan McGregor in the Amazon. I really enjoyed working with him because he was such an able student and a good person. As he learned, comfort in the jungle is a matter of mastering a thousand tiny skills – like how to put up your shelter.

For me, being with indigenous peoples has always been as much about listening as anything else. That way you can learn so much and start to earn their respect.

Making a birch bark canoe with Pinnock Smith and then paddling it myself was a dream come true.

I had to really fight to get the television people to make a series which would bring
the story of the Telemark raid in World War II to a much wider audience,
so it was a special privilege to meet five surviving members of that secret mission
and visit the memorial to the bravery of the saboteurs at Vemork in Norway.

something caught Ffyona's eye. I stopped and she jumped out and ran through thick vegetation and into a gravel pit; she was searching for any evidence pointing to her having made her last camp there before leaving for the UK, and almost unbelievably she found it. There among the undergrowth was a damp, faded piece of paper – the packet of a used Sainsbury's chicken soup. We were right back where she'd left off.

The following morning, she started walking back to Kisangani and I trailed behind her in the Land Rover. She would walk what she termed 'quarters', each representing 16kms, and she'd aim to walk three quarters each day. I'd follow in the vehicle most of the time and generally look after her. Sometimes, I'd go a little way ahead, stopping at some of the villages on our route to engage with the locals. I'd make a point of talking to people, asking them about the trees and the plants nearby and what they used them for. I learned so much by doing that. There's a particular type of tree – they called it *kamba,* which is the Swahili for 'cord' – and its wood makes it a really useful medium for fire sticks. Almost all of the villages used it for that purpose, but it's a massively versatile plant and I talked to people on that journey who had all utilised it for a different purpose. In some villages they used its leaves as toilet paper; some used it for its medicinal properties . . . they even used the bark to make string.

It took us three or four days to get back to Kisangani but Ffyona was delighted because it meant she had picked up her walk from exactly where she had left off when she was evacuated. It also gave us a good opportunity to warm up for the walk proper and establish a rhythm, a routine with me in the support vehicle. We hit Kisangani on the Saturday morning, and that afternoon we bade a fond farewell to Mike and Johann who went off to join their ride – sitting on the roof of a beer truck to Uganda. We vowed to keep in touch and I was really sad to see them go – you form a close bond on expeditions like that, a really strong sense of camaraderie that is born out of shared experiences.

———◆———

That night, we woke to a loud banging on the door. That was highly unusual, so I was immediately on guard. I remember there was a huge tropical storm raging outside and the air was heavy. I quickly pulled some clothes on and guardedly opened the door.

In front of me was Johann, covered in blood.

'Christ, Johann, what's happened? Where's Mike?'

I shepherded him inside and he went straight to the bathroom where he threw up. We cleaned him up as best we could, tending to his wounds and then he sat on the bed:

'Guys, it was awful. We were on top of the beer truck with ten or so other passengers and assorted luggage. I think the driver had been sampling the merchandise because he was driving way too fast. The truck was completely top heavy, and we had to hang on to the sides every time we went round a corner.

'There was one particular corner that the driver was never going to clear; he'd been driving at 60 or 70mph and as he turned in, we knew we were never going to make it. I had a sick feeling in my stomach because we knew the truck was going to go over and I really thought that was it for me. Everything happened in a split second. I felt us going, and suddenly we were hurled to the ground among all the crates, tyres and assorted freight that had been stowed up on the roof with us.'

As he talked, he painted a vivid picture of the carnage that he'd witnessed. One guy had compound fractures of both his femurs, and a pregnant woman lost her baby in the most horrific way imaginable. Several of the passengers were killed.

Johann had been knocked unconscious when he landed and his back was absolutely peppered with glass shards. Mike had been hurt really badly; one of the spare wheels that had been up on the roof had broken one of his ankles when it hit him as he lay on the ground, and he'd also dislocated his shoulder. Johann had gradually swum back to consciousness and, under guidance from Mike, had relocated his arm for him – the pain from that would have been horrendous. With that done, Johann promptly dropped unconscious again. While this was happening, nearby villagers swarmed across the wreckage, running off with crates of beer that were strewn across the debris field.

Luckily for the wounded, word reached a nearby logging camp and a team from there with at least one medic arrived on the scene. They loaded the most seriously injured, including Mike, into a van and drove through the night to reach the hospital in Kisangani but there was little the doctors there could do to help as all the medicines had been looted during the rioting. They were on sale in the market place – grouped by colour, which was absolute madness. I'd seen a witch doctor ask for 'a red one and a yellow one'. Who knows how many people died after being administered lethal drugs simply because the witch doctor liked their colour?

We spent the rest of the night watching over Johann, pulling the glass out of his back and tending his wounds. The following morning, we found Mike amongst the filth in a local clinic, awaiting an X-ray on a rather enlarged, blue-coloured ankle that was the size of a basketball. After waiting an age, he was seen and it was no surprise to any of us that his ankle needed setting, but again, because of the rioting, all the plaster had been looted; there was none to be had anywhere in the clinic.

We couldn't leave Mike like that, so I fired up the Land Rover and headed through the town to try and locate some. Once again, fortune was on our side – I found some on sale in the market, and Mike's leg was set. That done, we did the best thing we could for him: we got him out of that dirty hole and into a French restaurant that – and you couldn't make this up – was serving frogs' legs, pizza and wine . . . on white linen table cloths. So we had an impromptu party. Mike probably thought he'd died and gone to heaven.

We were in the run up to Christmas by now, and just to complicate things further, we had to leave our hotel because they needed our rooms to expand the brothel. At least business was booming somewhere in Kisangani. Reluctantly, we packed up and moved to the main hotel in town, where we all spent a very merry Christmas together. But time was marching on and Ffyona's walk wasn't going to do itself, so a few days later, we said a big goodbye to Mike, who planned on remaining in the hotel until his leg had healed. Then with Johann, who had opted to come with us, we loaded up the Land Rover and set off to start Ffyona's walk proper.

———◆◆◆———

We soon established a rhythm: Ffyona would go on ahead, with Johann and me following in the Land Rover, and we made steady progress. I was the first up every morning and the last to bed because I had a responsibility to Ffyona – and I felt to Johann too – so it was my job to make sure everything ran smoothly and that we all got through safely.

Food wasn't always easy to come by, but we managed – sometimes only just though. At one stage, nobody would sell us chickens because the birds were just too scrawny, and I had to buy a tortoise so I could kill it and we'd have something to eat. Tortoises are an integral part of the diet in that part of Africa. It kept the three of us going for two or three days.

I was in my element because I learned things I could never have gleaned through any book. How much knowledge I acquired varied from village to village, but I always came away with some new skill or a piece of information to fill the gaps in what I knew. Seeing how people cooked things, the medicines, the plants, how they built and made things, and dealt with the tropical rain, it was all fascinating stuff. In some places I'd go to fill a jerry can from a river where the locals got theirs and the water would be crystal clear. In others, I'd do the same, but I'd look up stream a few yards and there'd be a guy washing his body in the water beside me. Sometimes, we'd come across entire villages that were deserted and I'd wonder what happened there. Was there a cholera epidemic? Had a massacre taken place?

I keep a tidy camp so I insisted that no matter how tired we were, we'd find time to wash both ourselves and our clothes each day. Johann and I would go down to the river at the same time as the men. We'd pick a point where they were washing, take our clothes off, and wash with them. They'd have a little stone there that you'd wash your clothes on. Of course, just when I thought we had a system going, I got it wrong one day and went down to the washing stone when the women were washing and I suddenly found myself surrounded by lots of men wielding spears. I had to play the 'I'm Johnny Foreigner' card to get out of that one.

On 31 December 1990 we crossed the Aruwimi River – where Tarzan lived, according to the novel by Edgar Rice Burroughs. That place sticks in my mind because Livingstone had a man speared to death there. Also, in the 1960s the daughter of a missionary family living there had come out from boarding school to stay with them, and one night she'd seen her whole family massacred by rebels. She was given a choice: become the bride of the rebel leader, or die. She bravely chose to die, suffering a horrific death after the rebels threw her to the crocodiles.

We didn't feel very safe that New Year's Eve because the local people tend to get very drunk, and things, perhaps unsurprisingly, were still a bit wild. On New Year's Day – 1 January 1991 – we stopped to stock up on food and provisions, and there were a lot of youths milling around. They'd run out of alcohol – they made their own from palm oil but once it was all gone, they'd be on the hunt for more. It's a pretty familiar scenario the world over, I guess. They started to surround the Land Rover while Ffyona was outside and I felt distinctly uncomfortable. They were drunk and unpredictable, and you could have cut the air with a knife. One of them, who I assumed was the leader, approached my door and made it quite clear that he wanted to have sex with her.

There's no easy way to deal with a situation like that but you have to seize the initiative because events are balanced on a knife edge. There's a crowd of them, Ffyona's outside, and there's just Johann and myself inside; we're already at a disadvantage before we start. I'd learned a bit about how to deal with the locals when we'd walked earlier, so I invited the leader of the guys to come closer. I had my window down and as he leaned in, I showed him the machete that I held in my hand down by the door.

'If you want to sleep with her, you'll sleep with this first,' I said, smiling as I looked him straight in the eye.

He got the message loud and clear because he backed off and walked away. Importantly for him, I'd allowed him to save face because the rest of the group neither heard what I said or saw what I had in my hand.

That resolved that – you have to know when to be firm but just as importantly you need to know *how* firm to be. That's the difficult thing and a lot of people make the mistake of not being firm from the off. If you do that, you've shown weakness and weakness will be exploited. One of the key things in Africa though is that you have to allow people to save face. There's an equilibrium that has to be maintained, so you tread gently. We learned very quickly that we needed to be constantly aware of and sensitive to the background at all times.

8

Heart of Darkness

There were many occasions when there were difficulties. We frequently found people trying to break into the vehicle – both when we were outside it, and sometimes inside. Sometimes things unravelled very quickly, and it got down to us having to beat them off physically with sticks. I always made sure that I had an escalating level of force available – from my fists, through to sticks and ultimately, a very sharp and fearsome-looking machete. We did a good job of looking after Ffyona, although in an environment like that, unless we were walking alongside her at all times, armed with a gun, we could never entirely guarantee her safety. There was one occasion when I was a matter of yards behind her and someone punched her in the face because they wanted to steal her sunglasses. It was that desperate. You couldn't drop your guard at all, not for a second.

We were in unknown territory so, while there were a few things that we could anticipate, most of what we did was just thinking on our feet. There was no book to refer to because Ffyona was the first – no woman had ever walked across Africa before, and I have to say she was brilliant. Her planning was excellent; she did very, very well and she was incredibly brave. Most of the time, she got on famously with everyone she met but there were always these unpredictable scenarios and we never knew what would happen, so we simply couldn't legislate for it. One thing we had agreed from the off was that we wouldn't pay any bribes; that was a given.

Nobody tells you the truth before you get to Africa – all I'd heard before I got there was the good stuff: the beautiful scenery, the pared down existence of the people who lived there and how stoically they coped with having almost nothing to their names. I didn't know anything about the aggression we'd find, the sheer bloody-mindedness, the *violence*. You'd walk through the villages on a Sunday and all the men would go to church. Afterwards, they'd go to a little *shebeen*, which invariably consisted of a hut and a bench to sit on, and they'd drink their palm beer. They'd get very drunk and then the beer would run out. Come the evening, all you would hear was the sound of children crying because the drunken fathers had come home and beaten their children. I met missionaries who couldn't stand it. Nobody tells you these things; nobody mentions the bad stuff, the things you have to do.

There was one very dark period that lasted about three weeks where we were quite literally attacked every single day. People were either attacking Ffyona or they were trying to get into the vehicle and attacking that. Most of the time, we were crawling along at no more than 10 to 15mph. To keep Ffyona in sight, and be within easy reach of her, I was driving at the sort of slow speeds where we could have been overtaken by continental drift, so we were an easy target.

There was one particularly nasty scene in Aketi. We knew there were problems there because we'd met a few overland trucks coming through and they'd all had issues there with corrupt officials who had tried to get money out of them by saying that everyone needed to have their profession shown in their passports, which is complete nonsense – maybe thirty years ago they would have done, but that disappeared in the early 80s.

We decided that we'd aim to reach Aketi at around 13:00hrs because at that time, everyone's enjoying a siesta. We planned on Johann and I holding back in the Land Rover, with Ffyona walking through the town, then we'd come through separately and we'd be gone. It wasn't perfect, but it was our best option.

There was a bridge as we approached Aketi and as we got closer, we saw another Land Rover approaching from the other side. It was occupied by two independent travellers like ourselves, so we pulled alongside to talk with them. It transpired that as they'd driven through Aketi they had seen a barrier erected across the road; for some reason or another, they hadn't stopped – they'd actually crashed through it, and they were worried they'd get arrested. This worried me because I could see us heading into a storm that wasn't of our making. They were driving away from the mess they'd created; we were heading straight into it, in a vehicle that looked just like theirs.

Aketi looks like a town straight out of the Wild West. As we drove in, it was deserted; there was only one woman on the streets and she had a little fire going on which she was cooking dough balls. Ffyona had seen them too – ahead of us, she pointed and mouthed, 'Get some,' so I pulled up.

Ffyona carried on – she had to turn right, cross a railway line, and up to a roundabout. Johann hopped out and went over to buy some dough balls but as the woman was bagging them, he realised he didn't have any small change. So what should have been a quick, simple transaction felt like watching infinite monkeys as they tried to produce the full works of Shakespeare. While Johann was trying to sort it out, I noticed a man in a green uniform approaching. He looked vaguely official but when I looked at him, something struck me as odd. Then I realised what it was: there was no insignia on his uniform.

Johann arrived back at the Land Rover and climbed in just as the man in the green uniform arrived at my open window and started waving a pink chit at me. He looked slightly deranged and I felt immediately on edge. The last thing I wanted to do was to get bogged down in some long, drawn-out argument so I pretended I couldn't speak French. Then I adopted the classic Englishman abroad stance, shouting, 'Jolly nice to meet you, old chap. Sorry, can't stop, places to go, people to see,' and with that, I shoved the gear lever into first and went to pull away – which is when he upped the ante and grabbed the steering wheel.

I was younger then and a bit more hotheaded but I felt seriously threatened by him doing that. How dare he try and take control of the car? So I pulled my arm fully back and slammed him in the face with my elbow. He went down and I floored the accelerator, trying to make a break for it. We flew across the railway lines at speed, causing everything in the back that wasn't strapped down to become temporarily weightless and float for a second before unceremoniously crashing back down. Ffyona heard us and looked back as I signalled at her to up her pace a bit. Then I backed off – I wanted it to look as if we were nothing to do with her. Then I heard a squeaking sound; as I looked round, it was the man in green again, trying to catch us on a rickety old bike. So I started shouting in French, trying to raise a commotion.

'*Voleur, voleur, voleur!*' I said, pointing. *Thief, thief, thief!*

That elicited no more than a disinterested look from the few locals who woke up at my shout; their faces said, 'Yeah, and so what?'

As I turned the corner, ahead of us was a military base with an armed soldier at the front. I shouted at him, 'Arrest this man, arrest this man, he's a thief. I insist you arrest him.' That's when I looked ahead and saw Ffyona being chased by a group of people.

Suddenly, out of nowhere, more people crowded around the vehicle so I floored the accelerator again. Just as we shot forward, Johann shouted, 'There's a guy on the roof!' so I slammed hard on the brake, pulling up on the handbrake to bring us to a sudden stop more quickly. Physics took over then and the guy who was on our roof suddenly learned how to fly without wings, shooting forwards like an Exocet missile and falling to the ground some 10ft ahead of us.

Ffyona had started to run, so I accelerated after her, which is when I noticed a man run out from a hut along the edge of the military base with a brick in each hand. He pulled his arm back, making as if to throw one at us through our windscreen, and then I did something that tends to work in Africa – I looked him in the eye and extended my arm to point at him.

For some reason, Africans really don't like that so he froze on the spot and I immediately turned the wheel to drive at him, forcing him to jump out of the way.

While this was going on, the man in the green uniform had somehow overtaken us on his rickety bike and as I looked ahead, he had caught up with Ffyona and was wrestling with her. This was beyond ridiculous – we only stopped to get some dough balls. The man in green had broken away to move in on Ffyona so I seized the opportunity and accelerated. I used the Land Rover to push him against a fence and pinned him there; that was him dealt with at least.

Then someone who appeared to be the head honcho came over to my window. I looked him in the eye and told him, 'This has gone far enough. Back off! We're just trying to leave this place.'

He insisted we go to the police station a short distance away (in reality, just another hut). So Ffyona, Johann and I, the head honcho and the man in the green uniform all made our way there. When we arrived, someone decided they wanted to search our vehicle. I knew this was happening because of the trouble they'd had earlier with the guys in the *other* Land Rover that we'd spoken to as we crossed the bridge to Aketi. For some reason – mistaken identity, or merely the fact we were all white too, and we had the same make of vehicle – the locals took all their frustration out on us.

It transpired that the guy in the green uniform was a police officer. So I said to him, 'If you're a police officer, why do you have no badges on your uniform identifying you as such?'

His response?

'I'm a secret policeman'!

Honestly, you couldn't make this stuff up.

In the end, they let us go in return for a bar of soap – because Ffyona had apparently 'dirtied the guy's uniform' when he wrestled with her – plus an umbrella and two aspirin. No, I've no idea why the umbrella, either. But the aspirin? They were 'for the headache you've caused.'

Our 'adventure' in Aketi was like a low-rent, poor man's version of Indiana Jones, written by Kafka and acted out by idiots. It was really very funny when we looked back on it. Whatever they'd thought when we arrived, by the time we drove out of Aketi, people were waving at us. I think they were sorry to see us go. We weren't sorry to be leaving.

All joking aside, the incident in Aketi could so easily have turned serious. Like so many of the incidents that we were involved in, it could just as easily have fallen the wrong side of the knife edge and who knows how things would have finished? That wasn't the only 'incident' to befall us on the walk, although some, such as the following account, were mere annoyances by comparison. This one took place in Gemena, near Zaire's borders with CAR and Congo.

As we drove into town, we were once again stopped by a 'police officer' who asked me for our papers. We'd been given a letter to present for incidents such as this by the British Consul in Kisangani. It said that we were in Zaire as the guests of the government for Ffyona's world record attempt and we should not be delayed by any persons, but afforded any assistance we required. I thought it might be a good time to present it, but I had an idea of what we would be up against as soon as I handed it to him – he held the letter upside down. He couldn't read. I interrupted him and said, '*Écoutez-moi!*' and pointed at Ffyona. 'This woman is very important and she is here under the protection or your embassy in London. She's *extremely* important and when she returns, she will be asked, "Did you have any problems in Zaire?"' and Ffyona piped up and said, 'Yes, Gemena!'

And the guy couldn't get away fast enough. He all but saluted us as he left, but it was a prima-facie example of just another day in Africa. So much faux authority; the best way to deal with it was through bluff, smoke and mirrors. It meant we were living on our wits throughout the trip, which is enormously tiring on its own without even taking into account everything else we had to deal with. It became part of the background noise, just something we had to do each day to survive – a bit like eating or drinking.

Don't get me wrong, I have a very healthy respect for the African people we met but the corruption that we – and they – had to deal with felt really pernicious. It destabilises everything and reaches into every stratum of society, so it's like a cancer eating away at respect for authority. Most of the people we met were lovely, really hospitable, humble and full of warmth. On the occasions where we'd driven ahead of Ffyona, we'd go into the backstreets of villages, into the real back edges of towns that most travellers never get to see. These are the places where they grow the plants and herbs they need for midwifery; I saw funerals, and people driving their cars into rivers to wash them – all the bits of African life that you never usually get to see. I found that really interesting, really educational and enriching.

We'd made good progress and soon it was time to leave Zaire for CAR. There's a border river crossing at Zongo that takes you across to Bangui and it was here that I learned the rules of a popular game in the African heartland which is called 'Try to Make the White Man Go Red in the Face'. It seemed that whenever we tried to do anything in Africa, a crowd would quickly gather. It's amazing what passes for entertainment there and I guess we were a break from the norm – something for the locals to look at, and laugh at. I was trying to reverse our Land Rover onto the ferry but every time the crewman tried to give me directions, the crowd would shout and drown him out. And I quickly realised they were trying to get me to blow a fuse so they'd see me lose my temper. That was the aim; so I stopped, got out and laughed at them. They laughed, and then we got on much better.

Once we landed at Bangui we had to clear customs and immigration, so Ffyona went in to deal with the paperwork while Johann and I stood outside by the vehicle. We'd heard there was often trouble while you waited for clearance, so we'd both got out armed with sticks, and in retrospect I'm glad we did.

We'd been warned beforehand that there are groups of thieves who hang around outside the border control offices in Bangui. They prey on the unwary, stealing their vehicles or otherwise disabling them while their owners are inside the offices dealing with paperwork. Their brazenness was astonishing, given that Johann and I were both standing beside our Land Rover – there was a group of between ten and twenty people milling around and the aggression coming off them was incredible. One of them broke away from the crowd and, calm as you like, approached us. Given his stance – and the tools he had with him – it was clear that he was determined to break into our vehicle. He must not have seen me, because he gave Johann a wide berth and made for the driver's side of the car, which was where I'd stationed myself. Both Johann and I adopted an aggressive stance and pointed our sticks at this guy, threatening him. He realised he was beaten, so he slunk back into the crowd.

If we thought that was an end to it though, we had another think coming. As the crowd absorbed the aggressor, they started drawing their fingers across their throats and ratcheting up the aggression. It felt like they'd have happily killed us, given the opportunity. It didn't help that Bangui was a Foreign Legion garrison so the level of violence there was of an order several times higher than elsewhere. All we could do was brazen it out. You cannot afford to show any weakness whatsoever. We stood there on the corner of the vehicle pointing our sticks at individuals in the group and shouting, 'You!' again and again at various people. They hate that; it's really intimidating to them, so they kept their distance.

A short time later, Ffyona left the office with our clearance and got in to the passenger side of the car. I thought that was it, but as I went to pull away, one of the gang obviously decided he wanted to show how brave he was to the crowd. He ran at the passenger side at full tilt and tried to slash at the tyre with a razor blade. He was easily dealt with – I turned the wheel towards him and accelerated. It's difficult to focus on anything other than getting out of the way when you've got two-and-a-half tons of Land Rover bearing down on you.

Although we escaped the border point at Bangui with our vehicle – and our lives – intact, the trek came to a halt when we reached the town proper. Bangui became our temporary home for seven weeks while we waited for the next tranche of Ffyona's sponsorship funding to come through.

There was one occasion not long after we arrived that Ffyona had to go to the Sofitel on the other side of town to use the phone. Sadly for us, this meant going past the checkpoint at the border crossing again, so we deliberately chose a time of day when we knew it would be quietest – generally, the locals siesta in the afternoon, so many of them would be asleep.

But again, after Ffyona got back in the car, one of the guys ran at us, and this time he reached through my open window. I was in no mood to negotiate so I grabbed his arm and put him in a wristlock. He wasn't expecting that, and I held him in place for a few seconds, and then quickly wound the window up, trapping his arm at the top. Then I hit the accelerator and drove off. I soon left him behind.

We found out later that the trees near this border checkpoint have razor blades embedded in the bark so that the thieves always have them to hand. Their plan is simple, and in most cases effective: while the vehicle is unattended, or your attention is diverted, they slash your tyres. Then, while you're occupied changing the wheel, they'll rob you. The police are in on it, so if you call them to report what's happened, they'll find some non-existent or invented infringement and then they'll rob you too. Twice at this border point was enough – after that trip to the Sofitel, we found another place where Ffyona could make phone calls. We weren't going to put ourselves in the firing line if we could possibly help it.

While we waited for the funding to come through, we planned the rest of her walk. She wanted to take the expedition up through Chad and on through Libya, which was the quickest, easiest and most direct route north. It wasn't without its risks though, so I started to analyse exactly what they were.

9

Out of Africa

Chad was well-known for its Zaghawas insurgents. They'd made a number of attacks on people over the previous year, so I made a point of plotting the locations of all the attacks on a map. Having done so, I could see a pattern emerging. They were coming into the CAR down the river and then attacking people along the roads either side, morning and evening, but always leaving themselves plenty of time to escape back the way they'd come.

My questions soon attracted the attention of a certain US intelligence agency. After all my hard work plotting and planning, I was called in to the US Embassy to meet with the CIA's head of station, who wanted to know what I'd discovered. In the process of tracking down the intelligence I needed to draw conclusions about the best time for us to travel and avoid the Zaghawas, I'd been asking questions all over town, so I guess the CIA soon got to hear about it – intelligence is its business after all, and there's a massive interest in that part of Africa due to Zaire's vast untapped mineral wealth. The French had a huge embassy there, too. Back then, Africa was a great big chessboard where the Cold War was played out.

After meeting with the CIA head, I managed to secure a meeting with General Canal, the then commander of French forces in Africa, because I thought he may be able to help with information on how we might get into Libya. He explained there were secret roads into the country and showed me where they were. Afterwards, I paid a visit to the Libyan Embassy and I was told we'd be safe in Libya (but then, they would say that, wouldn't they?). They said that the road was metalled for most of the way and we'd be taken care of. Finally, with the money due any day now, it looked like everything was falling into place.

But as if to prove that in Africa you can't take anything for granted, the French performed a complete about face two days later. I was called in again by General Canal and told that if we tried to go through Libya, we'd be arrested. The Lockerbie bombing was still all over the news and there was a very real prospect that if we went ahead we'd become hostages and the Embassy didn't want that to happen – let's face it, Libya was having enough bad press. So after all that hard work and planning, we were forced to reroute through Cameroon.

Finally, the last tranche of Ffyona's sponsorship funding came through, so once again we loaded up the Land Rover and travelled up through CAR. Because of the Zaghawas' attacks, I decided that it would be safest for us to travel at night and hide the vehicle in the bush by day, so that's what we did. We travelled in the cool of the night and tried to rest and sleep in the heat of the day. It was tough going, but it was different, and it worked – our drive through CAR was largely uneventful.

Did you know that you always, always, shake hands *with* respect in Africa? To do that, you place one hand over your wrist as you extend your other hand forwards. It was one of the subtlest and perhaps most important things I learned while I was there. Very few visitors to the continent know anything about it, but it's important that you always shake hands in that way, to show respect. It's all about being polite, friendly and genuine with people.

One day in CAR we had no food and, in desperation, I drove ahead of Ffyona a short distance and stopped at a village at the foot of a hill. Looking around, I saw a man who had some chickens, but they were scrawny and I knew from previous experience that he'd probably be too ashamed of them to sell one to a Westerner. So I went up to him and shook his hand in the traditional, polite African way, placing one hand over my wrist, and he seemed genuinely moved by that. I asked him if I could buy one and he agreed. I know for sure had I not shook his hand in the way I did he'd have said no; that's why it's so important to find out local customs and traditions before setting out on any kind of expedition.

But while I was paying him, I became aware of a noise behind me. When I looked, it was Ffyona and she looked distraught as she ran over to the vehicle.

She was in such a state; her T-shirt was torn, she had scratches on her face and arm and she was struggling to get the words out, but eventually I heard, 'Ray, somebody just tried to rape me.'

I was frozen in horror at the enormity of what she was saying, but all I could do was hold her until she stopped shaking, telling her it was all right now, she was with me and she was safe.

After a few minutes, she told me what had happened and that she'd managed to get away from her attacker. I'd heard of this kind of thing but had never had any kind of experience of it. I immediately took control; first, I'd need to find somewhere she could sit quietly, away from the general hubbub so she could collect her thoughts. The man with the chickens asked what happened, so I told him in French what Ffyona had told me. He was horrified as I explained it all and quickly organised a group of the villagers to try and find the perpetrator. He also had one of his huts cleaned out so that she'd have somewhere private to sit and recover from her ordeal as it was quite clear she was in shock. It was a very kind thing for this stranger to do for us, and a short time later he came back to ask me if she was OK. As he approached me, he extended his closed hand forwards and opened it, palm up in the respectful manner. Secreted inside was an onion; a tiny onion about the size of a shallot. He was giving it to us; it was his gift. I mean, what would that mean here in the West? Nothing? Less than nothing? There though, it wasn't what he was offering, it was the gesture. And in that context, the gesture was enormous, his gift to us was massively significant, and I believe it was all down to that handshake when we first met.

This whole episode epitomises African life and to be close to that means we got to understand it in a very African way. Tourists who travel to Africa have never had these experiences so, in essence, they can't really *know* that side of the continent. Those kind of experiences colour and inform your understanding at a fundamental level and when you work that intimately with African people, if you've had these experiences, they feel it and they understand that you know something more of their world and so there's a certain respect for you; they treat you differently.

Sadly, we never did find the man who'd attacked Ffyona, and it was just one more incident that she had to chalk up to experience. It is a mark of her strength that she shrugged it off and the following day was back on the walk, each step putting distance between her and what had happened, each stride taking her closer and closer to her objective. Yet again, Africa had humbled us and shocked us in turns. Yet again, violence and aggression had come from nowhere. To me, each attack, each incident highlighted just how much bigger Ffyona's task was than just the miles she had to walk to cross Africa. It was an expedition fraught with danger.

Finally, we crossed the border into Cameroon. My time with Ffyona and Johann was coming to an end because I had to get back to London for the publication of my second book. I had mixed emotions about leaving: I was loving my new relationships with Africa and Johann, and I knew I'd miss my relationship with Ffyona. We were together over a year and while we hadn't rekindled our romantic relationship during the trek across this wonderfully diverse continent, we'd shared something special. That said, all good things come to an end; that aspect of my life was over and I knew it. Life had to go on and I had my book launch to think about, so when we reached Douala I bid them all a fond farewell and caught a flight back to England.

That trip with Ffyona took almost seven months of my life, and it was a hell of an expedition with experiences and lessons that had a huge impact in shaping the man I've become.

Ffyona went on to complete her challenge, which was an amazing feat – a truly incredible achievement. However, she was treated abominably by the press on her return – castigated and censured when she should have been praised and held up as an inspiration. I think the press set her up. They saw her as a spoilt rich kid because she spoke nicely and was the product of a private education, but what difference does any of that make? Considering the upheaval of her childhood, I don't think her background conferred any advantage on her at all. None of it lessens or otherwise tarnishes what was a stunning triumph.

A lot of the animosity she faced stemmed from the previous trip that took her across the US, during which she had some awful problems. She became ill and was in danger of missing media calls set up by her sponsors – an astonishingly busy schedule of media appearances that would have stretched her when fit, let alone sick. Because she felt obligated, and because she didn't want to let her sponsors down, she ill-advisedly accepted a number of short lifts from her support driver – 15 miles a time, three or four times over a 1,000 mile stretch of her walk. She felt guilty about it so she went back and walked across America again, then wrote about all of it in her third book. She was attacked by the press for her admission. Had she been American, she may well have been criticised but it wouldn't have overshadowed her achievement. Here in the UK, though, people seem to want to knock anyone who aspires to be better, anyone who achieves success.

———◆◆———

Looking back, I learned several things on that trip. One of them was knowing when to be firm. I think this is something a lot of people who travel like that don't understand – they want to be all things to all people and you can't; you have to know where to draw the line, when to be firm, when to be friendly, how to be polite and respectful towards the people you meet.

They say the people you meet colour, shape and inform you – change you in certain ways – and in that regard I feel lucky to have met both Johann and Mike. Johann had this saying, which always made me laugh. If something went wrong, or if something broke, he'd say, 'Ah, it's OK, it wasn't a good one, anyway,' and I've hung on to that. He had a great sense of humour, and he was a really solid guy, a good man to have on your team. That made the man from Malmö a brilliant partner to travel with. In fact, it was a privilege.

As for Mike, I learned when I got back to England that he'd got his bike, which had been severely bent up in the crash, and repaired and welded it back together. You can do that sort of thing in Africa – there's always someone able to do whatever it is you need. Then he cut off the plaster because it was 'bothering him', put a bandage around his ankle and cycled to Uganda. There, he had his ankle re-broken and reset. I met up with him in England a few years later and it was really good to see him; we had a lot of laughs. Johann, though, dropped off the radar and I never saw him again after Africa. I often wonder what became of him.

The downsides? There weren't many, and even the incidents, the aggression and violence we encountered were all instructive in some way. Bad as they were at the time, we came through each one unscathed and somewhat wiser. I think it's also important to view them in context. When I joined Ffyona on her walk, we were going through some of the most unstable regions of the African continent, and working our way through countries riven by years of violence and unrest. We were considerably younger than we are now, and we were both perhaps rather more naive than the people we've become. Despite the trouble we encountered in the heart of Africa, my overwhelming memory is of a beautiful place that would call to me and draw me back countless times in the years ahead, and of those wonderful local people of modest means who went so far out of their way to help us and show us kindness.

Oh, and how could I forget malaria – I contracted it not once but twice, both times when we were in the absolute middle of nowhere. It's really not pleasant at the best of times but there, in the wilds of Africa, was just the worst experience. It's truly nasty – I felt like I'd been beaten up by a Rugby team and I was running a temperature of 103. Waking up in the middle of the night with the runs when you're sleeping in the bush is an experience I don't really want to repeat. The worst thing for me, though, was that I could hear life going on around me but I was unable to take part.

We did have medicine – Halofantrine – with us to treat the disease. This consisted of a course of six tablets; the first two stabilise your temperature; six hours later you take the second pair, which bring your temperature down, and once you take the third two a few hours later you're starting to feel you can communicate with people again. Over the course of the following week, you feel better every time you go to the toilet. When I got to Zaire at the start of the expedition I weighed thirteen stone; when I left Africa seven months later, I was half the man I used to be – almost literally. I weighed just eight stone.

In terms of my future, probably the best aspect of that expedition for me was that it clarified my feelings about the direction I wanted to take in life, and I realised how much I'd enjoyed talking about, and learning, new bushcraft skills. It was such an education but also it validated so much of what I'd already learned, and legitimised it too. Things like knowing how to get safe drinking water, how to cook in the bush, how to take care of yourself – they were all vital skills but now I had seen them in their true context. As much as anything, it was also a test of me, personally. On that front, at least, I felt I could hold my head high.

10
Changes

When I left England for Africa in 1990, I was at a turning point – one of those forks in the road of life that confront you every now and then. When I arrived in Africa, I still wasn't sure whether I wanted to devote my life to photography or whether to focus on the bushcraft, but there were no two ways about it – when I got there, I was undoubtedly a photojournalist but I knew as soon as I hit British soil on my return that things were different.

When I came back in the autumn of 1991, I learned that *World* magazine had changed hands and Mark had moved on. Mentally, so had I – I'd been so close to the outdoors for so long that, even though I still took photos, I no longer felt like a photojournalist. *World* had ultimately become a victim of its own success; it was bought out by the BBC, which appointed a new editor who wanted to make his mark on the magazine. He started to employ people like Sebastião Salgado to do assignments for the magazine and it started to lose sales because Salgado's fine art photography wasn't what the audience wanted; they wanted a home-grown version of *National Geographic*. *World* and I parted ways.

———————◆◆———————

The publication of my book for Random House went OK, but it coincided with the peak of the recession that hit Britain in the early 90s, so sales were disappointing. Ironically, sales of the survival handbook I'd written for Haynes were rather healthier, although by the end of its first year in print it had been stolen from almost every library in the UK – perhaps it was down to the recession starting to bite. The Random House book was something of a slow burner though, because it's still in print now.

While I'd been in Africa, all of the things I'd been teaching had proved incredibly useful, so I came away with a renewed interest in the culture of the outdoors. I was hungry to build on that, so Woodlore became my sole focus.

I met Rachel on a foundation course that I ran quite soon after my return to England, and I just *knew*. We hit it off from the beginning. She was a scuba diver – she worked for a company that specialised in teaching people to dive in Israel's Red Sea – and she was really keen to learn new skills. She had my attention from the off. She was one of those people who lit up a room, so it was inevitable really; she had her own gravity, so people were drawn to her.

She had this wonderful dark curly hair but she wore it short and it suited her. She had the most amazing smile, just wondrous; she'd smile and it was like being bathed in sunlight. She had these beautiful, deep hazel eyes, and a really sharp wit – a great sense of humour. She was always up to mischief! We got on like a house on fire. And though I didn't know it, she was almost nine years older than me – not that you would have known by looking at her.

We took things easy at first – we were just good friends initially, but it was a feint really. We both knew how we felt about one another, so why pretend? A few months after we first met, we decided to go to France together and I guess that's where it became official – we cemented our relationship there and when we came back to England, we were a couple.

We went to Normandy and I remember we'd forgotten to

change the lights on the car so we blinded everybody coming towards us. We didn't bother with camp sites, so ended up camping on the banks of the River Seine and in the Brotonne Forest, while avoiding *gendarmes* with their mobile headlight-testing kits who were looking for cars just like ours. It was beautiful. We went to Paris for a few days and it was just magical. It was a great place to forge the bond between us – just incredibly romantic. We had a great time together.

Not long after we returned, we made a home together in Eastbourne; it was Rachel and me, plus her two young children, Nathan aged seven and Ellie aged five. Our house was on the coast, so the South-East of England where the bulk of my work with Woodlore took place was easily accessible. Then Rachel fell ill with a throat infection and the company she worked for got really uppity about it; they were concerned at how long it would keep her off work and kept pestering her to return long before she was ready. We were both really annoyed by this – she'd given everything to that company, she'd never let them down or so much as taken a day sick before, so it felt really petty for them to treat her so badly, and it soured things somewhat. On a whim, I suggested that she resign and come and work for me, running Woodlore from a bedroom at our house, taking care of the admin. That way, I could devote all of my time to running courses while she ran the business. She loved the idea and resigned the same day. And we never looked back.

I know not every couple is able to work together, but it came easily to us. We trusted one another implicitly and it was all just very, very relaxed and easy. Rachel was dynamic, and she was really good for me; a lot of things fell into place. I've never been motivated by money, but I appreciate you can't get very far without it. What makes the business work – and this is something I learned at the beginning – is that I don't chase the money, I chase my interests. If you chase the money as well as your interests, you break the spell, so it's always best to have someone else sort out the finances. From the day she started working with me, Rachel always looked after that side of things, which left me free to concentrate on my strengths – being outside and furthering my knowledge. After she joined, Woodlore started to grow really quickly. Before I knew it I was taking courses back-to-back. The company grew and became more successful because I had the energy to devote to it, and the belief was there. Rachel brought order and direction to the chaos. We were the perfect combination.

Things were ticking along nicely, and within a year or so I became the subject of a television documentary – I'd given a lecture and I was approached by someone in the audience who was a producer for TVS. I quite enjoyed making the documentary, and it brought in more business, but it also gave me an idea. As Woodlore had to support both Rachel, the children and myself, I needed to find a way to boost its income and TV looked like the perfect medium. So in late 1993, I found an agent to represent me and he organised a meeting with Collette Foster, a TV producer at the BBC's Pebble Mill studios, in Edgbaston.

I liked Collette immediately. She was warm and approachable, and had a good track record. She'd produced the BBC's massively successful *The Clothes Show* and had an idea for a magazine-style series on the outdoors. She thought I might be able to present three five-minute items within that series, so I did a screen test. It took place in the Malvern Hills and the director, Kath Moore, asked me if I could find three things to make or eat using natural resources within 100m, and talk to the camera about them. Thanks to my bushcraft skills, and the lectures I'd done, it wasn't too difficult. In the end I got the job and I've never looked back. The cameraman who shot that section was Barrie Foster, who was Collette's husband. Kath directed me, and the sound recordist was Sam Cox. In years to come, we all worked together regularly on various commissions.

Kath clearly liked what I did because instead of three five-minute things I ended up being commissioned to do six ten-minute pieces. That is how my first ever TV series, *Tracks*, was born and I took to it like a baby takes to water. First broadcast in 1994, *Tracks* was a great success and ran for six series. It was made at Pebble Mill under the guardianship of John King. I liked John a lot; he was a very intelligent man, one of several very capable TV executives in the BBC at that time who had an innate understanding of their business and made it work. John was something of a wizard at the Beeb in those days and, rather appropriately, he liked to dress completely in white – I called him 'Zeus'.

Tracks was well received, it paid reasonably well and I enjoyed doing it. Not because it was TV – I've never quite understood the whole concept of people being 'famous' simply because they're on TV. To me, TV is a medium, the same as books, newspapers, magazines and the Internet. It's just a more efficient and effective medium for getting a message out which, for me, means sharing the knowledge and skills that I've acquired with the widest audience possible. It was also good fun because I was lucky enough to team up with a director, Paul Watson, who I really enjoyed working with.

I was keen to do another programme and the BBC was keen to work with me again, but which vehicle? *Tracks* had been set in and around the UK but the Beeb wanted me to do something more adventurous so they pitched the idea of dropping me into remote places so I could show how to survive in them. The problem was that what viewers would have seen would have been me killing and eating things, which would have been a bit gratuitous and unnecessary just for the sake of television. Of course, several other networks have since gone down that path but I wasn't comfortable doing it so I declined.

Then I suggested we go and film indigenous people around

the world – the real masters of living in the bush – engage with them and really get a feel for how they lived. We played with the idea, refined it a little and settled on filming in these places when they would be at their most inhospitable – at a time when no other film crew would even consider venturing there. I liked that idea and it found favour with the higher-ups at the BBC so we got the green light.

What we produced was broadcast as *World of Survival* – two series of six thirty-minute programmes filmed in some of the world's most extreme places. Those series were broadcast in 1997 and 1999 and we had literally weeks to make each film. Television was a different business then and, in the context of today's programmes, it was a simply unbelievable amount of time to invest in each episode. What it did do was enable us to really get each one absolutely right.

Having a budget that enabled me to do what I had been longing to do was a tremendous opportunity for me. My focus was on making sure I did a good job for the viewer. I wanted to make sure I did a good job of honouring the indigenous people that I went to see. But it was also an opportunity for me to go and meet people and ask questions that I didn't believe were being asked by anthropologists. I had a practical interest in the way they lived in the bush. Dr Johnston said that those who go in search of knowledge must first acquire it. To my mind, if you don't know anything about the lives of the people you meet then they will be inclined to treat you like a child, but if you can hunt, if you can make fire, if you can make shelter and you know how to take care of yourself, they see this; they know the time it takes to acquire those skills and they will treat you as an adult. From that, they might involve you in conversations that you would not otherwise have. That is what I wanted to try to tap into.

I don't think there's anything worse than a presenter going somewhere and acting like a complete idiot. It's a peculiarly

British disease and it's disrespectful of the people they're reporting on. But at the same time I didn't want to appear to be too pompous or too macho; I wanted to make the subject accessible to people.

World of Survival was great, a very special series to make. Through my involvement in it, I learned a lot about myself, a lot about television and a lot about what's needed to make films in remote places. All of the different hunter-gatherer groups that I ended up working with gave me the most amazing education. Looking back now, with over twenty years of television under my belt, I think somebody at the BBC was really smart in green-lighting that project, but at the time I just didn't realise how special it would be. Those programmes documented cultures that have now all but disappeared. The elders we filmed were the last flickers from an ancient fire. Because what we didn't realise then, was that the indigenous people we'd end up filming were, in many cases, part of societies and cultures that sat right on the precipice of change. In the years following, many of them made the step into a more modern world, and the changes that occurred were irreversible. Some skills that had endured for millennia were lost within a generation.

Making those sorts of programmes is incredibly complex so it's absolutely essential that you have the right people in the crew. I was lucky in that Kath Moore, who'd directed me in my screen test, was the series producer for *World of Survival*, so I trusted her and she got where I was coming from. I said to Kath right from the start that when we went into these communities it would be a two-way exchange. We'd be taking something away, but we would also be leaving something of ourselves behind so it was imperative to choose crews that were sensitive to that, because television can be very harsh; it can walk in and trample over everybody. Kath listened; she was brilliant and we selected our team accordingly. It's interesting that the two cameramen we chose – Barrie Foster, who'd also been involved in my screen test, and Alan Duxbury – were the two cameramen I'd work with on almost every programme I made over the following sixteen years.

Barrie was as accomplished as they came; a consummate professional prepared to take risks; there was nothing he couldn't achieve in filming terms. Alan Duxbury was also one of the best cameramen I'd ever work with – he was known as 'Steady Al' because he could hand-hold the sort of shots that most other cameramen used a tripod for. Alan would go to the ends of the earth to get the right shot. He was as hardy as hell, prepared to endure everything that the weather and the environment could throw at him if it meant he could film exactly what he needed. Both Barrie and Alan were very special people and we would go on to become firm friends in the coming years. We would soon realise that *World of Survival* was to be a real learning curve for us all.

For the first series, we filmed between late 1995 and early 1997 and we focused on six locations and their indigenous people. Episode one took us to Baffin Island with the Inuit for a film about the Arctic; episode two took us to Arnhem Land to meet the Aborigines who live in Northern Australia, with its high temperatures and humidity. For episode three, we travelled to Siberia to meet the Evenki nomadic reindeer herders of the Taiga Forest. Episode four looked at life on the island of Savai'i in Western Samoa. For episode five we travelled to Namibia to see the survival skills of the Jo'hansi bushmen, and for the final film we looked at the Spice Islands of Indonesia and went to the island of Seram where we filmed the Nuaulu, a rainforest people who are historically head-hunters.

All of the trips were memorable for different reasons, though some more than others. The travel we undertook, and the places we stayed at to research and make each thirty-minute episode, made each film an expedition in its own right. The planning, the logistics, the difficulties we encountered just in getting to each remote location and the inherent risk in being there made them some of the toughest expeditions I've done to date. But putting ourselves in some of the world's most hostile and isolated environments when nobody else would go there made it some of the best stuff I've ever done. In part, that's down to timing; it was a perfect storm in TV terms, benefiting from generous budgets, time and forward-thinking producers who were prepared to take risks in pursuit of really good television. When you endure – and sometimes suffer – the same privations and hardships as the indigenous people you are filming, you develop a bond that is quite unique. It becomes something special, a 'happening'.

I learned so much in making each programme, not just in terms of bushcraft – the new skills and knowledge I acquired from these indigenous people could fill a book themselves – but in terms of what I learned about TV. There's a lot of maturing, a lot of learning and growing in the world of television, particularly with the sort of programmes we were making. There was no training course – nobody teaches you to do TV, you have to learn on the job. I didn't mind that because it's how I learn everything really – by doing.

What was really wonderful for me was that we were making principled films; we knew what we were doing, what we wanted to convey, and ultimately the people we were filming came first. I'm not sure that everything that came later was like that. *World of Survival* is without doubt, one of the highlights of my TV career.

It was tough on Rachel, though, with me spending so much time away either through filming commitments, or running Woodlore courses, so it was always going to be hard for us in that respect, but it's just the way it was. That said, neither of us was particularly clingy – we were a strong couple but we were both independent people and we got used to it. We always made the most of the time we did have together, and whenever I was away filming, we always had a sat-phone with us, so that helped too.

What follows are my accounts of some of the episodes from *World of Survival* that really stood out for me. Whether it's the people, the place, the smells, the ease with which the programmes came together – it doesn't really matter. These are the events that have their own special place in my head and my heart.

II

40 Below

We travelled to Baffin Island in February 1996. Baffin Island straddles the Arctic Circle and lies in the Canadian territory of Nunavut. There was a crew of four on this trip – Barrie Foster; Dennis Jarvis, the director; Sam Cox; and myself, which back then was the absolute minimum number required if you want to get the job done. Today, TV executives think you can do it with a single cameraman who'll direct, record the sound and film at the same time. You can't – at least, not if you care about standards. I firmly believe that these same television executives consistently underestimate the intelligence of their audience. Viewers are smarter than they realise, and will always see through shoddy production.

That trip was a real eye-opener for all of us. In planning the programme, I'd invested considerable time talking to people on Baffin Island, trying to establish which of the communities had the best traditional skills, particularly igloo building. At that time, there was a particular group of very skilled old men at Pond Inlet, on the northernmost tip, so it was a simple choice as to where we would go to make the film.

We flew from London to Toronto and from there we were due to catch our connecting flight to Pond Inlet. The weather had closed in though, and we ended up diverting to Iqaluit on the island's southern tip, where we got stuck for the night. We found a hotel and, after we'd checked in and dumped our kit, Dennis and I thought we might go to the hotel bar for a drink or two. We approached the receptionist and Dennis asked if she could direct us to the bar, but her response wasn't quite what we expected.

'You don't want to go to the bar, sir.'

'Sorry, let me rephrase that. We'd like a drink in the hotel bar, could you point us in the right direction please?'

'No sir, you really don't want to go to the bar!'

Dennis, who had, among other programmes, directed *Top Gear*, wasn't having any of that.

'Actually, we DO want to go to the bar!'

'Sir, I can't make this any plainer: you really don't want to go there. But if you insist, it's that way,' she said, pointing to a corridor. So we thanked her, and walked down this corridor where we came to a door, except this wasn't your average door – it was made of solid metal and was the sort of portal you'd find on a heavily stocked armoury rather than a bar. That should have served as warning enough, but we were thirsty for a beer so we knocked.

When it swung open to admit us, we were ushered in by a bouncer and one quick glance at him told us all we needed to know. Dennis and I looked at one another; the bouncer was 7ft tall and dressed in the armour that American football players use to protect themselves on the field. And behind him was the strangest bar I'd ever seen: the beer – in fact, all the alcohol – was kept inside a safe behind the counter.

It was packed in there but it didn't have the welcoming, gentle hubbub you'd find in your average village pub in Britain. Nor the jolly, well-fuelled revelry of your typical Irish pub or US bar. No, there was a distinct edginess to this place and the local people who were its denizens looked a rough and ready crowd. It was too warm by far; the humidity of so many bodies in one place was palpable, the view through the small windows obscured by condensation. It was also very smoky.

Still, it was too late to back out now, so we headed in and placed our order. We wanted beer, but they didn't have any of that, so we had to settle for a Budweiser. While we were waiting for our drinks to be drawn from inside the safe, somebody walked past us carrying a very large and very drunk Inuit woman on his shoulders. Sadly, alcohol is a real issue for many indigenous people around the world, partly because communities have often been relocated and some don't have the genetic make up to process alcohol efficiently. So alcoholism is a disease that blights many indigenous communities.

We soon received our drinks, but we'd no sooner taken a sip when we sensed, then saw, that the attention of the bar's customers had fallen on us. It was like someone had thrown a switch; whatever conversation or entertainment had been going on previously, suddenly we were the focus. The tension in the air was palpable. The receptionist was right. We *didn't* want to go to the bar after all.

I looked at Dennis. He looked at me.

'I think we'll drink up and leave, shall we? Like, now?' he said.

I took a quick look around the room. To be honest, even if we hadn't suddenly become the centre of attention, it wasn't the sort of place we'd have hung around in. I nodded.

'Good idea, Dennis. Let's do that.'

We swallowed our Budweisers and walked out. We didn't look back.

———◆———

At least nobody had a hangover to contend with when we awoke the following morning to bright sunshine and clear skies. Our flight to Pond Inlet was confirmed, so we headed to the airport. The check-in girl asked us where we were going, and when I said Pond Inlet she said, 'Oh, you're flying long haul.' I'm thinking, 'Long haul? It's only the other end of the island!' but then I remembered that the flight was six hours long – you could fly London to New York in that time. I think that's the first time it hit me just how big Canada truly is. You see it on a map and yes, it's large, but there's no context. When you're there, its diversity and sheer scale dominate. It's astonishing.

Things were just as bizarre on the flight; when the Inuit women boarded, a lot of them had babies with them which they carried in their *amauti* parkas, and they were all carrying kettles in their hands. The *amauti* is a unique garment: a huge windproof anorak with a built-in baby pouch just below the hood. The women were walking down the aisle to their seats and, as they sat down, almost every one of them banged their baby's head on the overhead compartment. Predictably, the babies made quite a racket as a result of this, although they very quickly settled down afterwards as if this was a regular occurrence. It was all rather charming – it was so different to anything you'd experience anywhere else and really quite lovely in a strange way.

When the cabin crew walked down the aisle with the drinks service, I asked what they had, and the steward winked and said, 'Would you like one of our special hot chocolates?' Apparently, the special hot chocolate is laced very potently with rum – it's their antidote to the fact that Pond Inlet is a dry community. I have to say, it was a great service.

We knew that Pond Inlet would be a difficult environment to work in the minute we stepped off the plane. It wasn't so much the temperature (at -30°C, it was actually quite balmy for February) but more the extraordinarily strong north wind that was blowing. We were lucky because temperatures in winter often reach as low as -50°C – that's 30° colder than your average home freezer. Despite this, and despite it being one of the most inhospitable areas on the face of the Earth, people had lived off the land there for over 4,000 years, using traditional knowledge.

We were met by Ham Kadloo, a lovely old Inuit fellow who we'd be working with, and I took an instant liking to him. He took us straight off to get kitted out in proper Inuit clothing, made from caribou skins. It was a nice touch, them dressing us in their clothes.

We had planned to spend two days or so filming on Bylot Island, which lies just off the coast of Pond Inlet. There's no permanent settlement there, but there is a seasonal hunting camp, so after a five- or six-hour crossing of the frozen sea ice by snowmobile we ended up in a hunters' cabin. I'll never forget it because some Inuit with a great sense of humour had written on one of the beams in the ceiling: 'O J Simpson was here on the night of the murder and that's the truth!'

The journey out by snowmobile was fascinating. I already had quite a bit of experience of riding snowmobiles but over nothing like the distance we had to cover here. The journey was tedious in the extreme as the sea ice was covered in pressure ridges that gave you a jolt every time you hit one. When the Inuit travel on snowmobiles, they have a sledge attached to the back that they call a *komatik*, and on top of that they build what is effectively an oversized dog kennel. Inside each dog kennel is a large mattress, and instead of sitting on the pillion seat of the snowmobile, whoever isn't riding it lies down in the kennel where they're protected from the wind. It's a great idea. Every 90 minutes or so, you stop and change riders – whoever was in the kennel takes over, and the rider gets to lay down in the warm.

I made a mistake on this expedition of assuming that the entire film crew would know how to take care of themselves, and that included the director. Now, some directors are very good at the logistics and organising side of things, whereas others are creative-minded and logistics, let's say, may not be their strong suit. But I think it's fair to expect anyone going on any kind of expedition to have the common sense to take enough food with them for the length of time they'd be there, plus some extra in case of an emergency. You certainly wouldn't dream of going out to the Arctic for two days with just a Thermos flask of chicken soup now, would you . . . ? (I still laugh about that.)

Fortunately, the Inuit had a plentiful supply of seals for food – they'd just go out to the sea ice and shoot one when necessary. Inside the cabin, there was a thin sheet of cardboard on the floor and atop it was a seal that had been sliced open. As we were working with them, they invited us to share their food, so we helped ourselves whenever we needed to. You'd just cut a piece of meat off when you were hungry, dip it in blood and eat it. It was great fuel for keeping you fired up and warm. They also made a delicious seal stew – I'd brought some ingredients with me, so they made liberal use of the Oxo cubes I had on me.

I learned quickly on that expedition that there was a difference between me going places on my own as I had in the past, and going as an integral part of a film crew. Dennis asked me to walk along the edge of the frozen ice to do a piece to camera. That was never going to happen – not before I'd asked an Inuit to test it with a harpoon to determine the thickness. While I was waiting for him to do so, one of the other Inuit guides, Jaco, walked over to where I was standing and pointed to where Dennis had asked me to walk two minutes earlier.

'Whoa, don't stand there,' he said. 'That ice is rotten!' That was a stark reminder that ultimately I would have to make my own choices when it came to what I'd do for the camera – an extremely important lesson.

One of my favourite aspects of that whole trip was the time

we spent with old Ham Kadloo. Most Inuit can build an igloo very well. It's part of their cultural identity so they have the skill but, just as in any culture, there are certain individuals that have a higher degree of ability. Ham was one of these individuals. It all stemmed from when he was a young boy, and he'd go hunting with the men. He was very lithe and they would get him to put the top block on an igloo – because Ham was thin and light and wouldn't break the ice blocks when he stood on them, he was able to make a slightly bigger igloo than all the others. I guess this sparked a desire to learn more, and over the years he became exceptionally skilled at building igloos.

We were going out daily to film with the old men on the sea ice and then coming back to our accommodation. Our hotel had a central congregation area similar to the main reception at a mainstream hotel, except this one was adapted for heavy-duty cold weather gear. I had one of those bizarre moments when I looked at us all sitting there one afternoon and laughed because the first thing everyone did when they got back was to remove their caribou jackets. So they'd be standing around in their caribou trousers, which were held up with braces, and it'd look for all the world like we were part of a convention for the rear end of pantomime horses.

Some young Inuit (and by 'young' I mean in their thirties) who were the hunters for the community we were staying in asked: 'Why are you interested in all this old stuff? We don't use igloos any more; we use tents and we've got Colman stoves and petrol lighters.'

'Well,' I said, 'I'm interested in that too. But it's important to me that we record the knowledge and the skills that the old guys have. When they die, a lot of what they know will die with them and those skills will disappear forever.'

They got that; they understood exactly what I meant, and it had an impact on them because they came over and joined us, and when we left to go to our rooms, they were in deep conversation with the old-timers about the skills they had that the younger generation didn't. That moved me; it all goes back to what I'd said to Kath about the two-way trade of information – that we take something away of them, but we leave something of ourselves too.

We went back on the ice later that day to film a piece with Ham on the use of a *koodlik* (a seal blubber lantern) and another piece with me dog-sledging. That was an amazing experience, although I did have a *bit* of a problem . . . obviously, with us being with the Inuit, the dogs only understood commands in Inuktitut, the Inuit language. Well, I could make the dogs go and I could make them stop. I could recall the command that Ham had given me to make them go left too, but out on the sea ice at full pelt, my Inuktitut pronunciation wasn't good enough to make them turn right. This had all the Inuit killing themselves with laughter because to get back to where they were on the right, I had to make a huge circle to the left. Eventually though, I managed to arrive back where I needed to be and we all had a good laugh about my pronunciation.

As we were standing there chatting with Ham, we heard the sound of snowmobiles heading towards us from the town. When the newcomers arrived and dismounted, we saw it was the same young guys we'd been talking to at the hotel – they'd seen us out on the ice and after what we'd talked about earlier, they'd come out to see what the older guys were up to and have a chat about it.

The old men were holding court and they were really in their element because suddenly, the younger generation were expressing an interest in what they knew. I watched Ham show them how he could make a quick snow-block wall to shelter himself if he was fishing or hunting for seal. When the Inuit usually build an igloo, they'd chink the gaps between the blocks, but here Ham was showing them a way of making the wall where no chinking was necessary; it was 'ready-chinked' as he made it. Even the old men with him had never seen that done, but the younger guys stood there in awe.

'Who showed you this?' asked one. 'When did you learn this?'

He told them how he'd learned as a boy, and that the older generation that had taught him skills and given him knowledge were effectively dying out even back then. It appeared that Ham was the last exponent of what he was showing them.

'Really, did he show you this? I didn't know that,' said another of the young guys. Just by being there, we had started a dialogue, bridging the gap between these two generations. I was amazed and humbled. It was tremendously important because while we were recording stuff, we had also created an opportunity for people within the community to remember lost elders and discuss skills that might otherwise have been lost to them forever. That was perhaps the most fulfilling aspect of the whole trip and it really affirmed what we were doing.

As well as seal, the Inuit's diet contains fish, but to go fishing in a freshwater lake in the Arctic means hacking your way through 6–8ft of rock-hard ice. It takes hours of back-breaking labour. The hole has to be about the width of a man's shoulders, and once you get past a certain depth, the only way to clear the ice is by standing in the hole you've dug. The breakthrough, when it comes, is quick – so you have to judge it just right and climb out to chip away at that last inch or so. When you break through, the water all but erupts and then settles as it equalises with the surface. If you're fishing on your own, you have your double-pronged kakivak spear at the ready and then dangle a lure of antler in the water to attract the Arctic char.

If there's a group of Inuit men fishing to feed their families, nets are used, and there are different methods used to cast them. One consists of cutting a series of holes in the ice and passing a line from one to the next, often by means of a long, straight pole. The line is then used to pull through a rope that, in turn, is used to extend the net beneath the ice. Another method uses an ice creep called a jigger, which is a sled-like wooden device that slides along the underside of the ice. The jigger is launched under the ice, towing a rope. When the rope is pulled, a lever is raised; when the rope is released, the lever springs back in such a way that it pushes against the ice and jerks the jigger forward. Another Inuit then listens for the sound as it creeps under the ice and, when it's gone far enough – a hundred metres or so – you clear the snow and then pour hot water or lick the ice with your tongue to defrost the surface. The ice is so pure that the Inuit can see the jigger through 8ft of it. All they have to do then is to repeat what they did at the start – i.e. dig another backbreaking hole to get to it. Once that's done, they can then thread their nets through the two holes and leave them there for six or seven hours overnight. If they're lucky, there might be as many as thirty or forty fish in the morning. If they're unlucky, there will be none and they'll have to repeat the whole thing at another location.

Because of the ambient temperature, the Inuit need to set up a tent for shelter, and a stove to heat food and drinks. It was fascinating to watch – not just the act of catching fish but how the Inuit organised themselves to provide the life-support system necessary to conduct the tasks. The patience required, their whole demeanour and the way they took everything that the Arctic could throw at them was truly amazing to behold. The Inuit are very different to us – it was like stepping into a totally different world.

That trip was special for a number of reasons, but being the first one we did, we all learned a few lessons over the time we spent with the Inuit. I knew Barrie was a good cameraman, but this trip really put his skills in perspective. It's an exceptionally difficult job to do in cold conditions because he'd have one hand holding the camera and the other supporting the lens. The lens is made of brass, which is a brilliant conductor for the intense cold, so for most of the time he was in pain while working out there.

We went out hunting for caribou with Jaco at one point and Barrie wanted to get a shot of him looking down the sight of his hunting rifle and swinging it round so that the barrel ended up pointing straight down the lens. I thought it might be a good idea to check that the rifle wasn't loaded and I got a rather indignant look back from Jaco when I asked him. 'Of course it's unloaded!' he said. I said that regardless, I'd still be happier if he just checked so he opened the breech and I heard him say, 'Oh my God, there's one up the spout!' If we'd carried out what we planned to do without checking, Barrie would have been looking down the wrong end of a loaded gun.

Some of what I learned was fascinating, but as ever, it's the small details that are most vivid. When Jaco shot and butchered the caribou, I saw how he pushed his knife into the meat when he wasn't using it – the snow is so deep that if he'd put his knife down on it, he'd have lost it. Nothing of the animal is wasted – not even its body heat. I watched Jaco take the stomach and fill it with snow. He then knotted the top and put the stomach back into the caribou's carcass while he butchered it. As he did so, the warmth of the carcass melted the snow. It was thirsty work, so that when he was finished, he took the stomach and put two small blocks of snow in it, which absorbed the water. He then sucked on the snow, which acted as a natural filter as he drank the water through it. It was absolutely fascinating to watch.

My interest has always been in traditional skills and knowledge. I want to know how you live in any given environment.

I wasn't there because I was writing some anthropological thesis or a doctorate study; I was there because of a specific interest. I was asking questions of the Inuit that others didn't ask and it was a shame I didn't have longer, really – I could happily have spent months with them.

12

Mud, Sweat and Mears

The *World of Survival* series took us down under to focus on the Aboriginal people in Australia's Arnhem Land, which has been occupied by indigenous people for more than 50,000 years. They were still living a Stone Age existence until as recently as the 1930s. Its native Aboriginals are one of the oldest living cultures actively maintaining their traditional life in the world today.

The Arnhem Land Region is situated in the north-eastern corner of Australia's Northern Territory, about 300 miles from the territory capital of Darwin, and is truly remote. How do you measure that kind of remoteness? Well, in parts of Europe you might lose your way for a few hours; in America it might be a few days; but in Arnhem Land you could wander for months without seeing any sign of civilisation. That puts 'remote' into perspective and also explains how the Aborigines who live there can be so unaffected by Western life.

So, from this vast expanse we were focusing on a very, very small outstation called Jibalbal, which had only about four-teen people in it. They had broken away from the community at Maningrida, the nearest large neighbour, which had a popu-lation of around 2,000 people, because they felt that their traditional way of life was being diluted and becoming 'too Westernised' – spoiled by the effect of alcoholism.

We'd arranged to work with this particular group, but just

prior to our departure they decided they didn't want us to make the film because they were worried about the impact it would have on their community – I could completely understand where they were coming from. We were committed at that point though. After a protracted negotiation with them, I went on ahead with Joe Ahearne – the director – and Jayne Simons, an anthropologist.

We drove into Arnhem Land, and what an amazing journey that was: an eighteen-hour trek off-road and across rivers, with no maps of any particular worth. It was also my first off-road driving experience in Australia and while it wasn't quite as challenging as the drive across Zaire in support of Ffyona's walk, it wasn't far off. I loved it; hard off-road Land Rover driving is wonderful.

After being greeted on arrival at Jibalbal, I asked if there was somewhere we could set up camp. They showed us to a suitable location nearby and I then asked them where we could find some decent sticks that we could use to support our tarpaulins. They said the best place was a short drive away, so they jumped into a pick-up truck and asked us to follow them. We ended up driving through grassland where the grass was higher than our vehicle's roof – it was a good job we kept them in sight because I had no idea where we were. After a short drive, we arrived at a spot where we were told we'd find some good sticks.

The next thing, we were up to our waists in swamp following an Aborigine ahead of us armed with a shotgun that was so rusty, the whole thing looked like it had been painted scarlet. I immediately realised we were in danger, but Joe didn't seem to know why we needed the guy with the shotgun, so he asked me. His face was a picture when I told him we were wading in crocodile territory.

Fortunately, no crocs impeded us and we were able to gather up the sticks we needed so we went back and made camp. The community's chief came over and we shared the contents of our billycan with him, which was the beginning of the two days we spent forging our friendship. That was a very special time; building a rapport with these people was the most important thing we did, and it was real – not just for the cameras. Lots of films have been made since then but because time is money in TV, you often don't have time to do this and it really is a shame. But we'd made a genuine connection and really got to know the people in the community we were filming. The corollary of that is that the indigenous people were much more forthcoming in terms of what they were prepared to share, and that meant I could do an honest job in depicting their lives, which was important to me. It's not about what we're taking, but what we're leaving of their world. In order to work this way, you need a crew made up of people who are worldly enough and humble enough to understand that if you give, then you receive; if you just take, you get nothing back. We had that in Barrie, Alan Duxbury, Andy Morton and Sam Cox, which is why we collaborated on so many programmes over the years. Hopefully the results speak for themselves.

While we were forging this bond with the local community, the rest of the crew had the most horrendous journey out to join us. They flew from Britain to Darwin, which in itself is a hell of a journey. It's an exceptionally long flight, and they'd arrived in the early hours of the morning and transferred to the old Darwin Hotel (let's just say it doesn't exist any longer and nobody who stayed there at that time will have mourned its passing). Barrie and Sam had eighteen silver boxes of gear with them and they were exhausted after husbanding it all the way from the UK – they just wanted to get some sleep.

Two hours after dropping off, they were awoken by a knock on their door by Rafferty Finn. Rafferty is a superb guy, one of the best local guides and fixers I've ever worked with. He was going to bring them out to join us and I think Barrie and Sam were just so tired, they didn't know what day it was so they just went along with it when Rafferty said to load their gear into his 4x4 so they could drive over to join us. I think they assumed the journey would only be an hour at most, so you can just imagine the look on their faces after Sam asked how long it would take to get to the camp and Rafferty replied, 'Oh, only eighteen hours or so . . .'

It was fully dark when they arrived and I remember there were so many insects buzzing in the beam from the headlamps that if you'd taken a bucket and pulled it along the beam you'd have filled it. There were Aborigines coughing, dogs being sick, and the air was so thick with mosquitoes you almost had to cut your way through them. Actually, the mosquitoes in Arnhem Land are like nothing I've ever encountered before – they can bite through the thick hide of a buffalo and can get at humans through two layers of clothing. They're really something else.

Barrie and Sam looked in a state of shock as they crawled under their mosquito nets, delirious with tiredness and needing sleep like a junkie needs a fix. They can't have been best pleased when they were awakened by the rising sun just a few hours later, accompanied by the sound of kookaburras calling above their heads. I did feel for them, I have to confess, but it was quite funny from afar. The point wasn't lost on me though that while for me it was all a great adventure – and my *raison d'être* – they were a professional film crew and the organisation could have been better. To be fully effective, they needed to be rested so, again, it was all part of the learning curve for us.

Each morning we'd go down to a billabong to wash – it was a case of jumping in quick and jumping straight back out again in case of errant crocodiles. Then in the evenings, the Aborigines would go down to the creek and catch *yabbies* (crayfish). I noticed two of the youngsters using a bow and arrow, which was just the tool for the job (although it most definitely *isn't* a traditional Aboriginal tool). I asked them where they'd learned about the bow and arrow and one of them ran off. He came back a few moments later with an English book containing the story of Robin Hood. These two Aboriginal youngsters had read it, adapted the concept, and made a bow and arrow to catch *yabbies*. I found that truly remarkable.

The time I spent with the Aborigines at Jibalbal was like a university education in terms of the breadth and depth of what I learned from them. They taught me how to make the traditional spear shafts that they use; how to use a spear thrower; what plants you could eat; and what sticks you could use to make fire. I made fire there with a man whose advanced age meant he struggled to do it using a traditional hand drill because he couldn't get to the best sticks. They were out of reach to him because the flood waters hadn't receded following the wet season so he was forced to use these 'B' class sticks, if you like. I offered to get some for him and there was a group of three or more younger Aborigines nearby. 'No, don't let the Balanda (white man) help you, Grandfather,' one of them said. 'We are the ones who should be helping you to do this.'

The old man looked sagely at me. Then he turned to them and barked at them in his language, 'You had the chance to learn this and you chose not to. He can do this. You can't.'

In letting me help him over his own kin, he was sending them a strong statement that instead of listening to their Bob Marley records, they should have been learning their traditional skills. I felt humbled to have been included in that experience; it was a very great privilege.

The Aboriginals also took us to the mangrove swamp. Mangrove trees have roots which extend above ground, so crossing the swamp is like climbing over giant wooden spaghetti that can come up as high as your chest. The Aboriginals persevere though because mangroves are also teeming with food. And one of their favourites is the *teredo*, or mangrove worm – possibly the weirdest thing I've ever eaten. *Teredo* worms live inside wood rather than in the mud. Also known as naval shipworms, they tunnel into underwater piers and pilings and they're a major cause of damage to underwater timber structures and the hulls of wooden boats. In the eighteenth century, the Royal Navy resorted to covering the bottom of its ships with copper to prevent the damage caused by these worms, which is where the saying 'copper-bottomed' originates.

They're actually molluscs rather than worms – a species of saltwater clam – and in these mangrove swamps, they bore their way into rotten logs. They don't look terribly appealing – like a long, slimy, pallid grey worm. I thought they'd taste revolting but they are actually quite nice with a flavour somewhere between crab pâté and smoky clam. They're a delicacy to the Aborigines, and they're also very popular in Asia.

Being there with the Aborigines, being welcomed into their community the way I was, was both humbling and remarkable; remarkable insofar as it was just like stepping back in time. I guess it's the closest thing we've got to time-travel at the moment. There were many events that made me think this, but one of the things I witnessed was how, when they used tools, it sometimes looked as if they didn't know how to use them. Take a knife, for instance. Hard as it is to believe, Arnhem Land has only had metal for the past 200 years, so the Aborigines might hold it by the wrong part and use the sole of their foot as a sort of chopping board to cut down onto. It struck me that when I was watching them demonstrate a skill or show me the way they do something, they were doing so according to their cultural practice, which is, de facto, their law. In effect, there is only one way of doing something for them and that's the way it's *always* been done. When I was being given a survival skills demonstration, for example, it took me a while to fully realise the implications of what I was witnessing. I was seeing how their people had always done it, in many cases for tens of thousands of years. I've seen this many times since in Australia and it's like you're pushing the 'replay' button on the way it was done the very first time. I'm not sure I fully understood that in the beginning.

There was one trip I did with one of the elder men in the community – a lovely man with a huge shock of snow-white hair on his head. I can't use his real Aboriginal name because he's no longer with us and once their people have passed away, it's seen as disrespectful to use their names, so I'll call him John. Besides, Aboriginals often have a 'white' name as well as it's easier for us to pronounce, and in most dealings with people, they prefer to use their white name rather than their Aboriginal name.

Anyway, I'd been out with John and his wife digging up edible yams. We were driving back, and they were sitting in the back of the truck talking away for ages in their native tongue when John suddenly said, 'Ain't that right, Ray?' like I'd been involved in their conversation all along.

'What's that, John?' I said, using his Aborigine name.

'Ray, you've got the same story as us – you know, about the man in the moon?'

While it's true they do have the story about the face in the moon, it's slightly different from ours – even so, it was a cultural connection. Those were really charming moments, the moments when you realise how closely we all are tied by the things that bind us together rather than separate us. That to me was profound, because when I started making that series, I was convinced that what I would see were the things that made us all so different.

Another funny moment when we were filming with John happened while we were on the coast looking for mud crabs. John was poking in muddy holes with an Aborigine crabbing hook, which is rather like what the Cornish fishermen use.

The sun was setting and the whole scene was beautifully filmed; it all looked rather romantic. Every time John looked for a crab in the hole he would come up with nothing. This happened over and over again to the point where we thought we'd have to stop filming. However, his wife and children were watching and decided to have a go themselves. Lo and behold, each time one of them poked in the same hole as he did, they'd pull out a crab. It was quite remarkable and genuinely funny. Aboriginal people have a finely developed sense of humour very similar to our own and they enjoy taking the mickey out of one another.

Eventually we made fire, and sat round it cooking the crabs with the sun setting behind us. Although the camera was rolling we were all aware of the beauty and significance of the scene and I was in another world to the camera crew. To me it was a 'real' experience with this man and his family, and it was the same for them, too. Once the camera stopped rolling, John's wife took a couple of crabs, wrapped them in some leaves and gave them to me. I was very touched by it.

We were welcomed with open arms into the homes of the people of Jibalbal and I found it really hard to leave. They were very special people. We spent just under three weeks there in total. Today, to make the same programme, we'd be lucky to have five days.

On our way back to Darwin our 4x4 broke down, so Barrie and Sam got back ahead of Joe and me. They'd also booked themselves into a much swankier hotel without telling us, so when they eventually got to town, instead of heading for the old Darwin Hotel, they were dropped at the Grand Marble, replete with gold door and air-conditioning, while Joe and I eventually rolled up at the nightmare that was the old Darwin.

When we arrived a party was in full swing but we were told it would finish at 1 a.m.; however, it was still rocking the building at 4 a.m. I got to my room and turned on the air-conditioning – it didn't work. So I went to turn on the fan and it made a terrible clunking sound as it turned. 'I know, I'll have a shower,' I thought – it was broken. So I sat on the bed and, just when you think things can't get any worse, I heard a creak and a groan . . . and it collapsed under me, throwing me onto the floor. So there I am, in abject misery after this horrendous journey back from the bush, thinking about Barrie and Sam in their palatial luxury, feeling oh so sorry for myself. I looked over at the dressing-room table and there was a comments card in my room saying, 'We know that the old Darwin Hotel – the "Raffles of Australia" – is somewhat the worse for wear but please help us to rectify things by telling us what you found.' So looking for some humour to tranquilise the discomfort, I wrote: 'You should bulldoze it to the ground and rebuild it.'

The funny thing is that a year or so later, that's exactly what they did. What I didn't know then though, was that things hadn't exactly gone to plan for the camera crew, as we learned when we left for the airport the next day. Barrie and Sam got to their air-conditioned hotel and got all their gear out. They were smelling their lovely soaps and feeling their soft fluffy towels and marvelling at the walk-in power showers, thinking how great it all was that they could have a proper wash, no doubt enjoying the fact that we were back in the Darwin Hotel. They cleaned up, relaxed and had just settled down to a good night's sleep in their respective rooms when the fire alarm went off and they were paraded out into the street in their dressing gowns. They didn't get back to sleep that night, so there was justice after all. As I told them, it's those sorts of experiences that bond a team.

13

South Pacific

Our next shoot in the series took us to Savai'i, Western Samoa. We thought it best to take the same approach as when we first met with the Aborigines in Australia – Joe and I went in first to establish a relationship with the community while Barrie and Sam would follow on later.

Western Samoa is about as far from Britain as it's possible to get; it's one of the tiny Polynesian islands out in the Pacific Ocean, way east of Australia. In my quest to find traditional survival skills, I was headed to the tiny coastal village of Falealupo, situated at the west end of Savai'i island, about 20 miles from the International Date Line. Due to its location, it was often described as the last village in the world to see the sunset each day – although since then, the International Date Line has been moved so it no longer has that particular claim to fame.

The islands have only been settled for about the last 1,000 years and, despite the stunning scenery and location, the environment is far harsher than it looks. The Pacific Ocean breaks on the island's coast with terrifying ferocity and there are treacherous currents just offshore. Cyclones regularly sweep through – there'd been one shortly before we arrived and it had flattened a concrete church completely – so it made good sense for the community on the islands to retain their traditional skills, although these are a curious marriage between the traditional and the modern, as they've integrated electric ovens and chainsaws into their old ways.

The Samoans are a very proud and self-reliant people. They work on the principle that while ships and aircraft arrive with supplies on a semi-regular basis, the prospect always remains that maybe one day they won't. So it helps to have fall-back skills and experience.

A good example of this is in the traditional houses they live in, called *fales*. *Fales* are designed to stand up to cyclones, torrential rain and strong sun. They're the most common house-type in the village, built straight from the forest. A simple yet effective design, each house is supported by several hibiscus uprights and open-sided, with the frame and rafters tied together with the bark of one of the trees used in its construction. Coral from the beach is used to make the floor, which is then covered with woven coconut leaves to make it hygienic, and also to keep the sand out. Woven coconut leaves are also used for the roof – two layers provide waterproofing, and their natural curvature (side on, they look like the cross section of a wing) allows rain water to drain away. They can be used to make an effective drop-down blind for the open sides too, keeping the wind out on a blowy day.

When the recent cyclone struck, traditional *fales* stood up better than most of the modern houses; the open sides allow the air pressure inside to equalise when a shockwave hits, whereas most closed structures just explode.

The Samoans live from the sea, but they make plentiful use of the forested centre of the island, and the incredibly useful coconut palm trees (known by Samoans as the Tree of Life) that delineate the edge of the forest. These provide fronds for roofing, flooring, baskets, plates, hats, beds, roofs, and have a million and one other uses including a water supply, in the form of unripe coconuts, or food and milk when the coconuts mature. The Samoans on Savai'i make their living from the island and there is nothing they don't know how to use.

One of the first things that struck me on arrival was the melodic singing. If you want to really hear singing, then you need to go to a church in Samoa and listen. It stems back from when the first people arrived there – they knew they'd found paradise and they've been singing about it ever since. It is just the most beautiful place with the most beautiful people.

A few days after Barrie arrived, he and I had a bit of a falling out. I'd spent the day building a canoe with the islanders – whether it's a traditional house or a canoe, they like to complete everything in a single day.

With a project like a canoe or a *fale*, every able-bodied member of the community works together to get the job done. We had gone down in the morning with a chainsaw, cut down a tree and run back to the village with it on our shoulders. I was helping and they were all shouting at me. I thought they were saying something to do with me not carrying my weight and wanting me to carry more but what they were actually saying was, 'Bend down a bit, we can't all share the weight because you are taking too much.' Anyway, we'd made this canoe and I was paddling it along. Barrie had wanted to put the setting sun behind the boat, but I couldn't place it where he wanted because what he couldn't see from his position on the shore was that there was a reef there and no depth of water for me to clear it. He thought I was being awkward, and once I got back to land we ended up having a bit of a set-to.

We were both trying really hard at the end of what had been a long, hot day to do the right thing, so tempers were a little stretched and we went back to the accommodation not speaking to one another. It shows the measure of the man though, because half an hour later there was a knock at my door and when I opened it, there was Barrie, standing with a perfectly mixed gin and tonic in each hand. I'd had it in my head to go and see him to sort it all out too, so I knew right then and there that we would be able to work together for years to come, because he understood that tempers may flare but the bigger picture is more important. I've never forgotten that – with people like Barrie in the crew you can achieve anything.

Diving for clams was one of the most amazing things we did there. To swim past the razor-sharp reef and out into the deep sea, the locals 'read' the waves and wait for just the right one to come along. I wouldn't know it – you have to have local knowledge to do this. When they said: 'Now!' that was the signal for us to jump into the right wave. Next they grabbed their T-shirts at the neck and trapped air underneath, enabling them to float out on the wave until they were somewhere between a quarter and a half a mile offshore. Then they'd dive down and collect the clams from the sea bed, resurface, and eat them raw as they bobbed in the ocean. I joined in. Eating clams in this way is an experience I would like to do again. Watching them do this was incredible – the clams were buried under rocks 60ft or more below the surface. I was in awe. And they can go deeper. In just a pair of hand-made wooden goggles into which they glued a piece of glass, and a T-shirt, the deepest I watched one of them dive on that afternoon was an astonishing 70ft. Whatever the depth though, they don't seem to be in any sort of hurry, having the astonishing lung capacity which can only be built up over years.

When we got back to shore we stopped in a volcanic pool filled with rainwater. We took a couple of leaves from a fisao plant which, when rubbed on the rocks, produces a lather, and so we washed the sea salt out of our hair.

On leaving Savai'i we were escorted by Va'asilifiti Moelagi Jackson, a lovely woman who had been our guide while we were on the island. She was a real character. We were on a ferry travelling to the neighbouring island of Upolu when all of a sudden there was a massive rush of passengers to one side of the boat. When I say a massive rush, it was enough people that it caused the boat to list, so you get the idea. They'd moved because a school of dolphins was swimming alongside us. Va'asilifiti turned to me and said, 'When our people used to travel by canoe, they felt a connection, a relationship, with the dolphin because they were very close to them in the water. That connection is lost now because our lifestyle has changed, but the people still long for it. That's why everyone moved – they had gone to talk to the dolphins.'

As we watched, a couple of dolphins within the school jumped out of the water and turned round to face us. That was a very profound moment.

'Historically,' she said, 'our canoes weren't as developed as those on some of the other Polynesian Islands because our island was bigger, meaning we didn't need to travel as much as others.'

The practice of making long canoe journeys across the Pacific ended in the 1950s due to the number of people killed in the rough seas. Va'asilifiti told us about a centenary celebration that her grandfather was involved in when she was a little girl. He was crossing to Fiji – the mere thought of that is astonishing – and at some point, he'd dropped his paddle in the water. The others on the canoe had laughed and joked, saying, 'Ha, go and get your paddle,' and, although he didn't really want to, he felt pressured and had to save face. So he jumped in and retrieved it, but as he was swimming back to the canoe, unfortunately he was attacked by a shark. But what a brave man.

She also told us that on long crossings, they'd shout praise at the helmsman to keep him awake. You can just imagine being on a long, tedious journey across the ocean and someone in the back shouting out: 'Well steered, sir!' in Samoan. It worked though, as I can personally attest, as she would often shout it out while I was driving around the island.

According to local protocol we exchanged gifts with our hosts before we left and as the gifts were made, a man announced what they were in a very loud voice. You can imagine our astonishment when we discovered that we had been gifted an enormous pig, which had been roasted in a ground oven. This posed the problem of what to do with it; I couldn't imagine the airline flying us home would have allowed us to take it on board as hand luggage, after all. So we loaded it into the Transit van we were using as a production vehicle and left the rear doors open to accommodate the oversized pig's legs. We then drove around the island distributing meat to its many communities.

There are lots of incidents that never made it into the film and generally, the most amusing anecdotes took place off-camera. In television, sometimes you have to ask people to repeat what they do because there are myriad issues that can mean reshooting a particular scene – maybe someone messes up, the sound doesn't record, the camera isn't in focus or it may be that you need to shoot from another angle. Anyway, we were filming one of the guys chopping some hibiscus wood as a segment to go with the footage of the *fale* being built, and Barrie wanted to get a shot of this guy coming towards the camera, but he had to stop and ask him to do it again because he was moving too fast. So the guy went back to the starting position, Barrie started filming again, only this time the guy moved even quicker. So we asked him to do it again and he got faster still. By the fourth time the guy looked like a Whirling Dervish whistling past the cameraman with his machete. Barrie didn't even try to film it then – he was too busy taking cover behind his camera. It turns out the man had thought he'd look weak and less manly because we'd asked him to slow down, so he sped up instead. You just can't win sometimes.

There was another amusing incident after we'd been diving for clams. We were back on shore and Barrie wanted to check the footage to see what he'd got, because he'd been shooting underwater. It was a very bright day, so we put the tape into a unit on the Transit van. Sadly, we couldn't see the monitor that the tape was being played back on because a huge Samoan man who'd been diving with us was completely blocking the gap at the side door so that he was the only one that could see the screen. We found out later that he hadn't been wearing any underwear when he dived and he was just checking the film to make sure that nothing was on show that shouldn't be.

14
63°N 96°E

For me, the film that we made in Siberia for the fourth episode is one of the best films we ever made. It's hard to say why, exactly, but there was something magical about both the remote location we were in and the Evenki, the people we'd come to make the film about. I was also working with a new crew – Alan Duxbury was my cameraman, a genius behind the lens who was willing to get his hands dirty and do whatever was required to get the shot he wanted, plus Andy Morton as the sound recordist and Ian Paul directing. This programme came about largely due to the expertise of the late Thomas Johansson, a Swedish expert on primitive technologies I knew. His knowledge of the Siberian boreal forest and its indigenous people was unrivalled. Those of us who knew him miss him dearly.

I knew that Siberia was big, but after travelling for four days to get there, and flying over it for four hours, I started to realise just *how* big. It covers five million square miles, is one and a half times larger than Europe and encompasses a million lakes and 53,000 rivers. And trees – millions and millions and millions of trees. To reach it, we'd travelled in three aircraft and a helicopter, which delivered us to a truly remote spot not marked on any map.

The journey itself was like a mini-expedition. We'd flown from London to Moscow, where we spent a couple of days before catching another flight from Moscow to Novosibirsk and then on to Krasnoyarsk, which had been a closed city until four years earlier – it was where the USSR manufactured some of its nuclear arsenal. We then boarded a small cargo aircraft that dropped us in Tura, a real frontier town. We spent the night there, as the helicopter taking us to our eventual destination wasn't leaving until the following morning, so that night we were taken to a bar where one of the locals was having a birthday party. The vodka flowed, the crew started dancing – which was very popular with the women there because the Russian men don't like to dance – and then suddenly they were surrounded by said Russian men who were all getting very agitated. We were then told that if we didn't leave then, we might not leave with our lives. A very quick exodus ensued.

The next morning we went to the airport to get a helicopter to our final destination, where we discovered that our pilot was one of the revellers from the night before and was *definitely* the worse for wear. That didn't exactly fill us with confidence, but then we discovered he was navigating with a Michelin road map of Asia! I do sometimes wonder how we ever made it. Alan got to film out the open door as we flew. Now normally when you do this, the cameraman is restrained via a harness. In this case though, one of the crew had hold of the back of Alan's belt. Rather him than me.

I was there to meet with the traditional Evenki people – nomadic reindeer herders who live deep in the Siberian forest and whose lifestyle has remained virtually unchanged for the past 800 years. They live in family groups, or 'brigades', and we'd be spending two weeks living with the brigade Gyalski in their traditional *chums* (pronounced 'chooms') or tepees.

The Siberians have the *chum*, the Native Americans have the wigwam and Scandinavia's Sami people have the *lavvu* – they're all variations on a theme but they share the same DNA, as it were.

However, the Siberian version is not to be confused with the Plains tip which is constructed with twelve poles on a tripod with two short, one long pole – so it sits into the wind. The *chum* that the Evenki use in Siberia is the Asian version of the North Woods tepee, which is symmetrical – its conical shape means it's easily constructed and covered, and the top part allows for the drying of clothes or meat. North Woods tepees are used throughout the open boreal arctic forest – and the culture has remained the same because all of its inhabitants are related in one way or another. The boreal forest (or *taiga* – a Russian word meaning 'barren place') stretches around the northernmost part of the globe like a blanket, and is the largest land biome on the planet. It takes its name from Boreas, the Greek god of the northern wind. I've been to most corners of it and it's absolutely fascinating – I love it.

There are only six Evenki brigades left in Siberia, and their whole lives revolve around the reindeer. The herds provide transport, milk, clothing and most of the Evenki's food. I was there to learn the skills that have allowed them to live and flourish in such a huge, harsh, barren land.

The community had put aside one of their *chums* for me and the crew to live in. It was heated inside by a wood-burning stove that did a great job of combating the relatively balmy September temperature of -8°C.

We soon got into a rhythm, and having taught Alan how to make feather sticks and fire, he was always up first, getting the fire going every morning. In fact, we all became really well integrated with the brigade and I loved how Andrew, Alan and Ian all developed their own rapport with the Evenki, each one of them contributing something unique to the overall experience, making it really special.

All the expeditions we did together were special, though, because they were all so far removed from the life we lived back home. In some cases, it was easy to forget just how different life was, even at the most basic level.

As an example, on most expeditions, we got in the habit of bringing various small toys with us to give to the children in each community, and on this trip we'd brought some of those really bouncy small rubber balls. One of the guys – I think it was Alan – gave one to one of the girls and she looked at it as if to say, 'What on earth am I supposed to do with this?' Then we realised that there was no hard surface anywhere for over 1,000 miles; it was just moss everywhere. There was nothing to bounce it on, but you don't think of those things.

We'd go out into the forest with the local people to film each day, which of course I loved because the forest is my environment. To keep their reindeer from wandering off, the Evenki build a really effective and simple fence, which they put up incredibly quickly (they erected over 100m in just twenty minutes). They chop down only the trees they need, and the fence is a series of interlocking poles. No tools are required other than an axe to fell the trees and chop them to size; the supports push easily into the soft ground and no nails or other fixings are required as the cross bars just sit across the inter-locking sticks.

Evenki skills may look easy, but they're incredibly precise. They kill the reindeer with a swift, single knife thrust to the spinal cord and death is instantaneous. The reindeer are communal property so the meat gets shared among the entire brigade. The carcass is skinned with great care because every-thing has a use; nothing is wasted. In winter the temperature dips to -70°C or below, and the warmest clothes are made from reindeer skins stitched together. The intestines are used to make soup. The meat from one piece of a leg can feed one man for four days. Once the sinew is dried, it makes the best natural thread there is. The fur makes socks, hats, boots . . . it's all used.

They lay fish nets in a nearby lake and go out twice a day

to check for the catch, but it's a precarious task. Vitally and Vadim, the two brigade members who took me out with them, made their way out to the middle of the lake on the most unstable, rickety, home-made raft I've ever seen. The water is so cold that if they fell in, they'd only have minutes to reach the shore before hypothermia would set in. That would be somewhat academic in their case though – they told me after they returned to shore that neither of them could swim. There's a reason for that: the water is always too cold to learn.

The fish are a valuable supplement to the brigade's diet and make a pleasant change from reindeer. And like so many of Siberia's resources, the Evenki don't seem to make even a dent in the stocks. But then, with one person for every 600 square kilometres, that's hardly surprising.

They have to be self-sufficient because the handouts that they used to get – and on which they depended – evaporated almost overnight with the collapse of the old Soviet system. Under the communist regime, a helicopter would fly in once a week and the Evenki could send pelts and furs to sell in the local town, buying tools and summer clothes with the money they made. Back then, the helicopters were free but with the introduction of Siberia's market economy, they now need to pay – and the flights are hugely expensive. The good thing is, though, because they've retained the skills to live in the forest, the Evenki will survive whatever happens in Russia. That said, it's not an easy life; although the forest may look benevolent, the reality is that it's semi-barren and the ground is gripped by permafrost, solid ice just a few inches beneath the moss-covered floor. So yes, life is really hard for the Evenki, but they're Russian people – they're tough. Let's face it, what else can they do?

Reindeer, as with all grazing animals, eat everything in sight, and because of this they need careful management. Their diet is lichen, which grows incredibly slowly but the Evenki have become masters at knowing just when to move their herds on. On average, each nomadic brigade has to pack up and find a new location every month, so they're masters at doing so – as I watched, it took an hour from start to finish to dismantle and pack up their whole existence, ready to move to pastures new.

———◆◆◆———

When the time came for us to leave, it snowed very heavily and it occurred to me that if it snowed a little bit more, we would be stuck there for weeks. I have to say, the prospect didn't daunt me at all, but a betting man wouldn't have liked the odds on the crew's feelings on the subject.

As it was, I was the first to hear the helicopter coming to get us, and it was so quiet where we were, so remote, that I heard it forty-five minutes before it arrived. There's no ambient noise, none of the background aural wallpaper that defines life in an urban environment or even in the English countryside. This is the sort of quiet that you only get in truly remote places. On the sub-Arctic forest edge, on a cold winter day, sound travels for miles. The Evenki are a very tight-knit community of people literally out in the middle of nowhere – their nearest 'shop' was over 300 miles away. The nearest hospital was a week's journey by reindeer, so they almost never get sick. Just as well, really.

It's a very honest way to live: chopping firewood and bringing it back to the stove; no mortgage because you build your own house wherever you stop, from the wooden poles you chop from the forest; your reindeer provide transport, food, milk, clothes, thread, covers for the *chum* . . . The forest provides wood, lichen to eat, flora and fauna. The lakes are filled with pike and other fish, which offer a much-needed change from reindeer. The Evenki are almost entirely self-sufficient in one of the earth's most hostile, barren environments. That alone is incredible. That's very much how I try to live when I teach courses, so I felt very at home there.

All of us loved that trip and we felt that we'd forged a very special bond with the family we stayed with. Making a film like that is like an iceberg: out of how we live, what we do for each episode and what we experience, only about a third – maybe less – ever goes into each programme. There's so much you never see on camera – the singing in the evening, the rapport with the people.

Just before we left, Alan decided to put up a tarp to make a rudimentary cinema. We put a monitor under it and ran the tape to show the family some of what we'd been filming. As the film was running, one of the little girls came over. She looked at herself on screen and said, 'Who's that? Who's that there?'

Andy said, 'That's you.'

'No, no, that's not me,' she replied. She'd never seen her own reflection and didn't know what she looked like. 'Who's that little girl? I've never seen her.' She got all upset and she just couldn't accept that it was her.

I learned so much too, just by being there. We could always tell how many Evenki men are in a *chum* because they all left their axes outside – if there were three axes in the log outside, then there were three men inside. They never went anywhere without their axes. They make their own knives too – they have a single bevelled edge, and the Evenki have a special way of cutting where they'll have the knife in front of their knee and they'll pull the wood towards the knife. They have a very special way of tanning the reindeer skins too, using the soft, rotting, punky wood from larch trees. They're a very adaptable and capable people.

I remember Alan had brought a pack of cards with him,

but we never got to use them. That said, someone was using them . . . We'd go out each day filming and each evening when we got back, we noticed the cards were getting dirtier and dirtier but they were always exactly as he'd left them. Eventually we asked Sacha, the head of the family, and it turned out that every time we left the camp the children had been going in and playing cards. Of course, after that we got roped into playing their particular card game and I think Alan ended up losing everything but his shirt. To me, the way the children treated the cards was typical of their gentleness, the way they put everything back exactly as it was.

15

The Red Centre

I've always worked very hard at increasing my knowledge. Thanks to a combination of my formal education, parental input and Kingsley's mentoring, I learned to take a subject apart, look at the nuts and bolts, and then rebuild it. That's the only way you can really understand how something works. You have to *really* study your subject to know it inside out. And it's what I've always done, and still do. I've never stopped because there's always something new to learn. So I'll attack an area of knowledge that I want to become familiar with and I mean really attack it – a peripheral acquisition of knowledge is never enough. Once I've done that, I'll think about it from the perspective of my own particular requirements and then re-evaluate whether I've got the information I need to answer the questions that I'm asking. If I have, then I'll look very carefully at it, reformulate the knowledge that exists to suit the need that I have, test it, and if I'm happy I'll move on to the next thing. There is *always* something; I'm never idle in that regard.

One of the limitations of TV is that you can only ever show the tiniest fraction of whatever subject you are trying to tackle. That applies to any skills that I have too; having been a student of bushcraft for over forty years, there's only so much of my repertoire that I can present in a thirty-minute film. But, by going back several times to make a series about the same place,

I can bring to bear different aspects of my skills and knowledge. More importantly, my underlying understanding of a culture improves massively so I can ask better questions when I'm there. Nowhere is this more evident than the time I've spent working with Australian Aborigines.

We were lucky to have had the length of time we did in order to make the film about them for the first series of *World of Survival*. These days, we're always under pressure to make a film in the shortest time possible – that's all down to budgetary constraints. But the time we invested in the early days of my TV career paid dividends in enabling me to build relationships and to better understand the people we were filming.

For the last episode of the second and final series of *World of Survival*, we returned to Australia, this time to its Central Desert. This is the red heart of the continent, some 200 miles south-west of Uluru – or what we in the West know as Ayers Rock. It's indicative of the vastness of Australia that the coastal rains hardly ever reach there, so drought is common. Don't be fooled by the trees and shrubs that dot the landscape – they're specially adapted to desert conditions. The same goes for the Pitjantjatjara Aborigines, or Anangu as they refer to themselves, who inhabit this part of Australia; they've had over 40,000 years to acclimatise.

The earliest explorers of Australia were astonished by the Anangu's ability to travel with impunity across land that they believed to be devoid of water. The secret was that their elders had told them stories about the landscape from childhood, detailing the location of every source of water to be found. That said, if those early explorers had been standing on top of the water, they might never have known it; many of the water sources are below ground. The water they contain seeped off the landscape when there were rains and ran down the rock into a sort of basin under the desert floor. The basins are filled with sand, which protects the water from evaporation by the sun. When you dig down to the rock, the water starts to bubble up through the soil. The Anangu place grass over it, which acts as a filter. What they collect at first is a brownish colour but once this is done, the well begins to produce crystal-clear, perfectly clean water.

We were there with the Pitjantjatjara because I wanted to focus on their spiritual and religious beliefs, something that, despite our best efforts, we weren't able to do in the first programme. There were several reasons for this: firstly, the interests of the director of that film didn't seem to lie in that direction. If you're not interested, it comes through in the end product. This is an important and often overlooked factor; the director *has* to have an interest in the subject for the film to be effective. You see that in movies all the time. If you look at the work of my favourite movie directors, the Coen brothers, the depth of detail in their films, the deep characterisation and the mood they build is a result of their own personal interest in them. And the same is true in television.

Another reason we had trouble was that, in Arnhem Land, modern Australia is largely shut out. Contact with the outside world is controlled by the Aboriginal people themselves and this has enabled them to retain their culture. They're excep-tionally protective of it, so they are reticent about even discussing their belief system with outsiders. In fact, the law by which they abide – their tribal and cultural law – prevents them from doing so.

By contrast, the Pitjantjatjara have had much more frequent contact with white Australia over the years and, because of that, they have had to confront the issue of how to commu-nicate their belief systems with outsiders. I thought that gave us a much greater chance of recording this information and we'd also be able to show the viewer a different Aboriginal people in a different place. Too often, people think Native Americans and Aborigines are all the same, and of course they're not – they're very diverse and very individual and for me it's very important to show that.

I was keen that we should avoid, wherever possible, using 'white' words to describe the Aboriginal belief system while we were there. This was important because I had come to realise that almost every description of Aboriginal beliefs was constructed by Western societies and that none of the terms seemed to do justice to the complexity of what they were describing. In the past, people covering this have spoken about 'song lines' and 'dreaming tracks' and 'the dreamtime' but I was very keen to avoid such clichéd terms because they're meaningless, really. Those words don't portray anything of what's involved in how indigenous Australians live their lives. We were very lucky in that we worked with a group of people there who were able to provide definitions for concepts, in English, that they were happy with. That said, when I'm trying to tell a Westerner about it, it's sometimes helpful to call it something 'white' for ease of reference. It's a shame that I have to do this, but often we just don't have a word or phrase that truly explains it, so 'as-near-as' has to suffice.

Very early on in our stay I had a conversation with one of the elders of the community. I explained that I'd worked with Aboriginals previously, and he knew the name of the tiny outstation in Arnhem Land where I'd filmed the earlier episode. But he wasn't finished.

'That oul fella der?' he asked, in the strange but rather delightful pidgin English that they use.

'Yes,' I replied, amazed. He actually knew the name of one of the old men we'd worked with there. I was astonished. This man was of a different tribe, thousands of miles away, in the tiniest community I'd ever come across anywhere. It was the equivalent of me knowing the names of everyone in the phone book for the Isle of Arran. I was completely blown away. As incredible as this was, it also helped because once the elder realised I'd worked with another tribe, he was different with me. It was like kicking off from where I'd left off in Arnhem Land, so I didn't have to start building a rapport right from the beginning.

———◆———

The Pitjantjatjara have lands that cover an area of almost 40,000 square miles, and a population of 3,500. We were filming among the 500-strong community of Amata who, while they still fiercely maintain their religion, are also forward-thinking. They have a clinic and a school because they want the younger generation to benefit from healthcare and education. But, conversely, Anangu families still return to the bush because of their religion. They believe that at the beginning of time, creatures both human and animal wandered over the land, shaping it. They believe that the landscape they inhabit – the hills, the rocks, the lakes, the pools, the canyons . . . everything – was created in the 'Dreaming' (to the Anangu it's known as the *Tjukurrpa*) by ancestral beings (or ancestral spirits). In most stories, these beings came to earth in human form and invented everything, not just the rocks, animals and plants but also the relationships between groups and individuals to the land, animals and other people.

Once this 'Creation' was done, the ancestral spirits became trees, stars, rocks, watering holes and other objects that are the 'sacred places' of Aboriginal culture and hold special properties. This means that the ancestors never disappear but remain on these sacred sites, linking past and present, people and land.

As an example, you might look at a cave on a hillside and this might be where a particular ancestor slept one night; then three days' walking distance further along you'd see a cluster of large boulders where this ancestor may have eaten too many onions and vomited them out. These stories are very, very important and are tremendously significant to Aboriginal people. They pass on vital knowledge, cultural values and belief systems to later generations and it's done through story-telling, song, dance and art.

And they have so many meanings and uses. One of the things that the community use them for is to navigate. This is their map, so if you're an Aboriginal person in your tribal territory you will know the stories of your spirit ancestors in your territory; you will know where all the sacred sites are and where not to linger in case you might fall ill. Traditionally, each sacred site will have a caretaker – a responsibility handed down from their ancestors – and this is as much a part of their way of life as is breathing. I remember reading a quote somewhere and I think it was from a clan elder. It went something like: 'Our story is in the land . . . it is written in those sacred places . . . My children will look after those places. That is the law.'

There will be some stories in your territory for which you are the traditional owner, and you will have the responsibility for looking after the animals associated with those stories and the ceremonies and the songs that go with it. You will pass down what you were taught and what you have learned to your children, and so it goes on.

Traditionally, Aboriginal people would migrate through the country, moving in an annual round – or biannual sometimes, if the distances were too long – travelling from site to site to site, performing rituals and ceremonies to ensure stories of the Creation and the Dreaming stayed alive, living off the land as they went.

Finding food is a complex thing in Australia – it isn't like finding it in Europe. In Europe and most of the Western world you can predict by season and by habitat where you'll find a blackberry or where you'll find a sloe berry, but in many parts of Australia this is very difficult. A bush in one area might be ripe while the same bush nearby might not be. So it's traditional, long-held experience and the knowledge of the elders that enabled the Pitjantjatjara to move to the right place at the right time. There's a very subtle relationship between the landscape and their lifestyle; being settled in one place for too long could break that connection.

So, as you can see, the *Tjukurrpa* is absolutely fundamental to Anangu life. It contains the knowledge of how to survive in their country and is the law that binds them both physically and spiritually to the land. Law is a 'white' word though – in Pitjantjatjara terms, it means so much more.

It's such a hard thing for us in the West to comprehend, because these stories depict the very essence of existence for these wonderful people. They are all-encompassing: traditional knowledge, education, religion, responsibilities, behaviour, law – it's all in there. The *Tjukurrpa* is their law and their tradition; it's their heritage, and it's a concept, and it's more expansive than any word we have in our lexicon. *Tjukurrpa* is the spiritual focus of the people, their spiritual guidance; it's also their history; it's their very essence, really, and it's multi-dimensional. Notice I said it's partly the 'law'; by that I mean if you break any of its tenets, the consequences are severe and potentially life-changing. Respect for the *Tjukurrpa* is so strong, it can be a struggle for some Anangu to even talk about it. Given that breaking it can mean they or their family may be ritually speared and killed, it's no surprise really.

When I was working with them, I'd say: 'I want to ask you a question now. If you are unable to answer this question because of your responsibilities, just say you can't answer and I will try to rephrase it in a way that you can.'

And so with a great amount of very painstaking effort, we would have conversations that could then be recorded to enable us to capture something of the essence. It's very difficult because television is a medium that was created by 'us', in 'our' world, and my experience of working with the Australian Aboriginal people is that they see the world in a multi-dimensional way – that's the only way I can describe it. Time is a more fluid concept for Aborigines than it is for us. Maybe they're string theorists, but I think that modern physical theory regarding the concept of time certainly has some resonance with an Aboriginal perspective.

When we were making that programme, there was an old woman (who's passed away now, so I cannot use her name) who was very concerned that the young weren't taking on the knowledge of the past. So she was more willing to talk to people outside of her culture who were interested because she was worried that the knowledge would disappear.

Anyway, this old woman enabled us to go down what we might previously have called call a song line or dream track; it's a pathway, a story pathway left by a very important ancestral spirit. One of the places we went to told the story of the Perentie lizard man. The Perentie lizard is a big monitor lizard with round circular markings on its body, and we followed this story. For me, it's important to engross myself in these things in an Aboriginal way and not question or try to put the story in a Western context. I find even talking about it now is difficult because I have to use our words to describe something that is much more than our words are capable of describing.

Anyway, she took us down this track, we filmed it and we eventually came to a place where there was some bedrock – about the size of a breeze block – sticking out of the sand. To find that in the desert, even with the benefit of eight-figure GPS co-ordinates, would be tricky enough. At this rock she wanted to perform a regeneration ceremony and she asked me to perform the act of rubbing this rock. On its side, it had the same marking that you find on the Perentie lizard. It wasn't made by people, it was a geological formation, but this to them was the Perentie lizard man and, by rubbing it with another rock, there would be a regeneration of a part of the story that was associated with an edible mistletoe that is found in the desert there. We could not stay there for more than twenty minutes, or she said we would fall ill.

So it was a one-take special. We did our bit, I said what I was expected to say to the camera – under her direction (for which I got a thumbs up) – and we left. Part of the purpose of these regeneration ceremonies is to ensure the continuous abundance of the resources associated with them, and about three days later, when we were filming again, I had a little bit of time where I wasn't involved. I just happened to be looking to my right when I realised I was looking at a mistletoe bush and realised it had just come into fruit in the time we had been there. Of course, I made the connection between this and the regeneration ceremony. And then I looked to my left and there was this old woman watching me, and she smiled and just gave me the thumbs up again, almost as if to say, 'You understand.' That was a very special moment for me.

———◆———

There were many times when we were filming that our hosts would take us to sacred sites of significance. Initially, they'd tell us we couldn't film but they'd add that they'd like to involve us, as it was about getting the message across. This is one of the reasons why I feel it's so important to have the right crew on these films – people like Barrie and Sam, who were with me on this trip, or Alan and Andy; people who would respect these privileges, who wouldn't laugh about them and who wouldn't in any way denigrate them. In taking part, we were then better able to communicate what they were actually trying to show us. As budgets and time constraints narrow, film crews are less and less able to connect in this way.

Leaving the Anangu was a bittersweet moment for me, and I think for Barrie and Sam too. With them, the other crew of Alan and Andy, and Kath Moore, who produced both series, I'd forged a strong bond. We'd been on a journey together that was as spiritual as it was physical. We'd racked up hundreds of thousands of air miles over the course of the two years it took us to make both series, and while I was on a learning curve that filled in some of the gaps in my knowledge of bushcraft, so too were they; they were learning a great many outdoor skills through osmosis – often without them realising. Our strength as a team would see us all the way through to the present day.

16

Reflections

After twenty-six hours of flying, three planes, a Jeep, a hydrofoil and finally a canoe trip, we arrived in Seram for the Spice Islands episode in the second series of *World of Survival*. Seram was home to the Nuaulu, the most feared tribe of headhunters in the world. The Dutch ran these islands for over two hundred years, all the while trying to pacify the warrior peoples of the jungle interior, and the Nuaulu eventually stopped taking the heads of their victims. That was the theory anyway; in reality, the current chief was in jail for beheading someone during an argument just four years previously.

When we finally arrived in the rainforest, it took us most of the afternoon to set up camp. We rigged our hammocks about a mile from the village we were filming in and, just as it was getting dark, our interpreter showed up to tell us there was a problem.

As the chief was in jail, a man from the village was nominated as his stand-in. This upset the chief's brother who felt that *he* should have been appointed as interim leader, especially as we were paying the Nuaulu for allowing us to film them. He'd come to the village and was threatening to find us and 'have a word'. The interpreter said he couldn't quite understand the brother's intentions, due to the nuances of the Nuaulu language, but he suggested it might be advisable for us if we didn't camp out as the brother had been drinking heavily. He was also armed, as all Nuaulu usually are, with a razor-sharp machete.

The interpreter wasn't panicking; in fact he was very calm, which made it worse in many ways. He very calmly told us there was a risk that we might be attacked by machete in the middle of the night.

It took us less than five minutes to de-rig, load up the vehicles and get out of there. Luckily, we established good relations with the brother the following day and moved back into the jungle. It wasn't the most auspicious start to that episode, though.

Alan filmed the Nuaulu collecting palm grubs that were burrowing in a rotting sago palm. They're a popular food for the Nuaulu, packed with protein. The director asked me to eat one, which I did, but I didn't want it to make the final film because I didn't want to get a reputation as someone who is famous just for eating strange foods for the sake of it. I was always very selective about which bush foods I'd eat, simply because I think there's a propensity to show gratuitous 'bug eating' which doesn't add anything or inform the viewer – it's all about entertainment, and to me that's never good because it drowns out whatever message you're trying to get across.

Another episode of the second series saw us filming in Tanzania, where we were making a film about the Hadza who live in the Great Rift Valley. This enormous fissure is visible from space and extends over 6,000 miles, all the way from Mozambique, through East Africa and into Turkey. Numbering fewer than a thousand people, the Hadza are one of the last remaining tribes of true hunter-gatherers left anywhere in the world.

We'd followed some of the Hadza boys to get some footage of them practising their hunting skills, shooting at birds and lizards with their bows and arrows. On returning to the vehicles, Annette Martin who was directing, leapt in to our Land Rover and locked the door when it was pointed out that there was a snake on the path directly by her feet. I love the fact she instinctively locked the door after her – as if the snake could have opened it when it was unlocked! One of the boys shot at the snake, but he missed. Ever the director and always thinking of the next shot, Annette wound down the window:

'Alan, why don't you move the arrow so you can film it?' she said, pointing to the arrow lying just a few inches from the snake.

Alan had no idea whether the snake was poisonous or not but, given our location and the numerous poisonous snakes in the region, I suspected he wasn't about to take any chances.

'You're much closer than I am, so if you want to move the arrow, I'll be more than happy to get the footage.'

That made her think twice. Strangely, she decided that particular clip wasn't so important after all . . .

Then there was another moment when Gudo, who was the main Hadza contributor, was demonstrating how to make poison for his arrows. He did this by mashing up desert rose root, squeezing the juice from it into my mug, and heating it to concentrate the liquid. Gudo got the juice boiling then walked away, leaving Alan to film a close up of the liquid bubbling away. As he moved in, the interpreter came over.

'Alan, be careful!'

He said that the fumes are more poisonous than the paste that's left behind!

Sometimes, it's nice to know these things in advance.

One of the things that struck me about that was that after they'd boiled the liquid up in my mug and given it back to me, they told me that not only had they washed it out, they'd also tested it by drinking from it to make doubly sure that it was now safe to use. I was really touched by that.

Before we left, I presented Gudo with a bow and some arrows that I'd had made by Christopher Boyton, my old friend and perhaps the world's greatest living bowyer. Gudo was delighted with it and sang to it as he carried it away, patting it by his side. He returned a short time later and said it shot like a rifle, and that it was much more powerful than their native bows. I was over the moon that he was so pleased with it, although I felt a little deflated the next day when we learnt that he'd sold it to buy some beer. Alan and Andy had a good laugh at that. Me? I was sanguine about it because even if Gudo wasn't using it for hunting, somebody somewhere sure was.

That reminds me of an incident when we went on to film with the Maasai for another episode in the series. I built a temporary *boma* from thorn branches for us to sleep in overnight. The thorns were huge; I actually had one pierce my hand and come out the other side, but that was one of the reasons we used them – their sharpness and size meant that they afforded a degree of protection to us against predators of the night.

There were two Maasai guys with us and one of them was dressed in traditional Maasai robes so he really looked the part. The other Maasai was a ranger and so was dressed in the appropriate uniform and carried a rifle and rucksack. Something was lost in translation though because for some reason the Maasai in traditional robes thought I'd built the *boma* for fun; he was quite taken aback when I told him we would be sleeping there because although he looked the part, he was completely unequipped to sleep out.

For a further episode of *World of Survival*'s second series, we also filmed in the Amazon rainforest with the Sanema, who live in the jungle near the headwaters of the Orinoco, close to Venezuela's border with Brazil. The Sanema are hunter-gatherers and their lifestyle has remained almost unchanged for over 10,000 years. Their only concession to modernity is that they've incorporated agriculture into their way of life and cassava has become their staple food.

We had to take a small plane from Ciudad Bolivar to the Sanema's settlement and missionary station, and I'd flown in with director J.P. Davidson ahead of Alan and Andy. Alan was very excitable when they arrived a few days later.

'We had to leave some of our kit behind, Ray,' he told me.

'Oh?' I asked.

'Yeah, when Andy and I got to the airport the pilot looked at our equipment and told us we'd need to leave some of it behind. I know you think we carry too much with us, but we actually travel about as light as is possible for a film crew. Everything in the excess baggage that we travel with on each expedition is necessary.'

I smiled. 'Go on . . .'

'In the end, I had to leave some camera batteries behind as well as the monitor so we won't be able to watch the footage back. The pilot said that the landing strip we were using also doubles as a football pitch for the local villagers, who remove the goal posts whenever a plane needs to land. The strip is on a bit of a slope, and to take off the aircraft has to accelerate down the slope and then make a sharp left once airborne to avoid a ridge immediately to the front and across the river. If we hadn't left some of our kit behind, we wouldn't have been able to gain enough height to clear the ridge. To ram the point home, as we took off, the pilot pointed out the broken aluminium fuselage – complete with grass growing through it – of a plane that didn't make it.' Obviously, travelling light has its advantages.

As it happened, towards the end of our time with the Sanema, J.P. wanted to play back to the villagers some of what we'd captured during our stay, but as Alan had had to leave the monitor behind all we had was a 2x3 inch square LCD screen that we used to check colour. One of my enduring memories from that trip is J.P. inside a hut before some sixty or more villagers. They were all looking up, trying to see the tiny screen he was holding aloft in his hand, and it looked for all the world like he was some kind of alien god and they were all looking towards him for guidance.

Some god! Somewhat ill-advisedly, J.P. had a tendency to wear sneakers in the jungle and he ended up with an infection in his foot. It turned out to be jiggers, which are tiny parasites that burrow into the skin and lay their eggs. Removing them is relatively straightforward and painless and involves using a needle in much the same way that you would to remove a splinter just beneath the skin. I know the sole of your foot is sensitive, but even so I was a little surprised that J.P. yelped as I held his foot to hook the egg sack away. Especially as I hadn't started yet. That really made Alan and Andy laugh. J.P. saw the funny side too . . . eventually.

We got in the habit of bathing in the river and using an eco-friendly soap that we'd brought with us. There was a young Sanema boy who followed us everywhere. We nick-named him 'Chatterbox' as he would talk to us constantly even though we had no common language between us. He'd also stand in the doorway of our hut giving a running commentary to the rest of the village; he never, ever shut up. Then one day, he asked us for some of our soap while we were bathing in the river, and before long it seemed like every boy from the village was in the water with us, washing. The soap we were using lathered up really well and all the boys started sporting foam beehives on their heads. It had us in hysterics because they looked for all the world like Marge Simpson.

———◆◆◆———

Whereas every other film we made focused on remote indigenous people, we did a film in India for the second series that was unique in that it focused on a rather congested area. We were filming on the Coromandel Coast on India's Bay of Bengal and what's different here is the degree of intimacy in terms of how people live. This is the heart of the caste system and every person in the village has a single skill. They all live cheek-by-jowl on the beach, sandwiched between the sea on one side and a main road on the other. Conditions weren't great – there was no privacy whatsoever and we were watched constantly day and night.

There was a short opportunity before sunrise to go to the toilet without too much attention down by the water's edge. Unfortunately, everyone else goes there too, so when Alan was out filming the fishing boats being launched, he said he would sometimes be aware of something in the surf running across his foot. It would invariably be a human turd gently rolling along in the waves.

———◆◆◆———

I'd really enjoyed my work on *World of Survival*, so I was delighted when the BBC offered me the chance to make a series called *Extreme Survival*. This reunited me with Alan, Barrie, Sam and Andy on a number of shoots that took us, once again, all round the world to some of its most remote and little-known locations. The series was broadcast in the run-up to the new millennium and, after we were back in England and settled, I invited Alan and Barrie round one evening for dinner. It's all well and good reflecting on the stand-out moments on your own, but together we'd often trigger other memories in each other as we talked. Fed and watered, we retired to my lounge with some fine whisky.

———————◆◆◆———————

Alan kicks things off, and the conversation goes something like this:

'Remember when we were in Alaska filming the story of the Wortman family at Rose Inlet?'

'Yeah, I remember that,' I say. 'That was on the site of a dilapidated, remote canning factory from Victorian times. We stayed on a boat and were able to go out on the dinghy to fish at the end of each day and have a beer or two.'

'That's it!' Alan says. 'That was where I caught that large salmon that you cooked for us on camera in your own inimitable way. Remember, Dan, the captain would say, "It doesn't get any better than this . . ."?'

'Yes,' I interrupt, 'except it did. The next day we saw a bear by the water's edge and Dan said, "It doesn't get better than this," and it became something of a mantra. Every day it *did* seem to get better, but I don't think anything topped us seeing a whale dive a couple of times, raising its tail out of the water. That was something really special.'

'Barrie,' says Al. 'When Ray and I did the expedition in Costa Rica, the director wanted me to film a sequence with Ray using his *parang* to hack his way through the rainforest.'

I laugh as he says this. 'It was completely ridiculous because nobody ever hacks through the jungle like that – it's the sort of thing Bogart might have done in the movies back in the 1940s. Neither do you walk through the rainforest with your face spattered with mud. You look for game trails and walk through them, not hack your own path through the vegetation! Honestly, the things we have to do to make an image.'

'So he did it in the end, Barrie,' Al continues. 'He's walking through the vegetation with a razor-sharp *parang* in his hand cutting and slashing the thick vines and branches as he goes. Sam and I had climbed up a slope slightly ahead of Ray and the plan was for him to stop as he got to us.'

'Yeah, I know,' I say sheepishly. 'You told me to stop after I'd made several strokes but you suddenly shouted out, "Ray, watch out! That's Sam's audio cab . . ." and you said it just as I brought the blade down and cut what I thought was another vine in two.'

'Yeah, except it wasn't another vine, it was the cable from Sam's portable mixer to his headphones. Ray looks up and there's Sam looking baffled and twiddling knobs on the mixer because he couldn't hear anything!'

'It looked just like a vine,' I say defensively, 'and he *did* have a spare.' Barrie and Al laugh at the recollection.

'I did a shoot with Ray in Arctic Sweden,' says Barrie, 'and it was one of their coldest winters. It was -40°C and I was shooting from a helicopter in the usual position, door open, feet on the skids.'

'It must have been -70°C with the wind chill,' I tell him. 'Wasn't that when my Ski-Doo packed up? It was just as well, as I recall, because your head cover had slipped and you had mild frostbite on your face!'

'That was painful, but you know us, Ray . . . anything to get the shot!'

'Wasn't that the gig where it was Ray's birthday in the middle of the trip?' asks Alan.

'It was. We were there to follow the Swedish Army Survival instructors' final test, where they have to survive for a week with just a sleeping bag and the means to light a fire,' I say.

'That's right,' Barrie offers, 'and afterwards, you were snug in the warmth of a Sami tepee interviewing your great friend Lars.'

'Yes,' I say, 'I thought it was strange that you had the camera mounted on the tripod – you'd have normally hand-held for something like that.'

'And you know why, don't you?' says Barrie mischievously. I smile.

'I had the camera favouring Lars, but with Ray in shot,' Barrie tells Alan. 'Rachel had told me it was his birthday before we left and she asked me to give him her present. That was why I asked Ray to cheat his eye line away from the camera slightly and then asked him to look straight down the lens. It was that moment that I pushed the custard pie in his face . . .'

'And said "Happy Birthday from Rachel!"' I say, laughing.

'I thought you took it quite well, mate, considering,' says Barrie.

Alan grins. 'Closer to home, one of my favourite memories is from when we were filming in the Forest of Dean. Do you remember, Ray?'

'Yes, I do. We went to a pub for our evening meal, and the place was empty until about five to eight when it suddenly filled up. We were playing darts and had to grab a table because it was quiz night.'

'That's it,' laughs Alan. 'We did quite well, Barrie, and we were in second place halfway through. The last round was via TV, with us watching a cartoon clip and answering questions about it afterwards. Because of our different disciplines we all noticed different things and scored full marks, winning a bottle of wine and four Snickers bars.'

'Yes, as I recall, the team next to us had been leading and were most put out.'

Alan laughed out loud: 'Yes, they asked us if we were coming again the following week in a tone that said we most definitely wouldn't be welcome!'

I look at them both. 'One of the things I like about working with you guys is how you're not afraid to roll up your sleeves and get involved in the nitty-gritty. Including, Barrie, your willingness to try most of the edible offerings I've tried.'

'Yes, you do enjoy your food, Ray,' Barrie replies. 'I think I've probably eaten everything that's been offered, including witchetty grubs – although I couldn't have done that with them alive and raw as the Aborigines do. They weren't too bad cooked.'

'Rather you than me,' Alan says. 'They're not my cup of tea at all.'

'I've eaten various insects,' Barrie continues, 'but the honey ants are my favourite. That sweet liquid that swells their abdomens is delicious. I'm trying to think what else I've eaten . . . there was porcupine, raw seal, emu, iguana – I was happy to try them all.

'However I did refuse one offer when we were filming Ray's first series in Arnhem Land. One of the Aborigines' favourite delicacies – you know, the teredo worm that lives in rotten wood in saltwater areas. I filmed Ray with the locals digging them out, taking hold of the head and biting off the raw white slimy body.'

'That's right, it's delicious – it tastes like crab pâté.'

'In your dreams, Mears!' is Barrie's retort.

When I finish laughing, he carries on, 'Hey Ray, remember the first shoot you ever did with Ben [Southwell]?'

'Yeah, *Tracks* wasn't it?'

'That's right,' says Barrie. 'He had just finished working on *The Clothes Show*, Al, and Ray told him that this was different – it was nature and he couldn't control it so he'd just have to go with the flow. We were filming fire lighting with a bow drill and of course at the crucial moment he got me to stop filming so that I could reposition the camera.'

'I'd forgotten that,' I say, smiling. 'The ember was lost and I pointed out that the hearth was now exhausted. Ben said something along the lines of, "Surely we could just get another bit of wood from around us?"'

'Yeah, we were in the middle of a wood, but hearths need certain types of wood to work, as you know, and there was no tree of that type anywhere near us. Ben ended up running all the way back to the vehicles to get a replacement hearth,' says Barrie.

I chuckle at the recollection: 'I think he was worried it could have been the end there and then, but we're still working together. What's that? Twelve years now?'

'One of my favourite memories,' Alan says, 'was when we were filming in Venezuela. We were right in the middle of nowhere and Matt, who was the associate producer for that programme, spotted a team of scientists studying the rainforest.'

'That's right, they were being resupplied and he got them to bring a cool box to us filled with chilled beers,' I add.

'Aye,' says Alan, 'that was quite something. Several days into a trip in the heart of the rainforest and we were able to have a few cold beers in the evening. Now *that's* perfection!'

'I forget where we were when we did this but Ben wanted a showroom dummy for a sequence to show the type of clothes you'd wear in the mountains,' Barrie says.

'I remember that,' I tell him. 'The dummy had a bendy wire frame so we doubled it over and bound it up so we could send it via the aircraft's hold. When we got back into Heathrow, everyone in the baggage hall took a sharp intake of breath because when it came out, it looked like there was a body on the luggage carousel.'

'Hey Barrie, did Andy ever tell you about when we played *Who Wants to be a Millionaire* in Morocco?' says Alan.

'No, I don't think he did.'

'It was funny really. It was really big on TV then and one of the guys – I think it was Matt, one of the researchers – had brought the *Who Wants to be a Millionaire* book with him for us to play round the fire in the evenings.

'Half of the book had the relatively easy questions in – you know, the £50, £100, £250, £500 ones and the last three pages of the book contained the £1,000,000 questions. We'd agreed among ourselves before we played that you'd have to take the first question on whichever page you turned to for that particular round – there'd be no scanning down the page looking for questions you knew the answer to.

'So we're sat around the fire one evening playing *Who Wants to be a Millionaire* and taking it in turns. You could ask the audience, which basically meant everyone around the camp fire, or phone a friend, which meant picking one person who you thought might know the answer. Matt knew about football, so if it was a football question, you'd ask him.

'Old Mears here just didn't want to know, though, did you?!'

'I was happy to play a part and answer as a friend or part of the audience,' I protest.

'Yeah, but that was in name only, generally,' Barrie replies. He goes on, turning to Alan: 'He didn't answer at all as I recall, and this went on for a couple of nights. Eventually I said, "Look, it's only a bit of fun – I mean Andy could only just about answer: 'Mary had a little . . . what?' so it's not like we're taking it at all seriously." Anyway, eventually Ray said he'd have a go, didn't you?'

I nod sheepishly.

'I kind of wish we hadn't bothered, to be honest,' says Alan laughing, 'because of course, you got all the way through to the £500,000 question and the first question on the page was "What's the Latin for hazelnut?" and of course, Ray knows most of the Latin names for all the flora and fauna so he went straight on to the £1,000,000 question.'

'Don't tell me . . .' says Barrie.

'Yep,' says Alan. 'The first question on the page was for

the Latin name of some obscure plant or other and he knew what that was so he went straight through and won the million! We'd been playing for three days and hadn't got anywhere near the top, and then Ray jumps in at the last minute and bang!'

'It was luck more than anything else,' I say. And it was really – I mean, what are the chances of the two last questions both being related to any area of the outdoors like that? If they'd been about popular culture or something, I'd have fallen flat on my face.

'Anyway,' says Barrie, looking wistfully at his empty glass. 'Who's for another one?'

I can see this evening isn't going to be ending anytime soon . . .

17

The Jedi in the Jungle

In 2001, the BBC invited me to make a one-off programme called *Trips Money Can't Buy*, which would involve me taking a 'celebrity' into some remote and faintly exotic wilderness. I wasn't keen on the concept, because I didn't want to propagate the myth that nature's harsh, and that therefore whoever I took with me was going to struggle. In reality, that's not how nature works. Yes, it can be harsh, but all you need are the skills to survive. What they had in mind was, I think, more about entertainment than education and I'm not a showman – I do TV because, as I've said, it's the most effective medium for me to teach and educate those viewers who are interested in bushcraft. I wanted no part in a programme that would take somebody well known out of their comfort zone and into the jungle so that they could be laughed at. That's exactly the sort of television show that I dislike.

That said, I considered how we might turn it around and still make an interesting programme and I thought, 'OK, these are intelligent people. If I give them proper tuition, they'll have a rich and enjoyable experience.' And I put forward the proposal that we should take a movie star to the jungle – it would be a tough trip but whoever we took would learn a lot.

Cue my agent Jackie. I first came across Jackie when she did some publicity for me. It also turned out she'd gone to the girls' school less than a mile from Downside, my prep school, so our paths may even have crossed when we were much younger. I'd had some agents previously but nobody who represented me as skilfully as Jackie. Over the years, she has become a dear friend.

Most people, including me, are somewhat naive when they first get into television. I'm sure the world thinks that you're taught to be a TV presenter, but of course you're not. Jackie's background was perfect – she grew up in television and has a long family involvement in that media. She's also a very nice person, very straight, and she has a clear sense of right and wrong and fair play. She is not a short-term player; she's there because she wants to make some sort of long-term contribution to the whole process. You hear of some agents out there who think that to be effective they have to be horribly aggressive and nasty. Jackie isn't like that. She's a lovely person, dedicated and very professional She also has great ideas . . .

Cue Ewan McGregor – Jackie got in contact with him and he was up for it right from the off, which was brilliant. We couldn't have picked anyone better.

It's important for me that I get across there was no artifice here; I don't do pretence – things are what they are, so I deal with whatever an expedition confronts me with, and that goes for anyone who is with me, so everything is done for real. And that's one of the things I loved about Ewan – he didn't gripe, there were no airs and graces on his part, no ego. He really bought into the whole experience and from the minute he agreed to take part, he just threw himself into it 100 per cent.

We met at my old stamping ground the Royal Geographical Society in Kensington and I guess he must have felt a sense of trepidation but if so, it was never noticeable – he really engaged. I thought it was a bold move for him – he was then, and remains today, a big box-office A-list actor. At the time, he'd just made *Moulin Rouge* and *Star Wars* so he was a hugely bankable star. He had no idea at the time how doing this gig would affect his reputation, but then I think that's one of the things about him that sets him apart from his peers. To him, acting's just a job much like any other, and he's got no interest in the red carpet stuff, the fame and the trappings. I think he sees himself as a regular guy whose job is making films. He enjoys it, but it's work, and when he's finished he goes back home to his wife Eve and their children, and he lives his life. I like that.

It was important to me that we weren't trying to catch him out; quite the opposite in fact. Also, it wasn't TV work for me, it was just another expedition, so I never felt like I was making a programme and maybe that comes across. I just felt like I was doing my job, which in that case was to take care of Ewan and make sure that he had the best experience possible.

There was a point to the programme – it wasn't just about Ewan and me walking through the jungle while Alan filmed us. We would be on the trail of the remains of an ancient civilisation so the journey would fall into two halves – down river into the heart of the rainforest to the site of some ancient artefacts, and then a three-day trek to a newly discovered archaeological site. For poor old Ewan, there was only one way out and that was forwards. We would have ten days to reach the helicopter landing site on the far side of the jungle, and they would prove to be ten eventful days, to say the least.

I was working with Ben Southwell, a director who is absolutely top rate, and a very, very talented guy. He's creative, he's got a strong visual style and a good editorial mind, so he brings all the tools that are needed for good, effective film-making. He's decisive so he always has a clear vision of the film he wants to make. He doesn't overshoot, he's very good on logistics and also very good with people. He doesn't have an ego that gets in the way – he's a real team player. It's not an easy job, directing, but it was a pleasure working with him.

Like any film of this nature, it's essential that you undertake a reconnaissance trip before you make the actual programme, in order to iron out any potential problems and get some idea of the sort of obstacles that you're likely to come up against. The bottom line was that, whether he likes it or not, Ewan's a valuable commodity, so in effect we were undertaking a risk assessment.

We flew out about five weeks before filming the actual programme – Ben, Alan, Andy and me – and did the trip exactly as we were planning to do it with Ewan. I chose Honduras for the expedition into the heart of the rainforest. It's a prickly sort of rainforest because cyclones are a regular occurrence and they disturb the forest, making it more 'spiky'. It's a tough environment to be in.

The weather was awful when we got there. It was very cold, which is not what you generally expect in the jungle. Ben suffered terribly and was verging on hypothermia at one point so we had to stick him in his hammock while I built a fire, and Alan and Andy fed him a steady stream of hot orange squash. It was a bit of a baptism of fire for Ben and also, I guess, something of a rite of passage in terms of him learning how to take care of himself in the jungle and how to stay warm. It's not something you'd generally expect to do in Honduran rainforest. It was a tough old journey.

We encountered several dangerous snakes, too. I was walking up a steep trail beside a waterfall at one point and there was a local guide called Racendo in front of me. Suddenly, he jumped while shouting, 'Aie, aie aie!' and as he was in mid-air he pulled his machete out, span round and there between us was this very large and angry fer-de-lance (a venomous pit viper). Pit vipers get their name from a pit organ between their eyes that sees in infrared so they are able to detect the heat signature of their prey in complete darkness. They then strike with deadly accuracy and it's one of the reasons you don't wander around in the jungle after dark. It doesn't have a rattle, but it shakes its tail in the leaves when it's annoyed – this is one snake you don't mess with.

That was a red flag for me, and a good heads up on what we could expect when we came back with Ewan. I could just imagine what would have happened if we'd had an A-list actor, halfway through filming the newest *Star Wars* movie, coming to grief by a venomous snake. So I made a note to make sure we brought our own anti-venom with us. Using anti-venom is never straightforward because it's not uncommon for complications to arise. These are far easier to deal with in the confines of a hospital, but not so simple when you're on a muddy trail in the middle of the jungle. The dose of the anti-venom we had with us meant you'd need sixteen separate 30ml injections into the thigh to combat a fer-de-lance bite. That's one very serious snake. In the jungle we'd be at least several days away from rescue once we started the expedition proper so we had to take all that into consideration. You have to ensure you've got literally everything you would need for every eventuality with you.

Ben was putting up his hammock one night and I shouted 'STOP!' – initially because he was going to use the 'wrong' tree but also because I'd looked up and realised there was an eyelash viper right where he was about to place his hands. There are a lot of snakes in Central America and this was just another warning that we'd have to be on our guard. It was things like this that made the fact-finding trip so vital; once we knew what we were going to be up against, we could plan for it to a degree. Forewarned is always forearmed.

It rained heavily for almost the whole time we were there and I remember one night being suddenly awakened by a noise that sounded like a tidal wave hurtling towards us. You know that strange semi-conscious world you inhabit on waking suddenly? I knew in my head that it couldn't possibly have been a tidal wave but semi-awake thought is no respecter of logic when your mind is seeking a rational explanation. It sounded just like a tsunami and the noise lasted for ages and seemed to be getting closer and closer . . . and then it just stopped. The next morning when we left the camp, we discovered a giant tree in the rainforest had come down and the noise was caused by all the vines breaking as it fell to the ground. When I say it was giant, it truly was – it took us an hour to cut a trail around it.

We were supposed to be extracted by helicopter but the weather was still so bad that it couldn't fly. We ended up staying in a small village in the middle of nowhere and spent days standing at the landing area listening intently for the whirring sound of rotor blades. We were running out of time because I had another commitment to undertake back in England and eventually we could wait no longer. A dugout canoe was found to take us down river where a float plane would pick us up and fly us back to the Honduran capital, Tegucigalpa. Of course, no sooner were we heading down river in the canoe and settling in for a journey of many hours when our helicopter buzzed over the boat, before landing on a pebble bank in a bend in the river. The way that the helicopter just appeared out of nowhere and landed in the middle of the river felt like something straight from a James Bond movie.

———◆◆◆———

Five weeks later, we were back with Ewan. We'd established a good relationship on the journey over and I'd seen flashes of his sense of humour on the flight, but I really knew we'd get on while we were waiting to have our equipment checked through US Customs so we could catch our onward flight to Tegucigalpa. Ewan was at the back of the queue with Alan and me, and apropos of nothing, he adopted the voice of Alec Guinness as Obi-Wan Kenobi in *Star Wars* and said: 'These are not the men you are looking for. They can go about their business, move along, move along.'

He had perfect comic timing, but it was the way he said it so drily and without warning. It was just perfect and I knew for certain at that moment that Ewan and I would get on famously.

When we finally got to Tegucigalpa, it was just like the start of any other expedition. There's a kind of surreal atmosphere that exists around the preparations because, even with prior reconnaissance, until you've got mud on your boots you're never really sure what you're going to be dealing with. The other thing is, you can't make a programme like this on your own – it's like a full-on expedition except with cameras, so when the helicopter dropped us off at the start site, we were met by a team of helpers and guides, all with experience of the Honduran jungles. They were waiting for us with rafts. And unlike when we'd been there previously on the recce, the sun was shining in a blue sky when we set off down river.

My plan was to make a base camp about twenty minutes downstream so Ewan could acclimatise for a couple of days. It was a nerve-wracking time because some people find the rainforest very claustrophobic and don't get on with it at all, but Ewan was brilliant – he embraced it from the off, really threw his heart and soul into it – and you could tell that he was looking forward to the journey that lay ahead of us.

The white-water rafting was great; Ewan loved that. I think it was about our third day on the river, and both Alan and Andy were in my boat trying to get some footage of Ewan in one of the others. As we were heading down the river, I could see a large rock ahead of us, protruding through the top of the water and, in the time it took for the thought to form in my head and for me to go to warn them, we'd already hit it. Suddenly Alan was six feet up in the air, camera in hand, with Andy not far behind. Alan landed first, but by the time Andy landed, the boat's forward momentum meant it wasn't there beneath him anymore. I turned round to look just as Andy hit the water. He struggled valiantly to keep his microphone aloft but it was a battle he was never going to win – he was in too deep and his boom mic and sound mixer disappeared beneath the surface with him. For anyone who's up on their Arthurian legends, it was like watching Excalibur disappear into the lake.

It was pointless carrying on at that point so I suggested we stop to allow Andy and his kit to dry out and then we could re-assess. Experience has taught me that normally if you have a problem like that, very often there'll be another problem you haven't noticed. When we took everything apart, a lot of the gear had got wet – the seals on our waterproof cases weren't all as intact as they might have been – and so we spent most of the following day drying our kit out under the sun. We got off pretty lightly, although some of Andy's microphones were banjaxed. We were all pretty accomplished at dealing with problems, although that one was about as bad as it gets: a day lost – as well as some mics.

When we eventually reached our destination, we hiked through the rainforest to some Mayan ruins. We had a Mayan archaeologist with us, from Arkansas, who'd been with us on the reconnaissance and he spoke just like the characters in the film *Deliverance*. Luckily, we'd all swotted up on lines from the film so the poor guy had a miserable journey as we went along with us all shouting out, 'Ain't he got a pretty mouth?' and 'Boy, you gone do some prayin' fo' me,' with a bit of 'Squeal like a piggy' and 'Looks like we got us a sow rather than a boar' thrown in for good measure. He was a great guy and took it all in good heart. He was a real asset in the rainforest – he knew how to take care of himself and I say that without equivocation.

On the pre-expedition trip, we had come across some people cutting down trees in the rainforest in a World Heritage site on the Mosquito Coast. We'd been shocked then; they were turning it into a coffee plantation. What really surprised and saddened me when we arrived at the same point with Ewan was that in the five or so weeks since we were last there, they'd cut acres and acres of it down and there were men armed with AK-47s guarding it all. The depletion of our rainforests is a real concern and to see it first-hand that day was a shock that upset us all.

Still, we were there for a purpose and had a job to do, and at least the sun was shining, but I'd a feeling it wouldn't be shining for much longer. By day four, the weather returned to what we'd experienced on the reconnaissance trip. Once again, the rainforest was very cold and very wet – the weather was highly unusual but Ewan was brilliant and took it all in his stride. The only moment where he had any difficulty was when Alan wanted to film him cutting up some wood from a carbon tree. It's unusual because you can cut it 'green' and it will still burn but there's a particular way of cutting it with a machete that is difficult even for someone experienced – it's a really skilful job. That said, Ewan was a quick learner, really skilled in fact, but he struggled with this and it frustrated him, so much so, in fact, that he dashed off into the forest and hacked away at a few things. I sat there patiently by my fire, waiting for him to come back and I said to him, 'Ewan, remember there are things out there that can bite,' although perhaps I should have done a Yoda and said, 'Ewan, things out there, bite! They can!'

'Yeah, good point!'

And he looked down at his feet and that was when he realised he'd cut through his boot. There was literally one thread of sock left between his bare foot and where the honed, razor-sharp edge of the machete had last been. That *really* got his attention – the machete I'd given him could have sliced off his foot before he felt it. Luck was really on his side that night. For me, it simply reinforced the fact that '*parang* rash' is far more common than snake bites.

Each night we'd stop to rig our camp about an hour before dusk, and Alan would film Ewan and I setting up, but that meant that invariably he and Andy had to put their hammocks up in the dark. Alan had lashed his hammock to a tall tree, which, unbeknownst to us all, was utterly dead. The roots had completely rotted so there was nothing to hold it up, which meant that when Alan sat in his hammock later that evening, the tree toppled over and he was rather unceremoniously plonked on the ground while the vines and lianas pulled against the canopy. It made quite a noise . . . as did our laughter.

One afternoon, a couple of days in, a thought struck me that we must have crossed the same river about fifty times as we moved through the jungle. There were mules a bit of a distance behind us carrying our generator and some other equipment, and as we were crossing the river yet again, they must have seen us crossing further up and decided to join us. Unfortunately there was a rapid between us, and we watched them stumble and lose their footing. Of course, the generator slipped off and the next thing we saw it was floating past us down the river. Luckily, the assistant director was an ex-Para and he dived in and managed to recover it.

There was another surreal moment a day or two later when we stopped in a clearing in the rainforest and Ewan used the satellite phone to take a phone call from Ridley Scott, who was calling to offer him the part of John Grimes in *Black Hawk Down*. That was kind of weird, the way our two worlds collided in that moment.

For all that though, Ewan didn't once act the film star. He was just Ewan, and a pleasure to be with. He pulled his weight and had real endurance. In fact, I think one incident really underlines the sort of guy he is and it's indicative of how far he'd bought into the whole thing. We were at a point where Alan had filmed loads – more than enough to make the programme. So Ben said to him, 'Look Ewan, we've got everything we need, you're more than welcome to put your pack on a mule – that's what they're there for, mate.'

And Ewan didn't even need to think. He was straight back, 'Thanks Ben, but I'm fine carrying it.'

And he did – right up to the very end, which only deepened the respect we'd all come to feel for him. Both Alan and Andy carried all their own kit too and that's hard, especially in a rainforest. Their own packs, plus camera kit and lenses for Alan, sound mixer and mics for Andy – that's a lot to haul around, all the more so given how slippery and muddy it was on that gig. We climbed something like 4,000 metres too, so it was one hell of a tough expedition and I was really impressed with how everyone dug in and engaged.

———◆———

Eventually, we reached our extraction point and the helicopter came. I have to say, it was really tough saying goodbye to the jungle at the end. It was a really emotional experience for Ewan too, I think – he had tears in his eyes, which told me that while he was glad to be leaving, he was sad about it too. He really got a lot out of it. Obviously he wasn't sure at the beginning how we would treat the whole thing, but he relaxed into it very quickly and I really enjoyed working with him.

He and I were the first out when the helicopter arrived and it felt very strange because we'd been in the jungle for twelve days and we were caked in mud; we must have stank to high heaven and we climbed into this lovely, luxurious cabin of the Squirrel helicopter with its white leather seats. Talk about feeling out of place!

It eventually put us down back on the apron at Tegucigalpa,

and we came out of a side gate at the airfield; it was weird – one minute we were in the middle of the rainforest, soaked through, muddy, living rough, avoiding snakes, and the next we're stood among the full fury of Tegucigalpa during rush hour. That was bizarre. There we were stinking, wet, stood in our green kit with our machetes and people were looking at us wondering, 'Are you mercenaries? Are you with the CIA?'

When Alan, Andy and Ben joined us, we hailed a cab back to our hotel. Of course, it was the height of luxury with a black and white tiled floor that we squelched across with mud oozing out of the drainage holes in our jungle boots. Picture the scene: five guys in the same jungle clothing that we'd had on for the last ten days or so, all unshaven, muddy and generally filthy. It wasn't a pretty picture. The receptionist later told us he thought there'd been a coup d'état and we were there to take over the hotel.

When I got into my room, I walked straight to the bathroom, switched on the shower and stepped into it, hat, rucksack, clothes, boots . . . the lot. I tipped my rucksack out into the water, socks off and into the bin – they could have walked there all by themselves – and then stood under a hot shower for the best part of fifteen minutes. It was delicious.

———◆———

It was a good trip, and I think that Ewan had come to understand the rainforest. A trip like that – a good, honest trip – can have a lasting, profound impact on a person. For me, it was just another day at the office, but for him it was a massive step to go from Hollywood into the snake-filled Honduran rainforest. I'll always have a deep respect for him for that.

18

Looking Up

Ifeel incredibly privileged that my work over the years has brought me into contact with so many amazing people. There are so many who stand out, and they cover every stratum of society and every age group.

We have an incredibly rich vein of young people out there and they're a long way from the myth perpetuated by some doom-mongering newspapers that paint a dystopian picture of a diaspora of teenagers in hoodies kicking around and causing trouble. Society has always had those, but they represent a minority. The ones you never see mentioned are the polar opposite and they are nowhere better exemplified than by those who aspire to the Duke of Edinburgh Award Scheme.

I've been asked to hand out Gold Awards three times and it humbles me; the stories are truly heart-warming. Presenting those awards is nerve-wracking for me because it's such a big thing for the recipients who have all made such a massive investment to get there. The organisation itself is remarkable in what it has achieved and I have the highest respect for the Duke of Edinburgh himself because his commitment to the award scheme that bears his name is astonishing.

What I love about it is that you don't even have to win an award to benefit. Of course, that's not to detract from those who've won the Gold Award and crossed the finishing line – it's a brilliant achievement – but like many things in life, it's the journey that's important. There are many who take part but don't necessarily finish but they are still enriched by the process and enjoy the time they spend on it. Yes, they may get a few blisters, but they learn something about themselves that they can draw on at other times and in other circumstances. I believe it helps to give these young adults confidence, which is a wonderful thing. The Scout Association, the Boys' Brigade, the Cadet Force – any organisation that empowers young people to take responsibility for themselves and support themselves engenders something unique to the greater benefit of society.

All the people I've given awards to stand out because they are all amazing. Even if it were possible, I think it's dangerous to single out people for any reason, because inevitably there are certain organisations that will look for somebody who's come from the most appalling and disadvantaged circumstances. As far as I'm concerned, their achievement is no less and no greater than that of someone from another part of society. Anybody who achieves a Bronze, Silver or Gold Award achieves it, and that's it. To my mind they are all amazing.

The Duke of Edinburgh's scheme is incredibly well run. The organisation of awards ceremonies at St James's Palace is truly spectacular and performs like a well-oiled machine in a way that only the Palace can do. The staff there are selflessness personified. The contribution they make and the demands made upon them are quite astonishing. As far as the monarchy is concerned, I do understand where the republicans are coming from, but I think they have departed from the path of wisdom because that part of our heritage isn't something that, if you change your mind, you can recreate. The overall cost of the Royal Family is minuscule compared to how much is gained; it's unquantifiable. You could see from the mood of the people during London 2012 that as a nation we are quite clearly massively pro-Royal, and I think that it's a measure of our democracy that we are prepared to listen to voices of dissent and give them space.

Someone else who graces my amazing person's list is one of our greatest unsung heroes. You know the type: someone who has done a wonderful thing for his country or mankind, but has lived their lives quietly, away from the glare of the media spotlight, and who you have to work very hard to track down. Well, the late Jim Bradley was one such man. I was lucky enough to meet and interview him, and when I did, he was the last man alive who had escaped from the Burma Railroad during World War II. He was a lieutenant in the Royal Engineers and, in the confusion of the early days of the Occupation of Singapore, he had made some escape preparations, just in case. He'd managed to get hold of an escape compass that was disguised as a collar stud and he had a false bottom welded into an Army water canteen of the day, inside which he secreted a prismatic marching compass. When Singapore fell to the Japanese, Jim was sent up the Burma Railroad as a prisoner of war and put to work on the project. At the time, the Japanese engineers who were in charge of the project were killing the labour force through overwork and starvation.

Cholera swept through the camp where Jim was based and he learned he was a carrier of the disease. As soon as this was discovered, he was put behind wire in a different part of the camp with other victims. There were no huts, no beds, and he and others were made to lie on the ground. When they awoke the following morning, they found they'd been sleeping on the partially cremated remains of other cholera victims. Can you imagine the horror? He was then given the job of organising cremation parties for those soldiers in the camp who succumbed to disease and died. He said he couldn't recall a single day during that period where there were less than four victims; sometimes he'd see men chopping wood in the morning and then being cremated on the wood they'd cut that same evening because they'd have died later that day. It was decided that word had to be got out so Jim and nine others managed to escape into the jungle. Weak, and with no food or other equipment and no survival training, they made their way deeper and deeper inside the jungle until some eight weeks later, when Jim and four others stumbled out alive. They built a raft and went down river but the raft broke up in rapids. They were rescued by local villagers who fed them, looked after them and promptly sold them back to the Japanese.

The Japanese had said they'd execute anyone who escaped, but Jim's life was saved by a British senior officer who could speak Japanese. He intervened on Jim's behalf and explained to the Japanese military that they couldn't execute him because it would be contrary to the code of *Bushido* (a Japanese concept derived from the samurai moral code encompassing frugality, loyalty and honour unto death). He invoked *Bushido* because, he argued, Jim had overcome the jungle which is something even the Japanese soldiers hadn't managed. That meant it would be seen as disrespectful to execute Jim. Instead, they sent him to Outram Road prison, which was the Kempeitai (the Japanese Secret Police) headquarters, and they tortured him. He couldn't describe what they did to him but it must have been terrible.

There were two occasions on which they went too far and expected him to die, so rather than have his death on their conscience, they sent him to Changi Prison, a hellhole where prisoners preyed upon each other just to survive. Word of Jim's exploits had reached there before him and, against the odds, he survived – both times. And both times he was sent back to the Secret Police. Jim became something of a legend at Changi because he held out against the Kempeitai. It's a remarkable story of endurance and stoicism.

When the war ended and the Japanese surrendered, Jim managed to get home in three days because his story had reached a lot of people: this is the man who was in the hands of the Kempeitai and told them nothing. What kept him alive throughout was the thought of seeing his wife and daughter again. That was his motivation. But what makes him even more remarkable is that he bore no grudges; he had no hatred for the Japanese who did so many terrible things to him. He even met some of his captors after the war. I find that remarkable. I also think, in some strange way, he'd won. I'm sure he'd disagree with me but I still believe he'd won because, despite their best efforts during the war, the Japanese couldn't even make him hate them. He was a truly remarkable individual. As with other remarkable people I've met, a light burned in Jim's eyes.

Which leads me on to another heroic story. Before I went to Arnhem Land for the first time, I read a book called *Whispering Wind* by Syd Kyle-Little, who was the first policeman to go into Arnhem Land at a time when the Aboriginal people were still quite warlike and would fight those who made them feel threatened, using stone-tipped spears. In the 1950s, he was sent in to track down a man wanted for murder. Anyway, the place we were filming was the same place that Syd went to and he had founded a police station when he arrived which became the centre point of a town that sprung up around it – that's Maningrida, one of the most important towns in the area. It's a fascinating story; Syd turns up and he's forgotten to bring a bedroll. There's just him and his two Aboriginal trackers in very hostile terrain. He describes how he injured his foot, which became infected and an Aborigine told him to put his foot in one of the billabongs where the little fish would come and eat away the infected flesh. He did this, and it worked. When we washed in the rivers there, that's exactly what happened – the fish come up and nibble away the dead skin on your feet. I believe there are places in England where you can pay to experience this now, without risk of crocodile attack.

That brought what Syd had written alive for me and I thought how much I'd love to meet him, but I assumed he was dead. He wasn't though, which was something I only found out many years later when I was back in Australia making another film. I was lucky enough to meet and interview him the day before he moved into a home for the elderly. What a man. He was like a tower of strength even then and he showed me some incredible photographs that he'd taken of the people that he travelled with, like his trackers and one of the medicine men that he'd worked with. Syd had always been a very fair lawman back in the day – he didn't use handcuffs and he told the Aborigines he arrested, 'If you run off, I'll shoot you.' He demonstrated that he could shoot straight, so they respected him for that.

He was one of those old-fashioned policemen, as stiff as if someone had put a broom up his backside, but he'd been absolutely true to his word, so he was the perfect representative of the State to work with Aboriginal people. Previously, white men had always looked down on the Aborigines as though they were somehow a lesser form of humanity but Syd didn't see them like that at all and dealt with them as equals. He administered the law fairly and equitably and treated the Aborigines as he wanted to be treated himself.

What I found interesting was that, on a personal level, it was the right time for me to meet him; if I'd met him on the first journey it would have been meaningless, but because I'd been to Arnhem Land several times before, when I finally got to interview him I knew about the places he was talking about and I'd worked with the descendants of the people he knew, so there was a real meeting of minds. He was a good bushman and he'd crossed Arnhem Land's Stone Country as well, which is an unbelievable feat.

Syd described receiving a phone call from one of his Aboriginal trackers who was on his deathbed; as soon as the tracker put the phone down, he passed away. He'd phoned to say goodbye, which really emphasises the regard in which Syd was held. I still find it strange that Syd never received more credit for his achievements; to me, he was one of the last pioneers of the Australian frontier. In 2012, Syd packed his swag and rifle for the final time and left the old people's home he'd been staying at, and this life, forever. I am certain that on the other side his trackers were waiting for him beside a burning camp fire at a billabong and, young again, they now travel the trails of the Arnhemland bush once more.

❖

Reading this back, I can see there are some common traits that all the wonderful people I've met share, but the ones that stand out for me are fortitude, selflessness and understatedness – these are the qualities I like in people. I've recognised another trait too that's common to all those I've met who have done amazing things: stoicism. They don't moan about the everyday hassle of mosquitoes or cold or whatever – there are bigger things occupying their minds; they have a strong flame burning inside them.

Another truly impressive man I was lucky enough to interview, this time for an episode of *Bushcraft Survival*, was Chuck Klusmann. Chuck was the first American jet pilot shot down in the Vietnam conflict. He flew US Navy fighter bombers from an aircraft carrier and after his aircraft was hit on 7 June 1964, he ended up ejecting over Laos where, upon landing, he dislocated his leg and damaged his arm. So he did what anyone would do – he simply wedged his leg in between some trees and pulled it back into position. What a guy!

When the Carrier force with which Chuck had been based learned of his ejection, they hit a wall; quite unbelievably, they had no plans in place for the recovery of downed aviators and I honestly think they didn't expect to be taking casualties of that nature. So, as US forces weren't supposed to be in Laos, they had to ring the White House, which had to get a Secret Service agent to wake Lyndon B. Johnson, the US President: 'Er . . . Mr President, one of our men is down.'

We wanted to film in Laos at the point where he'd landed, but the risk assessment wouldn't have got out of the starting blocks for that one – there were too many mines still there, which was a great pity. We ended up setting up camp in the jungle of Northern Thailand – about the closest we could get to Laos. I brought in a friend of mine, Tom Lutyens, who had been a survival instructor in the US Air Force during that period, to give us some contextual information.

We invited Chuck to join us in the jungle and tell us his story and I have to confess, my heart sank when I saw him arriving. He'd had quite an arduous trek into the mountains and when we'd arranged for him to join us, I hadn't really taken into account his advanced age; I was worried that the effort of getting to our camp might have given him a heart attack. But he's a tough bird, and he came out to the jungle just a little out of breath. So, we set him up, made him comfortable and that night he sat down by the fire and we started to record him. We didn't have to prompt him or ask him any questions; the story just poured from him like water from a tap – being there, the atmosphere of the jungle, the humidity, the sounds, the smells brought it all back for him in glorious Technicolor and we captured it all on film. It was incredible.

To rescue him, LBJ sent in helicopters belonging to Air America, the CIA's covertly owned and operated US passenger and cargo airline. That offered the US a face-saving clause of 'deniability' but the rescue bid was a disaster. Communist Pathet Lao fighters who were loyal to Vietnam (Laos was involved in a civil war in the 1960s and 70s) got to Chuck first, captured him and then shot at Air America's rescue helicopters, hitting one of the pilots in the head (fortunately, the round just creased his skull and he survived).

Chuck wasn't the sort of guy to just sit and take whatever punishment the Pathet Lao had lined up for him, so he tried (unsuccessfully) to escape. After that, his captors took his boots away; that wasn't too great a hardship for him though – it was so wet and muddy in the Laotian jungle that he couldn't run in his boots anyway because the design of the soles meant they didn't offer any grip. Fortunately for Chuck, he was aided by a Laotian prisoner who was sympathetic to his plight. He helped Chuck get his boots back and when he had them, he cut grooves into the soles to help give them grip. Then, with the Laotian prisoner's help, he managed to escape. Luck was on his side this time and Air America was able to launch a successful bid to rescue him. After he'd been extracted to a safe house, he realised he'd left some clothing behind on the helicopter.

The team that Air America despatched included one particular doctor who'd been a captain in the Marine Corps on D-Day; he was a real go-getter, a proper dyed-in-the-wool American Marine. This was the real deal, a granite-hard, crewcut Marine captain who'd been through the hell of the Normandy Landings. So he secured Chuck's clothing and kit from the helicopter and then he went to the safe house where Chuck was and knocked on the door. A big CIA spook with sunglasses on opened the door and said, 'Yeah, whaddya want?'

'I've brought these things for the guy who you brought here earlier.'

'There's no one here,' was the reply, and with that, the door was shut in his face.

So the Marine started hammering on the door – Bang! Bang! Bang! – and CIA Spook opened it again, but before he even opened his mouth, the Marine slammed his fist into the guy's chest and said, 'This is for the guy who isn't here.'

He went in and after giving Chuck his kit, he disappeared and Chuck never saw him again. But guess what? We tracked him down – he was living in Northern Thailand – and we were able to reconnect these two remarkable men who had played such a fleeting, but significant, role in one another's lives.

When Chuck eventually got back to Washington, he was invited to the Pentagon to give a talk about his experiences so that some of the US military's most senior officers could learn from them. As he was being cued up to go into the theatre and deliver his lecture, an Army captain came up to him and said: 'Can I just grab you here for one minute? I just want to know is there anything from your escape that could be of any use to other servicemen serving in theatre – is there anything you can tell me that might help us?'

'Well, actually, there is. I had a real problem with my boots so I had to cut these big grooves in the soles . . .'

Which is how jungle boots ended up with the panama sole with the grooves, because of Chuck's escape.

One of the things I remember most about Chuck is his sense of humour. Alan was filming for this programme and he's got a very dry and quick wit too. I like Tom Lutyens a lot but I was surprised by how very much in awe of Chuck he was. You know how it is in Britain, we have a bit of a chuckle and pull each other's legs a bit, but it's not like that in the US – they tend to look up to their heroes and Chuck was kind of uncomfortable with that. I'd made a table and a candelabra out of bamboo at the camp and so, this one night, we were all sat round it just kicking back.

'I've been to America a few times. I went to Memphis and I met Elvis,' Alan said apropos of nothing.

'Did you really?' Chuck asked.

And adopting his best Elvis impression, Alan says: 'Ah-huh-huh . . .'!

Chuck loved that. We all roared with laughter – except for Tom. Tom is a hard-core survival instructor who is absolutely uncompromising in his attitude to his chosen field. His training has undoubtedly enabled many US servicemen to return to their country and families alive, and with honour. Consequently, I think he just felt a bit awkward because he was so in awe of Chuck.

'C'mon Tom, you really ought to loosen up a bit there, fella,' Chuck said to him – and it clearly had the desired effect because from that point on, whenever anyone asked Tom anything, he'd reply, 'Ah-huh-huh . . .'!

19

Mission Impossible

The men who carried out the attack on the heavy water factory of Vemork in Norway during World War II had long fascinated me and I was keen to make a TV documentary about their exploits. Fortunately, I found a sympathetic ear in 2002 when I made a pitch to the BBC for a commission to do just that, so I was delighted when they green-lighted the idea. We tracked down the surviving members of the Norwegian Special Forces squad that showed extreme courage in a raid against the odds, and in early 2003 we flew to Norway to begin filming what became *The Real Heroes of Telemark*. The story is well rehearsed but no less remarkable for that, so I think it bears repeating. It was arguably the Allies' most important and longest-running mission of World War II.

Prior to the war, the Germans took an interest in producing a nuclear weapon but they failed in their attempts because they couldn't produce graphite that was pure enough for the necessary reaction. They worked out that they needed deuterium oxide – or 'heavy water'. It occurs naturally in nature but only in minuscule proportions, but the Germans found out it was being produced in a Norwegian factory as a by-product of an electrical process involving hydropower. The factory took its name, 'Vemork', from its location, near the town of Rjukan, at the foot of the Hardangervidda (which is the Telemark Plateau). It was situated in a very narrow gorge that today is a Mecca for ice climbers. Because no sun reaches the valley floor in winter and the waterfalls freeze solid, the darkness in the valley was serious enough that the Vemork factory had installed a cable car to transport workers out to the Hardangervidda to experience sunshine during the winter.

When the Germans invaded Norway in 1940, they had their eye on Vemork from the off and they seized control of the plant almost immediately. Churchill was aware of their plans beforehand though, and had arranged for all the heavy water that had been stored at Vemork to be secretly transported out of Norway and into the safekeeping of the Marie Curie Institute in Paris. Then, when the Germans invaded France, it was moved to Bordeaux from where it was sent to Scotland on the last boat before the port closed.

After the heavy water came an exodus of loyal Norwegians who left the country by any means they could and made their way to Britain, bringing with them all their outdoor clothing and equipment. The Nazis then forbade the possession of winter-proof clothing and outdoor equipment because they knew the Norwegians were so accomplished at travelling around in the mountains. They wanted the population where they could see them rather than in the mountains where they couldn't, and there were very severe penalties if you didn't do as you were told.

Once they arrived in Britain, the Norwegians were vetted by the security services to make sure there were no German spies among them and then all the outdoor equipment was gathered in and stored centrally. The fittest and most capable men were selected to join Kompani Linge, the Norwegian Special Forces, and sent to the West Coast of Scotland for training. There was a worker at Vemork named Einar Skinnerland who was owed some leave and, as he wanted to escape the German occupation, he left a short time later under the guise of taking a break and made his way to Scotland on a ferry. He was swiftly identified by Allied Intelligence as a significant potential asset and when he arrived, he was asked if he would go back to the factory and act as an agent for the Allies. When he agreed, he was given rushed training and two days later he parachuted back into occupied Norway and made his way back to the factory.

The Allies knew they had to do something to stop the Germans producing significant quantities of heavy water, but they didn't know what. There were real problems because any opportunity to carry out aerial operations in Norway was severely limited by the weather, so this made conventional operations very difficult. Also, the factory was so well defended by its position in the gorge that attacks from the air would be ineffective, and so the task fell to Combined Operations, who came up with the concept of a commando raid on the factory to destroy it.

They looked to the Norwegian Kompani Linge for men they could put on to the ground to act as a receiving committee for whatever mission they put together. So before they even had a plan, four men, known as the 'Grouse' party, were parachuted into the area: Jens Anton Poulsson was in charge; Klaus Helberg was an accomplished skier; Knut Haugland was the radio operator; and Kasper Idland was a strong all-rounder.

Combined Operations then trained two teams to be taken in by glider and dropped on to the Hardangervidda and then make their way down to the factory and destroy it. Everyone knew it was likely to be a one-way trip – as escape and extraction afterwards were thought to be too difficult, the only option the guys had was to try and make their own way out by any means possible. It was quite desperate.

The two teams had been trained on a mock-up of the factory and awaited the signal to go. When it came, they boarded two gliders that were towed by Halifax bombers. Sadly, the weather turned once they reached Norway and both gliders, plus one of the Halifaxes, crashed. The lucky ones died instantly; those who survived fell into German hands and were either executed on the spot, or passed into the custody of the SS who made them suffer appalling torture before killing them and throwing their weighted bodies into a fjord. One group were sent to Grini Concentration Camp and later bound with barbed wire before being shot on Hitler's order.

The waiting Grouse party had laid out a landing strip in the mountains and were told by Combined Operations simply to lie low for the time being and 'go into hiding'. When I interviewed him, Haugland said to me, 'How? With what? We had no food left. We had nothing. It was easy for them to say, but what were we to do?'

The Hardangervidda covers an area of about 2,500 square miles, at an average elevation of 3,500ft. The barren, treeless landscape is dominated by rocky terrain and the temperature can drop as low as -30°C, so you can imagine how horrendous the conditions for these guys were. They ended up moving to a hut called Svensbu that's really remote and well hidden, and for the next few months that's where they stayed – with no food other than what they could scavenge from their desolate surroundings. That's what really interested me; I wanted to make a film purely about the survival side of the story. Eventually Combined Operations washed their hands of the whole affair, saying it was beyond their level of expertise, and it was taken over by the Norwegian Section of the Special Operations Executive (SOE), run by Colonel Wilson.

SOE looked at Kompani Linge and selected nine men to form a team who would go in on a mission known as Operation Gunnerside. They were led by Joachim Rønneberg with Knut Haukelid as the unit's second in command or 2 I/C. (I'd have loved to have met Knut because he ultimately finished the mission, but sadly he died before I had the chance.) The men were parachuted in, landing 18 miles from where they were meant to be, and Rønneberg had to hold it all together while they linked up with the Grouse party.

Despite all the obstacles, the two teams did eventually find one another and this brought renewed impetus to the mission, re-energising the whole thing. They undertook a reconnaissance of the bridge that goes across the river at the bottom of the ravine and into the factory. Not long afterwards, they climbed down into the gorge, got into the factory undetected and blew up the heavy water apparatus. Quite unbelievably, the Germans didn't even notice – the team set 30-second fuses on the explosives and Haukelid later said that the noise of the explosion 'was like two or three cars crashing at Piccadilly Circus and nobody noticed'. He later received a Mention in Despatches for having a Nazi soldier in his sights within three feet and not pulling the trigger; rather than risk alerting the Germans by taking the shot, he instead waited for the soldier to move away, demonstrating remarkable coolness under pressure, given the circumstances.

Astonishingly, the whole team got away – they re-crossed the gorge, made their way to the cable car and climbed the mountain underneath it. They reached the summit just as dawn was breaking and I had the privilege of taking the surviving men from that mission back up to the cable car. Every one of them had a wistful look in his eye as he beheld the view, remembering a mackerel sky clearing from the east. I knew that this was a sight they never thought they would see again. At the time, they had no idea how serious the mission was; they knew it was special but they didn't know just how special it was, or realise the full importance of it, until after the war had ended.

Once the Germans discovered what had happened, they realised the site at Vemork was simply too hot for them to continue to produce heavy water there, and intelligence reached the Allies that the Nazis were going to transfer the heavy water that they'd produced to date to a safer facility in Austria. To do that, though, they first had to get it out of Norway and that meant putting it on a train out of Vemork and down on to a ferry across Lake Tinnsjå from where it would be transferred to a ship and on to the Fatherland.

Of the original Operation Gunnerside team, most of them got out through Norway across the mountains. Only Haukelid remained locally on the Hardangervidda to watch over the factory. It was he who eventually planted a time bomb against the hull of the ferry on which the Germans were transporting the heavy water. When it exploded, it sank the ferry, taking the heavy water down to the deepest part of the lake. Had he not succeeded in his mission, there were several other sabotage teams waiting further down the line; there was even a submarine waiting to tackle the cargo if it had made it as far as the sea. Whatever else happened, that heavy water was never going to get to Germany.

Every single member of that team was exceptional; they were very remarkable men, each and every one. Klaus Helberg was well known in Norway for his work for the Norwegian Mountain Hut organisation, the DNT. In fact there is even a statue of him because of it. The Norwegians have a mountain huts system rather like our youth hostels and this is what he did as a job. He did it before the war and he felt that the Germans had taken away what, for him, was the best job in the world. He wanted it back, which was part of his motivation. Meeting Rønneberg and Poulsson was special; Poulsson, who kept the men of the Grouse party together for those months when there was no food, had gone out on a daily basis hunting for reindeer. He didn't manage to shoot one until 23 December and even then he missed with his first shot but eventually that day he managed to shoot a calf. He drank the blood from the carcass to give him enough energy to carry it back, and that Christmas they tuned in to the World Service on their radio, put their headphones on a plate as an amplifier and dined on venison. That was a Christmas dinner like no other.

Poulsson truly was remarkable. I asked him, 'Tell me about your time in Scotland when you were training there,' and he told me some of the tales of what they did. He said they used to catch salmon, which interested me.

'Did you spin, or fly-fish to catch them?' I asked him.

'Neither,' he replied. 'We threw hand grenades into the water.'

And it's true. Even on the estate today, water baillifs are still dredging unexploded hand grenades from the bottom of the loch.

They were all incredible men but Rønneberg was the one who seriously impressed me. He led the final assault. We were at the factory filming on the eve of the sixtieth anniversary of the raid and there was a reception in the factory for the men, but he wasn't with them; he was climbing the gorge again that day. Afterwards, he joined me and his eyes were aflame with the memories of that night.

These Norwegians were something else; their determination, their courage, their selflessness, their readiness to sacrifice themselves for their country – it was quite unique. You have to remember that Norway is even now just over a hundred years old. It was a young country then, but they were immensely proud of their independence and, as Rønneberg very eloquently said to me, 'In Britain, you never really understood what it meant to be occupied. We did, and we would have given our lives willingly to get our country back.'

When we hosted the men for dinner, he said something else that's stayed with me: 'I want to say something. It's important. When we were in Scotland training, we felt we were free Norwegians. We longed to be back in Norway. When we got back to Norway in the mountains, we felt we were British.'

That's how warm a welcome they had been given when they arrived here after escaping. That for me showed us at our best; it was a wonderful piece of wartime co-operation, and sixty years later, it was very moving to be around people like that.

20

Blade Runner

As I've grown older, one of the things I've noticed is how the public's perception of knives has changed. It hasn't so much evolved as reached a dead end. As society has become increasingly urban, the humble knife has been hijacked by miscreant youths from deprived city areas and used as a weapon to target other young people who they believe are guilty of 'disrespecting them'. Just because some young idiot wants to carry a knife and stab somebody, that shouldn't tar those of us who need to use one for legitimate purposes with the same brush.

When I first started running courses under the Woodlore banner on a regular basis, knives were an issue that came up again and again – except it was for a different reason back then. A knife is a vital tool in the woods because you can use it to make so many things. In fact, without one you're as good as helpless, so I'd ask students attending my courses to bring a knife with them. One of the first courses I ran was for some Adventure Scouts and Scout Leaders, and none of their knives were sharp enough or suitable for the tasks involved. It meant that my students weren't able to do some of the things I wanted to teach them, no matter how hard they tried, because they didn't have a tool capable of doing the job.

This was a real issue so I started to scour the UK market for a suitable knife and what I found really surprised me: there just wasn't one available – anywhere. There were lots of knives but they were the wrong shape and size, or they weren't sharp enough. What I was looking for was a small, sharp, strong and well-made knife with a blade no longer than the width of my hand. But I couldn't find one.

I'd had some involvement with Wilkinson Sword when I was first starting out and I managed to get a piece of sword steel from them; I set about designing exactly what I needed and then made a sample. It was a very simple knife with a very simple shape and an antler handle. Sword steel is very straightforward to use and I had enough to experiment a little, so once I had the sample, I refined the design and made several others – one with a classic style of edge, another with a flat ground edge, and one that had a slightly convex grind which was very tough. They were very good and worked very well.

But as I used them, I came to realise that the design would work better if the blade had a slight drop for a guard at the front of the grip. I changed the blade shape to one that would be more suitable and eventually settled on what I call a flat, bevelled grind, which is typical of Scandinavian knives. I came across a couple of Scandinavian knives that students brought to my courses that cut really well, but the blades weren't thick enough and weren't as strong as I would like.

Having settled on a design that worked, I commissioned knife-maker Alan Wood to make me the first batch. Alan's an artisan – his work is flawless and the quality is second to none. I met him through Kingsley, strangely enough, at a fair in London and he was – and remains – the best knife-maker in the country. What he produced for me is what became known as the Woodlore knife and it's since been copied all around the world.

Alan can only make small numbers – as an artisan he doesn't like mass-producing things, which is fair enough because I think they'd lose something if that were to happen. I have commissioned some other experts to make them too, so we can meet demand without compromising on quality. Over the years, we've done various editions of the original design – for our twenty-fifth anniversary, for instance, we had a Swedish black-smith Julius Patterson design a special version of it.

Of all the things I've designed and used over the years, the Woodlore knife is the one I'm most proud of because it's so perfect for what it's required to do. These knives are exception-ally strong, razor sharp and versatile because they have to be: one minute you could be cutting something to hang your pot over the fire with, and the next you could be carving a canoe paddle – it is able to take all of that in its stride. Despite there having been a twenty-five-year span since its initial design, I still haven't found a knife I like better. Anyone who knows me knows that I would happily abandon my own version if I found one that was an improvement on mine because all I'm inter-ested in is the best tool for the job – and currently, that's the Woodlore knife.

I designed it so that the back of the blade has a slight curvature so that when you're splitting bark from trees, you're able to keep the tip of the blade out of the wood. You can also easily control the depth to which you push the blade so you can strip the bark off very easily. It also helps when you're skinning. The curvature at the tip is quite important; it has a gentle radius to stop it slipping off if the turn at the end of a cut is too sharp. I learned that the hard way while testing one of my prototypes, and I have a scar on my leg to show for it. Another beneficial aspect of that design is that as you sharpen the blade, it will retain its useful shape; in fact, the edge shape will improve as you sharpen it. Its strength means you can split wood with it, or hammer it through wood to split it and you can pry with it – it doesn't shift at all.

We only make the knives with the antler handle for instruc-tors at Woodlore because they're heavier; when they receive one of these knives, we tell them that it's a weight of responsibility that comes with the job.

---◆---

There are many things in the world of bushcraft that are easily accessible and people take for granted today, but those things just weren't around when I first started out. We use a folding saw, for example, and those first came out in 1995. We lend saws to students on one of the Woodlore courses, and over the years I don't think we've ever had a blade break – handles yes, but never a blade – they're that strong. And the folding saw makes life so much easier in the woods. There are many things you can do with it and although it can't replace an axe in every given situation, in many cases it's enough.

Over the years I have used a lot of axes and although there are some exceptionally good ones out there, none were perfect – at least, not perfect enough for what I was looking for, so again, I designed my own. As with the knife, I didn't design it because I wanted to sell it; I designed it because I needed a decent bit of kit. A few years back I came across an axe firm in Sweden called Gransfors Bruks Axes and back then, the company was unknown in Britain. I started to use their Small Forest Axe, which is a lovely size of axe and I liked it a lot. I'd previously been using a much lighter, Tomahawk-style axe when I was in the woods or a small felling axe and the Gransfors fitted in somewhere between the two. You could use it one handed, or two if push came to shove, so it was a great axe.

I used it for many years, but in doing so I noticed that it was weak in a couple of areas. I say weak, but it does what it does and it does it very well. Sometimes though, you want a different axe, something that will behave slightly differently in a given situation, or you could do with something a little longer, with a head that's a fraction heavier. The way Gransfors grind their axe heads means that sometimes, when you're splitting with them, they will stick in the wood. A few years ago, I met the owner of the company and he said: 'If you ever have any ideas for a different axe, let me know.'

And I said, 'Well, actually, I do.'

So I came up with a modification to the Small Forest Axe. I liked the shape and size of its head, but I wanted it heavier so the one I designed is slightly thicker and stronger, which means that you can use the back of it to hammer with greater security. The head has a slightly more obtuse edge angle – as axes used to have – and it's heavy behind the edge so it will split better.

If you're going to use an axe, as I do, for carving, you need to put magic into the edge and by that I mean you have to sharpen the edge back a little to give a better bite. You have to put the right edge on for whatever task you're doing, which is the right way because if you live in an area where you're only cutting softwood, you want a fine edge, and if you're in an area where there's knotty wood or tougher wood, then you want a stronger, more obtuse edge, so that's left up to the user. I don't believe you can make an axe for a beginner to use, in truth. The one I designed is not meant for beginners, it's meant for experienced users and they will know how to file on the angle as required.

The axe, the knife and the saw are the tools of my trade and the rest is all to do with nature. These are the things that make life possible on the trail. You can't just cut anything – you need to know which trees to cut and why so that you don't harm the forest. But these are the tools that enable us to go into wild places and to live there. We might carry heavier tools than some people, but we can carry fewer other things because we'll use nature to help us. And that's wonderful. It's a very organic experience. Bushcraft is an organic thing. Really, with a knife, a saw and an axe, you can do absolutely everything you need to. The only other thing that's good to have is a needle – you can manage without and make them from bone but metal needles are much better.

If you could see all the things I've made over the years – if I could mount it all up – we'd have a catacomb filled to the top. Many of the things I make get thrown on to the fire later on, so there's nothing tangible left behind, so perhaps people don't really realise the extent of investment we make towards learning at Woodlore. For the first fifteen years I ran the majority of the courses, living outdoors for an average of 250 nights a year. Today that responsibilty has passed on to my team. I don't think there's any other company that has their team out as frequently as we do at Woodlore and that's what makes us special. We have a real understanding of the craft. And I still find it all really interesting. I'm still learning. I think that's the joy of the subject. One of the things I can truly say about bushcraft as a whole is that the more I learn, the more I realise I don't know. The more you undo it, the more you find. It's like an onion – there are always more layers to be found within.

It seems to me that people today are in love with the idea of being an 'expert'. Personally, I would rather continue to be a student and keep learning than consider myself in that light. There aren't the same expectations placed on a student – in fact, your only expectation is to learn, and there are few subjects where there comes a point when there's nothing left for you to assimilate. There's always something to learn because life moves on and things evolve.

When you climb the ladder of knowledge in bushcraft, as with any other field, the rungs are fairly close together initially, and you make good progress. You can look out from your elevated position of knowledge as you climb, but the further you get up the ladder the further apart those rungs become, so the harder it is to progress. That's when you really start to see those who have the staying power and those who haven't. Every step up gives you a view back over the scenery before and sometimes you find quicker ways and easier ways of doing things, and sometimes you think, well, those rungs are strong and they're reliable but we can avoid those and take a big step past them if we do this instead. And that's the joy of climbing higher. But you should never rush the journey because to have a ladder with a bit missing is not safe.

I think the maxim 'it's about the journey, not the destination' is everything in this field. If people are starting out, they shouldn't try to know it all too soon but just enjoy the process, and enjoy what they're learning as they progress; if you're too busy focusing on what's over there, you miss what's here. And it's the here and now that's important in this subject.

Bushcraft takes a lot of dedication. It's a big subject to learn, in terms of edible plants, fungi and skills. One of the difficulties we've had, especially over the last few years, is that there have been a lot of people coming on courses who've been taught to eat this, that or the other, and there are people eating things that, in many cases, aren't edible. That's an aspect that's really changed because when I first started teaching bushcraft, you couldn't get people to eat anything – they were scared to. Whereas now the fear has gone to the wind and they think they can eat everything; and of course that's not true either. I'm afraid the reality lies in that boring, grey middle ground of learning what's edible and what's not. I've always been very careful about what I eat.

These are old-fashioned skills. Many of the early authors on bushcraft were North Americans writing in the late 1800s about how to live in the woods. There's a great following today, I think, among people who have rediscovered some of these old texts. But when you actually look at the skills described in some of these books, they describe what we would know as recreational camping. They don't describe the skills of the pioneers or the local communities. I know the woods very well; I have had to live on the trail and I've worked closely with indigenous people, and I see very little of the native skills represented in these early books.

Sadly, I think this is typical with the subject – people will over-complicate things for the sake of a woodcraft camp rather than keeping it elegant and simple, which is usually the native way of doing things. The earliest book I've found written on bushcraft, although they don't use that term, was one written by two Britons in 1875 and has the wonderful title of *Shifts and Expedients of Camp Life, Travel & Exploration*. The authors, W.B. Lord of the Royal Artillery and T. Baines of the Royal Geographical Society, were two extremely experienced explorers and their book remains one of the very best about the subject. They write well, and they'd been all over, so it's truly fascinating. Interestingly enough, Sir David Attenborough chose that very book to take with him on *Desert Island Discs*.

21

Close Encounters

When it comes to what you see, wildlife documentaries on TV have much in common with icebergs: what's visible is about a third of the whole. It's a risky business working with wild animals, and I don't mean from a TV executive's perspective. When all the risk assessments have been done, what it comes down to is man against beast and the greatest threat doesn't always come from where you'd think.

Whenever I make a film about dangerous wild animals you'll probably see me on screen armed with a rifle, and there's a simple reason for that. It's because when I'm tracking in the wild, it's real. We're not faking anything. I'll be moving very quietly and going wherever the tracks go. If the tracks go into thick cover, I go into thick cover and if I bump into a leopard, a lion or a black rhino, for instance, I need to be able to defend myself; if there's a problem, then me having someone beside me with a rifle is no good to me. A person beside me with a rifle is a person too far away to be effective.

I believe that when I make a TV programme, it's imperative that what you see on the screen is, wherever possible, completely honest and transparent. What I don't like are wildlife documentaries where the presenters don't have a visible means to defend themselves but they'll have someone with a rifle or some other weapon behind the camera to protect them. I don't think that's appropriate for a number of reasons, but principally because it's dishonest. It paints a false picture to viewers, who may go away under the impression that if they're ever in the bush, they can just bimble around without risk; they can't. Take Africa for instance; sure, the wild animals in some of the areas where documentaries are made are well acclimatised to the presence of humans, but in other parts of the continent it's a completely different story.

For me, a rifle is the most appropriate means of defence, and it needs to be a very heavy calibre. My own choice of calibre for self-defence is a .416 Remington Magnum. That strikes at a force of about five tons. And don't believe everything you see in the movies; if you're defending yourself against dangerous game, just about the worst thing you can do is to fire a warning shot. If you make the decision to pull the trigger, you're shooting to kill. So far, I've never had to, and I hope I never will, but you never know what's in the next bush.

Unfortunately we don't live in a Utopian world, and as beautiful as she is, nature isn't always friendly. You will never know whether the animal you bump into has just had an encounter with another animal and its blood is up, its adrenaline is flowing, and it's angry, fearful or annoyed. If you bump into an elephant, how can you know if it's got toothache? We get grumpy and irritable when we're in constant pain, and so do animals. The fact is, there are many influences – both physiological and environmental – that can change or affect a wild animal's nature, which means you can *never* truly predict its mood.

As with most things, the best option is to try to mitigate risk wherever you can. Prevention is better than cure and, yes, it's a cliché and it's oft-quoted, but it's no less true for that. I will always try to ensure that when I'm working in the wild with animals, I've done everything I can to avoid a confrontation. If I'm tracking, I have the welfare of the people with me to consider, so if we are moving into cover, I'm sharp and alert to any threat. However low the chances are of suddenly encountering a dangerous animal, it's imperative that should I need to, I have the means to take action. When I'm around bears I don't carry a firearm of any sort unless we're in the Arctic and there's a threat of polar bears. That's a whole different ball game because a polar bear will stalk you, hunt you and eat you. We're just an hors d'oeuvre to them.

It's not an easy thing to defend yourself with a rifle, so you need to feel comfortable with whatever weapon you're carrying. At close quarters, people tend to imagine that'd you use a pistol. However, with the sort of animals I'm likely to encounter, a pistol just wouldn't be effective. Firing a pistol at a charging rhino or elephant would be about as effective as spitting at it.

The rifle that I choose to use is a Blaser R8 made in Austria. It is an extremely accurate weapon and you can interchange the barrels so it fires different calibre rounds. That's important because the overriding factor when you use a weapon is the appropriate use of force. Many people choose to use a .375 Holland & Holland Magnum round which is perfectly good for some things, but it's not as reliable against a charging rhino or elephant as a .416 Remington Magnum, even though both rounds have a similar range.

The Blaser R8 has a short, synthetic stock, which is easy to carry, and a straight pull bolt, which means you can reload very quickly. It's almost the perfect hunting rifle. It's a beautifully engineered and manufactured weapon – you can dismantle it, reassemble it and it holds zero, for instance, which is astonishing. I use Schmidt & Bender optics for hunting – their Sniper Scope 3-12 x 50 is probably the most popular sniper scope in the world for that; it has superb accuracy and that's what you want. One shot; one kill. But if I'm using the rifle for self-defence in the bush, I use Aimpoint, which is a red dot sight that enables you to respond quickly to a moving target. It's extremely good; the batteries will last, turned on, for five years.

I'm not geeky about the axes, knives or firearms I have – to me, they are just tools. And as you've probably gathered, I don't just use the rifle for self-defence – I hunt too. Why? Well, it's not for pleasure. Let's look at deer. Firstly, I believe in management and control for the welfare of the deer population, which is increasing in Britain. Deer produce 25 per cent to 30 per cent more young than they actually need every year, and the traffic on our roads doesn't take out anything like the number that's required to keep the population under control.

We have to intervene because we've removed the predators from the ecosystem. If you have an area of land where the owner doesn't want the deer stalked, this allows the deer to breed uncontrollably and you end up exceeding the carrying capacity of the land, which leads to a subsequent decline in the animal's condition.

I have DSC (Deer Stalking Certificate) Level 1 and 2 and I have a Professional Deer Manager's qualification. Here in Britain we have the best education in the world when it comes to deer stalking. I was a Trustee of the British Deer Society for three years, so I'm very keen that we should manage our deer population, not just with the bullet but by other means as well, for the welfare of the herd.

Managing deer is an important part of looking after their welfare and British deerstalkers who have undergone Level 1 training are taught to inspect the animal for any signs of disease or ill health. In this way we have constant sampling of the whole deer population happening on a regular and ongoing basis. Generally speaking, it's a very healthy species but it needs to be monitored. In my experience, deerstalkers are some of the nicest and most mature people you'll meet in society. Deerstalking isn't like shooting pheasants. You can't just throw them in the boot of the car. It's a big effort, it's a lot of work to recover the animal at the end of the day, and of course, it's wonderful eating. I love deer; most of the people I know really respect the animals they hunt.

———— ◆ ————

When it comes to dangerous animals, there's something of a hierarchy in the animal kingdom and, as I've said, there are some surprises when it comes to the biggest threat. To use another cliché, 'it's always the quiet ones'. Well, at least some of the time. These are often the ones you can't legislate for.

I've been stung by a scorpion, and a rifle isn't much good in that regard! I was just brushing past a tent in France, of all places. That was painful; they sting with arachnid venom, which is a neurotoxin that they use to paralyse or kill. This makes it safe for them to feed on prey, without the risk of a struggle, but it's a bit inconvenient to say the least for the human that's just been stung. There's a fair bit of swelling around the site of the sting but it also really messes with your mind; other venoms don't do that.

Not all of the animals that people think are dangerous pose a threat. I'm thinking here particularly of the wolf. It's such a magnificent animal but it gets the most appalling press and that really bugs me. To me, the wolf is a brother of the wild, an incredibly successful predator and a social animal. To the native inhabitants of the Americas, for instance, the wolf was a creature of power to be admired and to learn from. But to the European settlers, the wolf was an evil creature to be feared.

I was asked to track a pack of wolves in Idaho for a TV documentary that I made with ITV. In 1995, thirty-five Canadian wolves were released into the Sawtooth Mountains and by 2009 there were estimated to be over 800 of them. The release had been sponsored by the Nez Percé Indians, and when

I interviewed them, they said that for thousands of years their ancestors had lived alongside wolves, in direct competition with them for food, but they didn't hate wolves; they revered them. They recognised their strength and qualities as a social animal and they respected them for that. They also respected the wolf's skill as a hunter.

Wolves are perfectly evolved. They're not dogs, they're wild hunters – the super predators – and perhaps this is what we don't like about them. After us, wolves are our planet's top mammalian land predator. They're an effective species because they work as a team and it is team effort that's key. Although some cats, such as lions, have learned to hunt co-operatively, they're not in the same league as wolves. A wolf pack will chase a herd of caribou; two wolves will start the chase and when they tire, there will be two more waiting to take over from them and so on. When the caribou are starting to slow, the pack is ready to pounce and finish them off. Then, the wolves that were there in the beginning will rejoin the pack and share in the spoils. They work through concerted effort.

There's more and more evidence that shows that wolves play an important role in the ecosystem. They have the ability to tell whether ungulates are ill by studying their posture. Scientists also believe that wolves can tell from the breath of their prey whether they are ill or diseased in much the same way as some domestic dogs can sniff out cancers in humans. They have found increasing numbers of cases where wolves have killed ungulates but not consumed them. When they've subsequently performed autopsies, they've discovered that the dead animals were in fact diseased. So it appears that wolves are in some way programmed instinctively, to act as a regulating force in nature. People ask why wolves kill sheep and then don't eat them all: if there are too many ungulates, wolves will kill without eating so they're just performing their regulatory role in nature.

One day in our schedule was set aside for aerial filming, so as I was not involved I set off on foot to explore a quiet canyon where I had seen tracks from an alpha male. I took some forensic plaster with me to cast the track, and after six miles I found really fresh ones and set to casting them. The plaster was supposed to harden in ten minutes but it took thirty, so I sat down in the sage brush to wait quietly; I could sense the air was full of possibility. After twenty minutes I felt a presence; peering carefully over the sage brush, I saw that there, just twenty metres away, was the alpha male standing alone, sniffing the air. In complete silence and not moving a muscle, I watched him for five minutes until suddenly he looked me straight in the eye. When a wolf looks, it does so in a different way to other animals; it looks deep into your very soul. It wants to know what you are from the inside out in a way that no other animal I have encountered does. I felt no fear, no threat, just respect. We stood looking into each other in this strange encounter for what seemed like an age but it was probably only two or three minutes. Then I smiled and the wolf, with great dignity, despite my having had the drop on him, departed. I consider that moment to have been of great significance; it was as if he understood my mission. I still have the cast I made that day and it shows that alpha male's track perfectly; it's the same size as a large human hand. I am told that since then all the members of that pack have been shot – by hunters whose hearts are filled with hatred rather than respect.

———◆◆———

At the other extreme are the animals that pose a genuine threat, and crocodiles are, as you would probably expect, a huge hazard. I remember being told when we were filming in Costa Rica that there were no crocodiles in the mangrove swamps.

Well, in my experience, there aren't too many mangrove swamps where there *aren't* any crocodiles or alligators – they're kind of synonymous with one another. Anyway, I'd built a raft out of giant bamboo and the director wanted to get a helicopter shot of me sitting on it in the mangrove swamp. So there I am on this raft, waiting for the pilot to fly overhead, completely unaware that the film crew had been delayed and the helicopter hadn't even taken off yet. And guess what pops up beside me? Yes, a crocodile. So much for there not being any.

That reminds me of another close encounter with a crocodile I had when we were filming an episode of *Extreme Survival* in Arnhem Land, Northern Australia. We were telling the story of a medical flight in World War II that had crashed near the coast of Arnhem Land, and the crew had ended up building a raft to take them to Elcho Island. I knew there were likely to be a lot of crocodiles there so the threat was real and I was wary. We filmed on this beach – there were very high tides at the time so the width of the beach was very narrow and, while we were there, I saw a rather large crocodile cruising up and down watching us. With crocs, anything above three metres or so in length will think about having a pop at you, and this one was about four to five metres long. It didn't trouble us while we were filming, so eventually we moved off.

That night, I was awoken by a noise and I instantly sat up – alert and on guard. We had a couple of snorers in the crew and I have trouble sleeping when there's snoring, so I'd moved my mosquito net a bit further along the beach, a few yards away from the main camp. I lay quietly for a few minutes and then I heard the noise again. As I looked over to my left, there was the same bloody great crocodile that had been watching us earlier. He walked past me slowly, but he was very close. I was lying prone on the ground, looking up at its body. You realise just how athletic they are when you see them like that. I lay there absolutely still with my hand on my machete. There wasn't a lot else I could do but I'd decided that if it made a move for me it was going to get it on the nose. Luckily, it ambled past and went on its way. Believe me, that's a position I never want to be in again.

Earlier in the day, I'd killed a stingray with a spear and spear thrower that one of the Aborigines had lent me, and along with some other fish and molluscs I'd cooked it up on a nice fire on the beach; we all sat round and had a great evening. I would have much preferred to cook it all in the shade behind the beach but the director insisted that we move instead to the water's edge. And the one thing about crocodiles is that they've got an amazingly good sense of smell, so cooking seafood on an open fire in the middle of our camp on the beach was probably not the brightest thing to do. It's a cardinal lesson, though, that one of the really important things you need to know about dangerous animals is: what's their sensory ability? What are the things that attract them? With crocodiles, it's their exceptional sense of smell. Of all the large animals on the planet, the salt-water crocodile is, for me, the most dangerous. Bizarrely, it's not the most dangerous *life form* on earth – that would most likely be a microbe or a mosquito. But I'm splitting hairs here – you need to take very, very great care with salt-water crocodiles, so you regulate your behaviour when they're around. If you're in crocodile country, you don't go and get water from the same place twice. And if you're collecting water from a river, you put the bucket on a rope and throw it in.

When we were filming for that same programme, we were going in and out of the mangrove swamp by boat every day, and because the tidal range is so high, there was a mud gulley that we had to push the boat up and down to get into the water. We'd been doing this for several days so there we were on the third or fourth day and, as we were speeding up to get up the gulley, the propeller hit what we thought was a log. It wasn't though. Of course it wasn't – it was another crocodile that had come looking for us. It had seen us moving and thought, 'I'll have some of that.' When you're on the water, what you need to look for are bubbles coming up in parallel lines. You have to be very careful though, because crocodiles are so quick; they're an ambush predator so they're infinitely patient. Often, they will sneak up on you and you won't see them coming. Not exactly my favourite animal, that.

------◆◆------

Dangerous animals vary, and a lot depends on what continent you're on. In Africa, there are several threats that you have to consider; firstly, if you're in buffalo country, you could be in a lot of trouble. Believe it or not, the Cape buffalo is a very, very dangerous animal. It looks at you with absolute hatred; get close enough to look one in the eye and you'll see it's full of menace. As a species, it's not had a very good experience of humankind so we're not on its Christmas card list. I'm always wary when I'm tracking in the bush in buffalo country, and I wouldn't think of not having my rifle with me, although even with the right round, if you don't shoot it in the right place, the buffalo would still be a threat because when its adrenaline is up, it's unlikely to stay down. To eliminate the threat, you have to hit it in the nervous system – either a round to the brain or the spine. And when it drops, you have to immediately fire a follow-up shot to kill it.

Elephants can be very dangerous too. They can be very quiet; in fact, you can be close to an elephant and not realise it. They are wonderful creatures, full of personality, but they can have terrible temper tantrums. They're like over-tired two-year-olds in that regard, except with the power of a locomotive, and if they have had a bad day, they will want to show off and that's when they can be very aggressive. You have to be very, very careful. When bull elephants enter musth, they're a real threat. Musth is a periodic condition which is characterised by highly aggressive behaviour and caused by a huge rise in reproductive hormones – a bull elephant's testosterone levels when it's in musth can be as much as sixty times greater than normal. There are signs if you know what to look for; one of them is that they discharge a thick tar-like secretion from their temporal glands.

Animals have an invisible boundary system – a comfort zone, if you like – and these zones are not fixed, they are flexible according to the circumstances. But it's imperative that you're aware of them. We tend to think that they're visual zones, but for many animals they involve more than just their sense of sight. It's important to be aware of the distinction as this will impact on how you use the wind when you're moving through the bush, because of how your scent carries. So if you have, say, an elephant cow with a calf, and she's standing on the edge of some mopani scrub looking out over savannah grassland, her comfort zone *towards* the grass may be quite extensive because she can see over a great distance. Her comfort zone *behind* her in the scrub will be much shorter, though, because she can't see so far, so anything that comes into this zone will pose a threat much more quickly. And if you were to walk across the savannah towards her on the grass, the first of these zones is when she becomes aware of you – we call that the sight zone; if she sees you, she can assess you and she has the chance to respond to you and move away if she feels it necessary. But let's say there's some cover and she can't see when you enter that sight zone, and then you pop out from behind a bush and you're a little bit closer – you have then moved into her flight zone, which means that if she sees you and has sufficient time, she'll run away. Alternatively, you might be walking through the bush behind her and the first time she becomes aware of you is when you're very close. If she senses, or mistakenly perceives, that you are a threat to her or her calf, you'll find that you've entered her fight zone and, believe me, that's somewhere you really do not want to be.

———•◆•———

You're probably wondering why I haven't mentioned lions. Well here's where they turn up. Lions have killed more people than any other animal on the planet because, unlike say Cape buffalo or elephants, which attack when threatened, lions are predators. They hunt, then they kill, and they eat what they kill. So if you want to stay out of their food chain, you need to be aware. The lion really is the king of jungle and is by far the most dangerous of all the cats. I get really irritated when I watch documentaries and in the voiceover or narration, the presenter describes them as being 'lazy'. If you were to take a camera and film a human being at 3 o'clock in the morning while they're in their bed, you'd probably say the same. In the mid part of the day, you might find that they're a short-order chef in a busy restaurant in London and in fact they're anything but lazy, and the same is true of lions.

At night, lions are at least four times more dangerous than they are in daylight. A lion wants to kill. It's a hunter, a predator, and it's built to do just that. It's a masterpiece of engineering and nothing is wasted. Every cell in a lion's body is there to make it an incredibly powerful, capable and successful killer, and it's just perfection to watch. If you look at the skeleton of a lion, there's a big head full of teeth, with a high-powered engine behind it. A lion bringing down an elephant, for example, is not an uncommon event. Very often wildlife documentaries will say that something is very unusual, but it's not – it's only unusual in TV terms because it might be the first time it's been caught on camera.

Of all the big cats, though, the leopard is my favourite; it's a truly wonderful animal. Leopards are very beautiful creatures and very brave, too. If you threaten a leopard, it will attack, so if you get close to one, it's important not to make eye contact with it because it may just think that you want to have a go. That said, I have done just that with one and I remember thinking at the time, 'I really shouldn't be staring into your eyes like this.' It was looking back at me as if to say, 'Maybe I'll take a pop at you . . . maybe I won't . . . Let's just see who looks away first . . .' They have so much personality and they're very complex creatures. I find them absolutely fascinating. I really enjoy tracking leopards – probably because it's such a challenge. They have the perfect camouflage in the scrub and they're most active after dark. When you find a track to follow, you see how they move through a landscape and you get a sense of their identity and personalities. That said, tracking doesn't tell you everything – going out and observing them is the only way to fill in the gaps.

If there are lions about, leopards have to be careful because there's really no contest – a lion will kill a leopard without breaking a sweat. They don't have dominance in the bush like lions do, so they need to resort to guile and stay hidden wherever possible. They'll use gullies to get around, and when you track them you can see which side of the gully they've moved down, where and when they chose to cross, what they sniff, what they're looking at, and what they've scent-marked – it truly is fascinating. Occasionally you might find a place where females have been with their cubs, but that's a novelty – usually that side of their life is well hidden.

A few years ago, ITV had asked me to go to Namibia, to the Erindi Game Reserve, just east of the Erongo Mountains, to look for a specific leopard. The game reserve used to be a hunting ground, but in 2007 it was transformed into a nature conservation venture, and this elusive leopard who'd been named Houdini because he'd survived the hunting era had been the older dominant male at one time, but I thought it unlikely that he would have still retained his dominance.

He had a very big track; by that I mean his front right foot. Some people measure length but I use width and anything from 9cm and over is on the large side. Houdini's was about 11–12cm. He fascinated me because he didn't skulk like the other leopards and he was, against all expectations, still the dominant leopard, so any other male coming into his territory would have to be careful. There is ongoing research into this, but the theory for leopard behaviour in this area shows that you have a series of females that each have their own territories and they are all contained within the territory of a single male. This dominant male will do a circuit, visiting all of them, so he's always on the move. The females will hive off part of their territory if they have a daughter – that will then become hers, but a male cub gets pushed out once he's independent, and he then has to find his own territory. I'm sure in time we will discover more things. There is wonderful research going on now to try to establish the animal's behaviour patterns.

Houdini was quite happy to move in the open but we had great difficulty filming him; he was a very elusive character. We had specialist film crews working with us, and eventually we managed to get some footage of him with night-vision equipment while he was visiting a waterhole that already had some lions drinking from it. He was completely nonplussed and just walked up without a care in the world, gave them a look as if to say, 'I'm going to take a drink. What are you going to do about it?' took his fill and left. That's one pretty bold leopard.

———◆———

Of all the animals I've tracked, studied or encountered, though, one of the most amazing experiences I've had in my life was getting up close and personal with a grizzly bear. I was running a trip in British Columbia to watch and study bears in 2003. Rachel had joined me for this trip and we were living on a yacht with two clients and two of the boat's crew. When you live on a boat, space is at a premium because you have to carry a lot of food and we were sailing a long way – along the Nass River from Prince Rupert up to the border with Alaska. After a few days we had quite a few empty boxes that we needed to get rid of, and the easiest way to do that was to take them ashore and burn them. I looked along the shore for a gravel bar so that I could make a fire and not set anything else, like nearby trees, alight. Having found one, myself and the client built the fire and threw the boxes on. They were burning nicely – and that was when I heard a crackling sound beside me.

I turned to my right and there he was: a male grizzly stepping into the river right beside me. He was stood upright and he measured in at around 8ft, so he was pretty big. He stopped and looked at me. Now I wasn't completely unarmed – I had some pepper spray on my belt that was specifically for defending yourself against bears – but he didn't look like he was going to attack me, so I just stood still and watched.

All the conventional wisdom says you should never stare a bear in the eye – and it's sound advice, but inordinately difficult to carry out because their eyes are absolutely hypnotic. But I managed to pull my gaze away from the bear and I said to my client, 'Whatever you do, don't stare at the bear. We're just going to back off very slowly and move away.'

So I turned my back on the bear – which was a very difficult thing to do because it's counter-intuitive, but it's vital because it's imperative that you appear non-threatening. I gently moved away, but when I was at a safe distance and looked back, I saw that the client was absolutely frozen to the spot. I don't know whether it was from fear or the excitement of the encounter but, regardless, he needed to get away, so I had to very carefully retrace my steps and grab him. Funnily enough, though, as I got to him the bear backed off. He took a few paces backwards, and then lay down and went to sleep, as if to say, 'Oh for goodness sake, leave me alone to rest here in peace.' So we did. That really was one of the high points of my life – just an amazing experience.

Sadly, bear encounters don't always end as well as ours did. I remember a series I made a few years ago about bears, wolves and leopards where I interviewed a lady from Alberta who had been attacked by a grizzly bear. She'd been out hunting with her husband and, for whatever reason, he was into shooting animals from a long distance. He used a .300 Winchester Magnum rifle, which is a fairly pokey weapon to use; he'd shot at an elk and wounded the animal and then shot again but hadn't seen it go down so he assumed he'd missed and it had gone into some willows. He'd arranged with his wife, who was also a keen hunter, that he would stay where he was at his vantage point so that if the elk showed up again he would finish it off, while she would go down to the willows and look for it. And that's what she did. She was also armed with a .300 Winchester Magnum rifle – however, she'd never got on with it.

Bears are quite canny creatures and in the area that they were hunting, the bears had learned to run towards the sound of the fall of the shot because they would often get a free meal; the hunter would do the work and before he could get there to recover the spoils, a bear would have beaten him to it. Well in this case, the man's wife never found the elk but she did find a grizzly with her cub running towards her. She stopped to chamber a round in her rifle but the chamber was empty. So then she was stood there, fumbling for rounds to load into a rifle she didn't like, and of course as she looked up the bear was right there in front of her.

She described the bear's eyes to me; she told me how hypnotic they were and how she couldn't help but stare into them. To a bear, though, that's a sign of aggression and the bear did just what bears do when they feel threatened. Most people assume that a bear would swipe you with its paw, but its primary means of attack is to use its mouth. The grizzly stood fully upright, placed its paws on the woman's rifle, and then bit her in the face. It then went for her breast, and as she dropped to the ground, the bear took a bite out of her hip. That's when she realised that she had to play dead to survive, so, struggling with excruciating pain, she lay stock-still. The bear then walked away with its cub and left her alone.

I imagine you think that the bear was trying to kill her, but that would be wrong; it was only trying to warn her off, so it did what it normally does with other bears and bit her. When a bear bites another bear, it's almost never fatal because it's really only issuing a warning and so not using all its strength. Also, a bear's skin is tough like old leather, whereas by comparison ours is like tissue paper. The lady was badly mauled and has since had very successful reconstructive surgery. She doesn't dislike bears, although her husband does. I look at the aftermath of that situation and the obvious thing is that if her husband hadn't shot the elk from such a ridiculous range, he would have killed it with one shot and, in all likelihood, nobody would have been hurt. Also, if his wife had been using a rifle that she felt comfortable with, perhaps she'd have been able to chamber a round more easily. Really, she should have had a round already in there with the safety on; an unchambered rifle is just a club where dangerous animals are concerned.

The .300 Magnum rifle that her husband was using was a powerful weapon to use against an elk, but not from where he was shooting. Also, it has a lot of recoil and his wife was small, which may well have been why she didn't like it. If she'd had her own rifle – a .243 – with her and had loaded it with an appropriate solid copper bullet, she would have had the means of slowing that bear down and would probably not have been injured. Just having the rifle chambered would have made a difference. The bear would have perceived the situation differently because her posture would have changed. So lots of lessons to be learned there.

Grizzly bears have quite a bad reputation that I don't believe they deserve. I think black bears are rather more dangerous because they're more gregarious and much more likely to sneak up on you. If a black bear was hungry, it would deliberately stalk you and try to eat you. With grizzlies you really have to go out of your way to upset one; they'll let you know if they don't want you around.

22

Dark Clouds

In 2002, Rachel, Nathan, Ellie and I moved house. We'd outgrown the property in Eastbourne that we'd built our first home in, and Woodlore was really taking off, so we needed somewhere suitable both as a home and a place from which we could run the business. I was still having to go away a lot, either with filming commitments, lectures or running courses for Woodlore students – although, because there are only so many hours in the day, I'd had to recruit people to run some courses in my absence. I had also started to offer courses further afield – in the Arctic, and in the rainforests.

Rachel found a bungalow with some land on the edge of a beautiful forested part of England, on the border between East Sussex and Kent, and it's where the four of us made our home. On the first morning after we moved, Rachel ran outside and did cartwheels on the lawn – in her pyjamas. We were happy there for a while, but eventually the bungalow had to go because it started subsiding, so over the next year or so we designed, and then built, our perfect home.

It was a good move. By early 2003, things were going well for Rachel and me, and for Woodlore – the company that I created but which we'd built up together. When I think back to its inauspicious beginnings, forged in the crucible of Operation Raleigh, it's hard to believe that things were going along so smoothly then. When I set out, it felt like I was the only person in the UK with an interest in bushcraft, and when Woodlore started, that was all there was. Yes, there were survival schools – but they didn't do what we did.

During the first twelve years of the company, I spent a lot of time developing my technical skills. I was experimenting with everything to try to find out what was real, what wasn't, what was the creation of woodcraft camps and what was genuine bushcraft, real native bushcraft from the wilds. That took a lot of sorting out, but by 2003 I really felt I was getting somewhere. Rather than teach thirty ways of doing something, I would rather teach five that people can use anywhere; five skills that are bombproof.

In terms of my personal life, things couldn't have been better. On the TV front, I was happy with where my career was going. I had several series to my name, and I felt that I'd started to get my message out. People were watching, and learning. I'd travelled the world making programmes that I hoped were of interest to the viewing public, but in doing so I'd also acquired a much better knowledge and understanding of indigenous cultures, and the skills used by their people to survive – in one or two cases, skills that had withstood the test of 10,000 years or more.

In July 2003, I had a commitment in London to do some voice recordings. It was a rare day off in many respects – a few hours in a studio recording the narration to one of my TV documentaries, but otherwise I had time on my hands, so Rachel came with me and we booked into a gorgeous hotel. The plan was to go out for dinner when I finished, a few drinks and then back to the hotel. A nice big breakfast the following morning – the full works – and then off to a travel agency to book the trip of a lifetime.

For years we'd talked about planning our own trip to Australia. It had been a long-held dream but it had to take a back seat while we built the company and established ourselves. Sure, I'd been there a number of times making TV documentaries, but I'd never had a holiday there and Rachel had never been to the continent. So we had made a decision. After lots of prevaricating, we'd settled on a holiday: just the two of us, in a country that I knew intimately and loved. We'd been putting it off and putting it off but something changed and on a whim I said, 'Look, let's just do this. Let's make it happen.'

So I went to London to work, and the next day we were going to book the trip. The voice recording had gone really well and Rachel met me straight from the studio. We walked back to the hotel together, but she didn't seem herself. It was when we got back to our room that everything changed. I shut the door; she sat on the bed.

'Come here. I've got something to tell you.'

'I've got something to tell you.' Think on that for a moment. Six words. But they're loaded; it's one of those phrases that you never, ever want to hear, isn't it? Those six words almost never presage anything good. My blood ran cold. My stomach flipped. I don't know what I expected her to say, but whatever it was, it wasn't what she said next.

'Ray . . . Ray, I've got breast cancer.'

And it was like the world stopped turning on its axis. Suddenly everything changed; everything was different – in an instant. Just like that. Four words. And everything changed. Forever.

It was as if I'd been hit by a sledgehammer. The room began to spin a little and for a moment I couldn't function. My head didn't feel like mine because there was nothing there. No words came, no actions came, because I'd no idea what to do or say. I just sat there, looking at her. I remember putting my arms around her but I couldn't tell you if I spoke. Actually, I don't think I did for a few more minutes.

The news left me reeling because I'd had absolutely no idea.

Not a clue. I didn't even know she'd found a lump. She had obviously suspected something, but she'd kept it to herself. She'd even delayed seeing anyone about it for a week because she wanted to see a female doctor. She had seen her that morning while I was in the studio.

We didn't stay in London that night – how could we? We checked out of the hotel straight away, the bed as pristine as when we'd arrived, and headed home. We'd come up on the train and I remember the journey back as if it happened yesterday. There was a terrific storm – thunder and the most extraordinary lightning. It was as if the earth was angry too; like it was mirroring how I felt.

The train was packed, so we took seats in First Class because there was nowhere else to sit. A ticket inspector approached us and got very aggressive when I told him we didn't have tickets for First Class, but were quite happy to pay whatever the fare was. But he was having none of it. That's when I lost control and let him have it. Poor guy, it wasn't his fault – but I told him in pretty clear terms that my partner had had some really bad news and to just take the money, give us the tickets, and clear off. It did the trick because he backed off and never said another word.

I was in the middle of filming a series of *Bushcraft Survival* the day our lives changed, and was due in Canada a few weeks later, but I don't remember much of what we did in the immediate aftermath. I put my own anger, my own feelings aside and did everything I could to reassure Rachel. She was a fighter, and between us we were determined to beat this horrible disease, but in the meantime we were stuck in limbo with no clear path ahead and no way of knowing whatever the future held. Woodlore and my filming commitments placed demands on us both that we couldn't escape, so it was with a heavy heart that I bade her farewell in early August and headed to Northern Ontario.

The filming went OK but my heart wasn't really in it – for

the first time I was looking forward to it ending so I could get back to Rachel. Towards the latter end of our time there, Ben Southwell, the director, suddenly changed the venue for the next shoot, saying he wanted to bring forward a scene he wanted to wrap now instead of later. So I did what he asked and found myself canoeing along the Missinaibi River, when I noticed a float plane circling overhead. As I watched, it made a final turn and began its descent, landing a few hundred yards downstream of me. I paddled towards it and realised he'd landed in some rapids, which I thought was bizarre. Then the door opened and I heard the pilot shout, 'I've come to pick you up.' I immediately thought he meant all of us, but then why on earth would he do that when we were in the middle of filming? I quickly realised the aircraft could only take two people at a time, plus one canoe, so I said, 'OK, but take the others first. I'm more at home in the bush so it makes more sense to come back for me last.'

'Are you the presenter?' he asked.

'Yes, I am.'

'Then it's you I've come for; get in.'

At that point I started to wonder what the hell was going on but I climbed in, took the seat next to him and, as I settled, he handed me a Thermos flask.

'Here, have some coffee.'

Except it wasn't just coffee; it had Baileys in it. And then I knew something really wasn't right. That's when I started to panic; Rachel, it had to be Rachel. Something must have happened and she needed to get in touch. The pilot handed me a satellite phone.

'Raymond?'

For a moment, I was completely thrown. It wasn't Rachel; it was my mum, the absolute last person I'd expected.

'Mum? Is everything OK?'

'Raymond, it's your father. He's been rushed into hospital.'

After that, everything seemed to happen in a blur. Within two hours of climbing aboard that float plane I was on a jet starting my journey home. I left all my gear – Ben and the rest of the crew brought that back for me.

And that's when I learned that my father had terminal lung cancer.

Dad's 'mistake' was being young at a time when smoking was so trendy. Back in the 40s and 50s everyone smoked – all the movie stars, the glamorous women, the icons, and so everyone emulated that. He smoked a pipe; he was part of that generation for whom, I guess, it was cool to smoke. He'd been ill for some time, so I can't say the cancer came as a great surprise but it was still a shock to realise that our long-held fears had come true. We'd always warned him about it.

The prognosis wasn't good. They gave him a year.

23

Down to Earth

What with my father's lung cancer and Rachel's diagnosis with breast cancer, it's difficult to see clearly through the fog that blanketed much of what I did over this period. The entire family seemed to exist by mechanically plodding onwards from one thing to the next without thinking about the future too much. It truly was a very difficult time. However, when it came to my work, I had no choice but to step outside of myself and wear a mask that I could present to the world. There's one day though, even through the all-enveloping fog, that remains crystal clear in my mind's eye. I can even remember the date: Monday 23 August 2004. I can be certain about the date because it's the day that I almost died.

———— ◆ ————

It's early morning, Wyoming, USA. I'm in a town called Riverton. I push through the door of the faceless chain hotel that's been home for the past couple of days and out into the street. It's a grey day – low cloud, light precipitation with very strong gusts of wind. That could be a problem; we've chartered a helicopter for this afternoon to use as a platform for some aerial filming.

I hear the door open again behind me, and Alan Duxbury steps out.

'Not the best weather for flying, is it?' I say.

'Touch-and-go I reckon, mate,' is Al's reply. 'I'll get Matt to give the pilot a call, find out where we stand.'

That'll be Matt Brandon, the series director who heads up the film crew for the episode of *Bushcraft Survival* that we're here in Wyoming to make. There's also our sound recordist Andy Morton, production manager Cassie Walking and researcher Mary Albion. They'll be out too any moment.

We're making a programme about local legend Jim Bridger. For me, Bridger was undoubtedly *the* most notable of all the mountain men, trappers, scouts and guides who explored and trapped the Western United States between 1820 and 1850. His was a fascinating story. He was a really interesting guy who, unusually, didn't die with an arrow in his back – it was old age that killed him. He managed this unusual feat because he understood the Native Americans and there was a mutual respect between them.

He also had a reputation as a great storyteller and one of his favourite yarns had him being pursued by more than a hundred Cheyenne warriors. He'd recount how, after being chased for several miles, he'd found himself at the end of a box canyon, with the Indians bearing down on him. At this point, he'd go silent, prompting his listener to ask, 'What happened then, Mr Bridger?' He'd reply, 'Why, they killed me!'

———◆◆◆———

The others step outside into the chilly August weather. I hear Al speaking to Matt about calling the pilot and watch as Matt steps away to make the call.

Al turns to me: 'That guy we filmed yesterday was amazing, wasn't he? What was his name?'

'Ah, Jake Korell,' I say.

'Yeah, that's him – "Trapper Jake".'

Korell is in his late 90s and another fascinating figure who still worked trapping beavers and shooting coyotes for the ranchers in the area. One of the reasons we'd filmed him was because as a boy he'd known people who had met some of the legends of the West such as Calamity Jane and Annie Oakley, so he was a living link with history. After we'd finished filming, the old-timer cooked for us all over an open fire in the bush, finishing off with a peach cobbler that really hit the spot.

'Days like that are priceless,' Al says, 'a real privilege.'

Just then, Matt comes across: 'OK, I've spoken with the pilot – his name is Lionel Lester. He says that provided the rain holds off, we should be OK. He's got to fuel up later, so he'll reassess then. If it's dry, he'll meet with us as arranged. If not, he'll call me from his satellite phone and turn back.

'What I suggest is that we head to Lander and meet Jeremy Washakie this morning as planned. We can wrap up filming some of Ray's pieces to camera and some of the more basic shots.'

Lander is a small town up in the mountains and the famed Oregon Trail runs east–west near there; the wheel ruts from the old wagon trains are still clearly visible and we wanted to get some aerial shots to illustrate that. Calamity Jane lived in it back in the day – apparently she had a whorehouse on one side of the main street in Lander and a dress shop on the other. As Jake put it, 'She was making money on both sides of the street!'

Jeremy Washakie is the great-grandson of Chief Washakie, a Shoshone chief who was another contemporary of Jim Bridger. Jeremy is a one-off – a Native American Indian who is also a cowboy. It means he's an excellent rider, which is one of the reasons we are meeting him.

We spent some time the previous week filming me on horseback in Yellowstone National Park. Now horse-riding isn't a skill I've ever had to acquire before this series, so I had to learn before the shoot. I feel privileged to have been taught by a Shoshone Indian, but I could hardly claim to be experienced.

We need some aerial footage of someone riding a horse by the Oregon Trail. Bring on Jeremy – the plan is to film some long lens shots of him riding.

Now until this point, things have really been going our way, even to the point of us filming wolves in Yellowstone when we'd been told emphatically that none were around. Despite all the problems back home, this was turning out to be a great shoot.

So, onwards to Lander where I spend most of the morning doing pieces to camera. There is still a large amount of cloud overhead, with exceptionally high winds and the odd bit of rain but we carry on regardless. It's only weather – you deal with it.

When we finish, Mary and Cassie go back to our hotel to organise our luggage for the move to our next location. When they come back, they bring some food so we all break for lunch and kick our heels waiting for the helicopter to arrive.

It's about 13:30hrs when I first hear the familiar whirring of blades, then watch as the helicopter settles into the hover and lands. The pilot shuts down the aircraft – a Bell 206B JetRanger – and walks over to us. He extends a hand.

'Hi, I'm Lionel. Nice to meet you.'

I return the compliment and we all introduce ourselves.

'Have you done any aerial filming before?' Alan asks.

'Yeah, a fair bit. I did two tours in Vietnam, logged over 16,000 hours on various helicopters, so whatever you want to do is fine by me, just so long as it's within the physical capabilities of the aircraft – and my own.'

I've no idea where it comes from but I'm struck by a feeling that something isn't right. It's not something I can put my finger on – call it a sixth sense – but I have a definite feeling that something is wrong. I can't articulate it any better than that. Events overtake us though, and conscious concerns overrule my subconscious. The feeling is buried.

'Obviously, it's exceptionally windy today,' Lionel says. 'For that reason, it'll be better if you film when I'm flying *into* the wind because I can control our speed better. If the wind is behind us, then we're going to be flying a lot faster and the aircraft won't be as stable a filming platform as it could be. Clear?'

Alan nods, and explains what we're looking to achieve:

'OK, if you've filmed before, you'll be familiar with this, but what I want to do is to get some footage of Jeremy – he's the guy on the horse over there – riding along the ridge.'

Lionel nods, and Alan carries on talking through the list of shots that he wants to achieve, while Lionel interjects with affirmatives and the odd, 'Sure, that's not a problem.' Lionel is affable enough – he appears to be exceptionally pleasant and seems keen to help us get the shots we want.

'I understand you want to take the door off,' Lionel says to Alan.

'Yeah, the left one ideally – I can just sit the camera on my lap and still see the viewfinder.'

'Ah, OK. Really, I'd prefer we ditched the right one so I've got you sat directly behind me.'

Alan demurs – at the end of the day, the pilot's the captain of his ship and wherever there's a conflict between what we, as passengers, want and what the pilot says is preferable, his decisions trump everything else.

Sitting on the right isn't ideal for Alan because it means that he has to twist round to see out of the viewfinder, but ultimately you have to play the hand you're dealt. It makes things more difficult, but not impossible – life's all about compromise.

Lionel removes the door and we agree between us who will sit where. Lionel is flying from the front right seat, so Alan will sit behind him. I want to shoot some stills, so I sit next to Al on the left side. Matt has never done an aerial shoot before, so we suggest he sits in the front left seat with his monitor so he can review what Alan is shooting. He'll also be able to hear Alan talking to the pilot, so it will all be useful in the future if Matt's to be involved in other aerial shoots.

Alan is wearing a five-point harness with a karabiner, which he uses to secure himself to the inside of the cabin – it's an additional layer of safety when shooting through an open door so he can lean outside without any worry of falling. Alan looks at me: 'Ray, if anything happens, this is where I'm anchored, just in case I'm trapped or unable to release myself.'

'It won't come to that. Come on, how many times have we done this?'

We both laugh.

'Lionel, if I ask you to do anything that you consider too stupid, unsafe or you're simply not happy about it, then don't do it. Just tell me and we'll find another way to achieve what we need. OK?'

'Affirmative to that.'

It's something I've heard Alan say to every pilot who's flown us – a tacit admission that he recognises that the pilot's word on any matter is final, Ultimately it's just Alan's way of saying, 'I know how this works.'

Lionel gives us a standard safety briefing and then fires up the Bell's engine. I watch him as he takes the controls, and within seconds we lift gracefully into the afternoon sky.

First off, Alan wants to get some shots of Jeremy riding across the plain. We accomplish this without too much drama, although initially Lionel is worried about spooking the horse, so makes a pass quite a long way out, thus making life difficult for Alan who has to shoot right on the limits of the lens' capabilities. Eventually, Lionel flies closer to the ridge and Alan gets the shots he wants.

The next shot on the list is for a close-up of Jeremy which Alan will then pull slowly outwards to reveal that Jeremy's sat on a horse. As he pulls back to the end of the lens, the shot will encompass Jeremy on the horse and show the whole of the plain with the mountains behind, the sky and the surrounding topography. It's a classic 'reveal' shot that gives the viewer a frame of reference.

Alan's contorting himself with one leg folded underneath him in an attempt to get the best position for the shot, and I'm sitting upright, watching everything around me, when Lionel makes his next pass. It's too quick.

'Can we make that pass again, Lionel?' Al asks over the intercom.

'Sure can, but it'll be at a similar sort of speed,' says Lionel. 'That wind's pretty gusty so I'm not able to fly as slow as I might. And I'll have to fly downwind.'

'Not a problem for me,' Alan replies. 'Now I know, I can set the shot up.'

The fact that Lionel says he has to fly downwind means nothing to us. None of us are pilots, nor are we particularly 'air-minded' so we don't realise that it means the aircraft will need more power to stay aloft, power that is in short supply as, unbeknown to us, the aircraft is within 1 per cent of its maximum weight given the full complement of passengers and our equipment, plus an almost full fuel load.

That sort of weight figure isn't a problem if you're flying point A to point B at altitude, but if you're flying any sort of manoeuvres – such as those required in aerial filming – then you need power in hand. This particular manoeuvre turns out to be a grave mistake that will have serious ramifications for all of us. And it's born of the fact that most of Lionel's 16,000 hours' flying experience has been garnered at sea level, flying to and from oil rigs. As it transpires, he's only recently started flying in the mountains, where the air is thinner. That has an impact on how aircraft perform.

Singularly, none of these facts present a problem. Combined though, they come together to create a 'perfect storm' that whips up all too soon.

Lionel makes the approach. We're 40ft or so from a ridge that forms the edge of the plain that Jeremy is on; I notice the altitude indicator on the instrument panel and do a double take – we're flying at just 20ft above the deck. I glance at the airspeed indicator – it reads 70 knots. The thought occurs to me that, with the fact we're flying downwind, our groundspeed is going to be somewhat higher than 70 knots.

Lionel makes a violent turn that leaves me utterly disorientated. I look out of my window and at first I can't work out where we are relative to Jeremy. Then I notice the ridge seems to be a lot closer than on our last pass. It occurs to me that the ground beneath us rises in a gentle incline – and we don't seem to have the altitude to clear it.

I sense we're drifting – there's a definite list towards my side, the left-hand side of the aircraft – but all of this is happening so quickly, almost simultaneously.

I see the ground beneath us and it's rushing towards me.

The thought, when it comes, is calm and rational: 'We're going to hit.'

As I think it, I hear an alarm going off in the cockpit. With it comes the chilling, certain knowledge that I'm about to die.

'Shit, this doesn't look very good,' is the last thing I remember thinking.

———◆◆———

Nobody in their forties lives without sometimes confronting the uncomfortable knowledge of their own mortality. I've often wondered how I'd die – I guess it's fair to say I've had a few close shaves before now, but none of them ever got to the point where I thought without doubt, 'This really is the end.' Always, in the aftermath, I'd think about how my death might pan out and the things I might do as my impending doom unfolded – maybe I'd pour myself a huge drink, listen to some music and make some calls as I readied myself for the moment. Author Chris Ayres says in his book *War Reporting for Cowards*, 'If drunk-dialling is bad, imagine death-dialling – that could really get you into some trouble in the morning if you were unlucky enough to survive whatever you thought was going to kill you,' so perhaps on reflection, I'd ditch the phone calls.

But I don't get a chance to do any of that.

Inside the helicopter, everything changes in an instant and a subconscious thought prompts me to adopt the brace position. I do so without thinking and I feel like a giant hand is forcing us down.

The skid on my side of the aircraft strikes the ground. The force is immense.

We bounce up, and I have the sense that we're almost clawing at the air. The tail rotor strikes the ground and shears off with the boom and I'm vaguely aware of it flying past me, past the cockpit, at great speed.

Then suddenly, we're upended and we pitch forwards, nose down. The Bell's rotor blades – the sole means of keeping us aloft – spin their last. They strike the earth ahead of us, then dig in and shear off with terrific force.

People in car accidents and other severe traumas talk about time becoming elastic and slowing down, but in this case it feels like the polar opposite. Time seems to *accelerate*. It is so, so violent – like nothing I've ever experienced before. The energy is phenomenal – like having hold of a giant elastic band at full stretch before letting go. The mass of energy, the torque that's involved in a jet-engined helicopter, is something to behold. There's an aphorism that says that a helicopter is really just 10,000 totally unrelated moving parts, bent on self-destruction, flying in relatively close formation. Let loose, those moving parts exert a force that's all but beyond words.

The cabin, by now orphaned from the other components that made up the helicopter we'd been flying in just a few seconds before, somersaults three times. We are inverted and I reach out to grab Alan, but as soon as my hand approaches him, massively violent g-forces snatch it back and we tumble over and over again, impacting the ground before finally, thankfully, sliding to a halt.

Gone is the iconic shape of the Bell; we're now suspended upside down in what from the outside must resemble a random collection of mangled, twisted metal. The debris field is huge, bits of our helicopter strewn across the plain like discarded litter. Even now, I can still hear the sound of the aluminium body as we crash, and it's a sound like the earth screaming. I can hear the gravel death-rattling as we slide along it at an altitude no aircraft should ever be in. It's a sound I never want to hear again.

———————◆◆◆———————

We've stopped and all I can hear is silence – it's deafening. It's as if the twisting, scraping, nails-on-a-blackboard noises that define the crash have created a vacuum in their wake.

My brain sends out questions to the furthest reaches of my body, and my nerves convey signals back that answer: 'All present and correct.' I feel all right, but surely I can't have survived that completely unscathed?

A thought: 'Maybe I'm injured but I don't realise it.' But no, I'm really OK.

I've survived. I thought I was dead but I'm alive. I'm filled with a sense of euphoria.

At that moment, I feel Alan move beside me. My sense of euphoria increases as I realise I'm not the only one alive; Alan is too.

'I'm alive, but my legs are broken,' he says. My heart sinks. I look across to him and his right leg is at a horrific angle, the bottom half at 90° to the horizontal. His feet hang uselessly from broken ankles, with all the rigidity of a rag doll. The tibia and fibula in both legs are smashed. He must be in agony.

'Don't move,' I say to him. 'You'll be fine. I'll get you out.'

My survival instinct immediately kicks in. I know exactly what to do. I fumble for my seat belt release.

And that's when something ruptures above us and we're immediately drenched. I smell it even before it soaks me. It's jet fuel – 250 litres of it.

We're trapped in the wreckage, soaked in fuel with no idea what to do next. This is what *real* terror feels like.

24

Zanshin

As I'm hanging there, soaked in fuel, a thought occurs to me and I remember something that Kingsley had said to me so many years before. He told me, 'Ray, if you're ever in an accident, try to relax. You're less likely to be hurt if you're relaxed.' What he said is a fundamental element of judo – you always try to fall relaxed rather than stiff, and that's what I did as we came down. I adopted the brace position, just trying to absorb it, and it appears to have paid off. I feel OK.

I release my seat belt and drop gently to what had previously been the helicopter's ceiling but is now the floor. I clear my head. I need to focus; I'm the only one that I know for certain has escaped this crash without a scratch. I need to free Alan; he's my first priority.

I exit the aircraft through a hole that has been opened up in the impact. I'm wearing a new pair of buckskin gloves that I bought locally; it turns out they're absolutely perfect for wiping jet fuel from your eyes, as they are incredibly absorbent. Who knew?

I get to Alan.

'Alright mate, I'm here. I'm going to get you out.'

I brace myself as I undo his seat belt; Alan's a big guy and I'm worried he'll fall back *into* the wreckage and on to something sharp. I grab hold of him but nothing happens. He's stuck.

'Ray, I know we're close but can we save the hugs until later?' he jokes. 'I'm wearing my safety harness, remember?'

My small folding knife is in my pocket. I take it out, unfold the blade and cut Al free with one hand, while supporting him with my other. He's 6'2", but I have so much adrenaline pumping I'm able to hold him by myself. That's when I notice Matt is stood beside me with Lionel, our pilot. I can't quite believe we've all survived.

'Here, let me help,' says Matt, and together, we remove Alan and carry him to what I assume is a safe distance. We place him gently on the ground. His courage and stoicism are amazing; I can see his left foot and ankle are all mashed up, and his right leg is still at an alarming 90° angle to where it should be. The pain must be excruciating but he's still making the odd joke. He barely complains. He has a cut on his head – there's always a lot of blood with those because of the number of tiny blood vessels in the skin there.

'I'm sorry,' says Lionel. 'I don't know what to say. I've no idea what happened.'

'Are you OK?' I ask him and Matt.

Matt says he's OK, bar a few scratches. I'm worried about Lionel though; he appears to be in profound shock. He's also stooping; he looks like he's injured in some way. However, it's Alan who's the most badly injured and it's him I need to deal with first.

Jeremy Washakie rides over the hill on horseback and Matt shouts to him: 'Jeremy, we're OK. Can you ride over to the girls and tell them what's happened?'

He nods and, turning the horse around, gallops over towards Cassie, Mary and Andy who are with the cars about half a mile away.

Matt and I make Alan comfortable. I put a coat under his head and use my knife to cut his trousers open from their hem up to the knees. He has a major deformity to his right leg above his boot; his tibia and fibula are clearly broken. His left foot is damaged too but his boot's providing support so I leave it in place. I check his pupils; no dilation.

While I'm doing this, I hear the production cars pull up. Andy, Mary and Cassie get out and come over. I can see the shock on their faces.

Matt walks over to greet them. I watch them walk towards the cars and return with some Pelican cases. I use them to make a windbreak to shelter Alan.

I'm worried about Lionel. His stoop has worsened. He appears to be in pain.

'Lionel, come on. Why don't you lie down?' I suggest. We need to keep him prone until help arrives.

I get the first-aid kit from one of the production cars. As it transpires, it's really poorly packed and as good as useless. I'm angry. A few years ago, I asked the BBC to put together a proper expedition medical kit, but of course it went off on other trips and never came back, so we're stuck with a bog standard one which isn't majorly different to what you'd get off the shelf in your local Boots store.

I end up using some gaffer tape and a Karrimat and I improvise some splints to immobilise Alan's legs. We can't put him in traction – the pain would be too much for him to bear – so I very carefully straighten his legs out and then wrap them. That way he's afforded at least a degree of protection.

Cassie and Mary are just brilliant. I get Cassie to make a list of the injuries that I've identified, and ask Mary to contact the emergency services on 911. As she's talking, it appears from what I can hear of her end of the conversation that they don't believe her – I mean it's probably not the sort of occurrence they're used to dealing with every day.

She hands the phone to me and I explain what's happened to the girl on the end of the line. 'Look, we've been in a helicopter crash. Everyone is alive but it was a serious crash with a lot of energy involved. There's one seriously injured person so we'll need an air ambulance to recover him – he has two broken legs and other injuries, including possible internal injuries. We also have one man complaining of back pain.'

I have a Garmin Geko GPS device in my jacket and feel for it; it's still there. I was worried it had been dislodged in the impact. I take it out and give the emergency operator a six-figure grid reference for our exact location. I then ask her to read it back to me, which she does. She confirms that help is on its way and then I end the call.

When I walk over to Alan, somewhat typically for a cameraman, he's only concerned with the tape in his camera and I hear him shout to Andy, 'Mate, get the tape out, get the tape out,' which Andy does. Then I remember I've left my cameras – a Mamiya 7 and a Leica M7 in the wreckage too. I recover them. The two filters I put on the lenses have both been smashed in the impact but, incredibly, the bodies themselves and the lenses appear to be in working order. I take some images of the crash site, as does Mary.

Things start happening pretty rapidly after that. First to turn up is the sheriff, who doesn't really seem to know what to do. Hardly surprising really; I can't imagine he's seen many helicopter crashes up to that point. So in lieu of doing nothing, he resorts to that law enforcement officer's favourite stand-by and starts taking everyone's name and address. Next, some 'amateur' paramedics arrive – one of them kicks Alan's leg, so you can imagine how well that went down. I don't really need to say a thing, though – Alan does *all* the talking needed. I have to say, I had no idea his repertoire of swear words was so vast.

Then a fire engine turns up. It looks utterly incongruous given our location in the middle of a great expanse of open plain. The crew look immensely disappointed that there's no fire. A short time later, a much more professional team of paramedics arrive and administer some much-needed analgesia to Alan. Lionel is placed on a spinal board with his neck immobilised and then he's taken off to hospital.

It's only when I see the air ambulance making its approach a few minutes later that it suddenly occurs to me that perhaps another helicopter isn't the best thing for Alan from a psychological perspective. It's no more than a passing thought though; he's severely injured, and a helicopter represents his best chance of getting to the appropriate level of medical care in the fastest time possible. The crew are a model of professionalism. They ensure Alan is comfortable, load him up and that's it, they are gone.

It's only now that everyone has been dealt with that I relinquish control and responsibility for the accident site; I find doing so really, really difficult because as long as I was co-ordinating the rescue, I was occupied and in control. Handing it all over means becoming a casualty myself. It has to be done though, and then I too am taken off to hospital, along with Matt, to be checked over.

———◆———

Looking back now, I remember that in the immediate aftermath of the accident, my overwhelming feeling was simply one of shock. For someone like me, that's massively frustrating because I just want to get on with whatever I have to do, but after the crash all bets were off. I felt completely discombobulated and out of sorts.

Almost unbelievably, aside from a few bruises, both Matt and I escaped injury. Lionel chipped a tooth and fractured a vertebrae in his back, and was in hospital for a week or so, but poor Alan remained in hospital for over two weeks receiving treatment and was eventually repatriated to the UK, where he was admitted to a top Birmingham hospital for more operations and rehabilitation. Unfortunately, although he did eventually go back to work, it didn't last – the legacy of that trip was that he was no longer able to work. It was terribly sad because he was a first-rate cameraman and a key member of the team on so many expeditions. He is also a good friend and I know that even now, he still feels the loss of his career.

Both he and Barrie are really special, just brilliant guys. I know other cameramen used to wonder why they got all the jobs, but it was simply because they were really good at what they did. Nothing was too much trouble for Alan and he never seemed to get tired. Before the accident he had boundless energy, and to see that stripped away from him by the ineptitude of our pilot that day makes me angry.

When you fly with good pilots, you *know*. I didn't feel that with Lionel. He had supposedly done two tours of Vietnam – although it later transpired that he wasn't out there as a pilot; he'd been a Chief Tech, so there's a massive difference. On paper, he appeared to be one of the best around – he had over 16,000 hours logged, which is a simply huge amount for any pilot. Sadly for us, he was completely inexperienced in both mountain flying, which was what we needed him for on the day, and perhaps just as crucially, filming – he'd done almost none.

I'm still angry about that, although in my more contemplative moments I do recognise that we're all enormously lucky to have survived that crash. We were lucky too where the fuel cloud was concerned. I mean we were all covered in it, but because of the way it landed on us – almost like a mist – we all breathed it into our lungs too and if it had gone up, we'd have burned from the inside out. It doesn't bear thinking about.

Sadly, for me, the accident wasn't the worst aspect of that trip to Wyoming. And although it's the day that I almost died and

I remember it for that, the following day delivered another massive blow.

It's the day I found out my father had died.

The morning after the crash, I hadn't long woken up and was in my hotel room, looking at my camera and wondering how salvageable it was and whether I'd be able to shake out all the broken glass and other debris from the crash.

The phone rang. I picked it up.

'Ray, hi. It's Dick Colthurst [the series producer]. I'm afraid I have some very bad news for you. It's your father – he died yesterday.'

However much you expect to hear news like that, it still knocks you for six. And while his death wasn't unexpected, it still felt like the bottom had fallen out of my world. The only plus for me was that he never knew about the crash and he died without knowing that Rachel too was battling cancer.

My dad; my lovely, patient, wonderful, warm and caring dad. Such a lovely man.

He lost a finger when he was a young man; it got caught on a rag when he was cleaning one of the printing presses and got crushed, but it didn't slow him down. His zest for life knew no bounds and he was extraordinarily patient. He was something of an engineer as I guess a lot of men from his generation were – I once saw him convert a friction-feed printing press to suction feed, and he made *everything* involved in that. He made the device that he connected to the gearing system to control the suction device; he machined the pistons and he even made the rubber suckers to go on those pistons. With friction feed you have a bar that moves forward over a stack of paper and pushes a single sheet in, but what his suction-feed machine had was two pistons that would pick up the paper and feed it into the printing press. That's not an easy thing to create, especially in a garden shed. He did that so that he could print envelopes with greater accuracy. He was a very, very clever man.

While he was at News International, he became embroiled in the bitter dispute that occurred when Rupert Murdoch abruptly moved his printing operation to a non-union plant in Wapping. My father kept his integrity and fought, but it was a hopeless battle that sadly the guys were never going to win. Murdoch had covered all his bases and he broke the unionisation that had dominated Fleet Street for decades. When the strike broke, my dad started his own printing business. It was very successful and he retired happy and content.

I still really miss him.

25

Into the Dark

After her diagnosis, Rachel was advised to have a mastectomy. That was when time became an issue: if her lymph nodes were clear, then they'd do reconstructive surgery then and there, and she'd be in theatre for a number of hours; if, however, she was in theatre for only a short time, that was a different matter altogether and something I didn't want to think about.

The day of the operation came around much too quickly, but it was imperative we knew what was happening. Sadly she wasn't in theatre for very long. The news was as bleak as we could have feared: the cancer was terminal. I heard the words coming out of the consultant's mouth but they didn't compute. It was like having one of those out-of-body experiences people talk about; like I was watching this from afar and it was happening to somebody else. Rachel? Terminal cancer? How on earth could that be true?

The trauma of learning that the woman I loved was going to die – and that we almost knew the date – was devastating and it affected my eyesight. I don't know how or why, and I can't explain it any more eloquently, but it temporarily damaged my eyesight.

She had two years. Two years. Twenty-four months. Seven hundred and thirty days. That was all it took. Two years to go from full health, a picture of vitality, to her death. We thought we'd book that once-in-a lifetime trip to Australia that we never got round to arranging when we went to London. But the most mundane of things put paid to that idea and it never left the ground. We never got to travel to Australia together and it was all down to travel insurance. One of the things we learned quite quickly is that once you're seriously ill, you can't get health insurance to travel. How cruel is that? You've got limited time to live, so you think, 'I know, I'm going to go to that paradise I've always wanted to go to with the one I love. Sod the consequences.' But you can't.

The cruellest twist of all, though, was how quickly Rachel fell ill. There are different forms of breast cancer and Rachel had the most aggressive. Her decline was as painful to witness as it was rapid. She was amazing in how she dealt with it, just amazing. She was so, so brave. Immediately after we found out it was terminal, she seized the bull by the horns and got straight down to business. She'd never made a will; she had one drawn up the very next day. Then we sort of came up with a strategy to fight it. Terminal? She wasn't going to just give up, she went down fighting and she fought like a tiger right to the bitter end.

It's almost like you're living in a parallel universe after the diagnosis, as if you've been hived off from the real world. You start going to these clinics and you meet all these different people with all these different types of cancer, all different degrees, and they're all fighting this battle and it's a whole world that most people, thankfully, don't know anything about. There's a whole new language and shorthand to learn – it's like a secret landscape within Britain, complete with its own population.

My memories of that time have taken on a strange ethereal quality, and there are periods where I just can't remember anything – it's almost as if it's just too painful and my brain's shut those memories down and denied me access to them.

Rachel underwent both chemo and radiotherapy – the chemo in particular was awful. But there was a wonderful period of sunshine where she seemed to be a lot better. Sadly, it turned out to be false hope.

Rachel was a proud woman. She wanted life to continue as normal for everyone else around her, so she hid the fact that she was in a lot of pain. I remember her taking Nathan to the airport one day and she held it all in until she got home, where she subsequently collapsed and I ended up rushing her to hospital. The staff in A&E were fantastic, just fantastic. She was admitted straight away and that's where her care came undone. She had private healthcare so she was under an oncologist, but the hospital consultant didn't notify him. He was a bully, this consultant – a real bully. And when he realised how far her cancer had progressed, he sent a junior doctor to tell Rachel that she was dying. If I were ever unfortunate enough to be admitted under his care, I'd pull the lines out of my arm and crawl out rather than allow him to treat me.

I drove Rachel out of the hospital and took her over the South Downs – I thought if she was going to die we needed to spend some quality time together out of the hospital environment, and it's what she wanted. She hated being in hospital. I think that was on the Friday. Anyway, come Monday I managed to get word to her oncologist and he was furious. He had her admitted to a private ward and he took control again. Your first reaction is to complain and boy, did I want to fight. I wanted to go down and give that bully of a consultant a hiding. I thought of getting the press involved – there were so many different ways I was going to show him – but in the end I realised what was important, and energy spent on fights like that is energy you don't have to deal with the real battle.

Terminal cancer – anything like that, something life-changing, something that is going to take away the person you love more than anything in the whole world – teaches its own lessons. There's a paradigm shift in how you see and experience life. But you have to survive; life has to go on because, ultimately, there's no alternative. You still need to get up in the morning; eat, pay bills, buy shopping . . . it's the sheer mundanity of it all, the realisation that it's the minutiae of life that keeps you going. And in some ways, I guess, it's a good thing – the routine, the structure. It's its own form of support because if you're not careful, something like that can utterly overwhelm you. It's such a big thing to deal with, I'm not entirely sure you actually *cope* – you seem to more blunder through like a ball in a pinball machine, bumping from one problem to the next. As for the pain, the fear – I think I've blotted it all out. I really don't have a strong memory of that time.

All I can say is that when you are confronted with something so enormous, there's a profound challenge to your personal philosophy. You only survive if you've invested sufficiently in that philosophy because I think at that point you're on auto-pilot – you're no longer able to have control of anything. You become a passenger to some extent and life just carries you along. You have ups and you have downs but . . . how can I put this? You learn to swim, and at a time like this you are in rapids – occasionally you rise above the surface and take a gulp of air, but most of the time you feel like you're breathing water and drowning. All you can hope is that you'll eventually find the strength that enables you to swim out of the current.

In my case, I was my own support network. I trust myself. I trust my own judgement. I can deal with things. That's how I am. I don't really get lonely. I've always enjoyed solo trips into the bush but when Rachel was ill, I didn't want to leave her.

Fifteen years we'd been together; fifteen years in which we'd ribbed one another mercilessly about getting married. It became 'our thing', we joked and teased one another about it all the time. I'd ask her to marry me, and she'd say no. She'd ask me and I'd say the same. Because we never needed to. We were so together, we had consummate, utter trust in one another and we were in love. We didn't need to be married; it didn't matter, it wasn't important.

It didn't matter. Didn't. Past tense. Then suddenly, it took on huge importance. Nothing else mattered. It became the most important thing in the world. We married at Eastbourne Register Office.

Lars Fält, a close friend from Sweden, was my best man. And the date? It was 7 July, 2005 – 7/7 the day of the London bombings.

And then, a short time later, everything unravelled. Suddenly, being married didn't seem important. We had a vision of the end, and I would have given everything I had to delay the inevitable. I'd sworn to protect her. And I couldn't. I wanted to mend her, make everything better. All my knowledge, everything I'd learned, and there was nothing, *nothing,* I could do.

We'd been sat in the lounge on the afternoon that everything started to spiral downwards; the day that flimsy wall we'd erected around ourselves crumbled to the ground and her illness unveiled itself before us in the most pitiless manner. There were a couple of steps at the end of the lounge, and another couple that led up into the kitchen. She had just got up to make a cup of tea; how mundane is that? And she tripped. I saw it happen, but it wasn't a normal trip like you or I would do if we got to a step and missed our footing. I could *see* – and her legs just didn't seem to be working properly. And I knew. I just knew something wasn't right.

Rachel rang her doctor and told him how she was feeling. Then I spoke to him and that's when he explained to me that the cancer had reached her brain. Sadly, medicine hasn't yet developed an effective way of delivering therapeutic agents across the blood–brain barrier to treat that type of cancer. That really marked the beginning of the end; we both knew that there was no way back from there.

The really awful thing about a terminal disease like Rachel's is that those left behind have time to prepare. There's an end point, a demarcation zone, a line in the sand. A part of you knows there's life on the other side for *you* but not for your loved one, yet your brain doesn't want to acknowledge it. It's an awful thing to say, but while Rachel deteriorated I had time to try – and try is all I could do – to come to terms with everything. You know that death is going to be a form of release for the person dying, but you don't want to let them go. My mind was awhirl with so many conflicting emotions, and for me it was one of the worst things because you can't help focusing on the end even though you feel awful doing so – it feels disloyal, like a betrayal of some kind.

There's no way Rachel was going to go into a hospice. I've nothing against them, but she wanted to be at home and I wanted her to be where I could take care of her, so that's what we did. I'm not even going to try and describe the last few days. She was aware, but she couldn't communicate by that stage so it was indescribably difficult. When she finally passed away, Nathan, Ellie and I were all there with her; the whole family was there in fact. It was 16 May 2006.

* ◆ ◆ *

Afterwards, I was in a really strange place. It affects everybody differently, the aftermath. I really wasn't in a very good place at all. Losing Rachel was almost unbearable. I spent two years caring for her and all of a sudden there was a void there, this Rachel-shaped vacuum where the person I loved, worshipped, used to exist. For the whole of that two years, we hadn't had a normal relationship but that's how it is – when the person you love and care about more than anyone else in the world is dying, you stop caring about yourself. For me, there was only her and I let myself go. I fell apart – physically as well as mentally. I wasn't important – she was. And then all of a sudden, I was on my own. Sadly, the immense strain of the whole ordeal, and the way that the effects of grief affect everybody, eventually tore the family apart.

I had so much resentment, frustration and anger inside me. I was angry at the world for taking her away. I felt lost. There was so much negative, poisonous emotion bubbling within me, yet I couldn't take it to the forest, which would have been my normal escape. It would have been wrong to take all that into the wilderness and get rid of it, almost like contaminating something beautiful. You have to rediscover your longing to go out again and so to take a problem outdoors would be to infect the outdoor experience with that problem.

I had to find another way to let it all flow out of me. After she died, I cried for three days solid. You have to let it out; you can't hold on to it. You have to let go. It's like in judo – if something's not working for you, you have to let it go, do something else. Judo philosophy is very powerful in that regard and it's a matter of finding a focus. You have to find a lifeline to grab hold of. And I found it, after a few months of floundering, in the gym.

The gym allowed me to create a routine, find myself something to do in the times when my mind was idle, when it would dwell on the things it shouldn't. It was very helpful – because it's so physical, it forces your body to produce endorphins and endorphins make you feel good and then you wear out as well, so you sleep, because otherwise you don't sleep. *That* was really important. The weights, the cardiovascular equipment, became the focus of my existence for a while and I took all the bitterness, the hurt and, the anger into the gym with me. I wore myself out and in the process, got myself fit – both mentally and physically. Mentally, because I had the time and space to process everything in my head, and physically because it was my body that benefited from the training.

I had something to get up for every day, and very gradually I started to feel better. It was good for me – you just have to cope, but you need a focus and that was mine. Coping is something I teach people on my courses – I teach them to cope in the wilderness, so I had to take some of my own medicine and turn those skills inward. I had to cope with the loss. Also, it got me out of the house; memories of Rachel screamed from every room so it was good for me to get out. And to be around people again. I don't mind being on my own, but the isolation you feel when your soul mate dies is just so traumatic. It's horrible.

Her death changed me in countless ways. I can't watch a soppy TV programme or film now without a tear coming to my eye – things like that never affected me before. It's made me a lot more empathetic. But the biggest change is in how I see the world and how I don't believe in wasting a single second of life. Filming involves a lot of standing around and kicking your heels and I get really frustrated by all of that these days. I want to do something with the time, so I'll say to directors, 'If you don't need me in the next hour, tell me because I can do something with that time.' I don't want to stand around – time is too precious.

In the aftermath, I had to close the door on my old life – the life I had with Rachel. I had to accept that it was over and the best way for me to honour her memory was to start something new – a new life. Life goes on. I decided I'd do all the things that I had denied myself before. If I was invited to any functions or events, I'd go – previously, I turned them all down.

I started a new chapter and was clear in my mind that I wouldn't make comparisons – what was before was before; everything that followed would be different. There is clear blue water between the two. I had to draw a line and it was important to me that I never made comparisons – either good or bad, between my old life and the new life I was leading. I needed to become a new person and to do that I needed clothes – clothes suitable for doing all the things I'd never done before. I didn't know anything about this – previously, I'd just worn green, all my attire was geared towards my outdoor life, my woodsman's life. That's still who I really was at heart, but I thought I should start doing all these other things too.

The irony is, I was doing publicity for a new TV series so it was the usual round of journalist interviews. One of the broadsheets wanted to talk to me, and the journalist – I won't name her, but she knows who she is – wanted to meet me in London, so I thought I'd dress appropriately for once. Instead of my usual greens and a fleece or outdoor jacket, I dressed in a good shirt with cufflinks, a smart jacket and slacks – you know, smart clothes, just what you'd wear for a decent hotel or bar in the capital. And the journalist made some snide reference in her copy about how I was dressed for the city rather than the woods. That was really hurtful and actually a bit of a cheap shot. She even had a dig at the fact that I didn't have a survival knife or emergency flares in my rucksack. The whole concept of dressing for, and carrying, what's appropriate for your environment seemed a bit lost on her. It was as if the clothes I was wearing detracted from who I am. Does dressing in a shirt really negate the fact I've dedicated my life to what I do?

I had bent over backwards to make myself available for

that interview. I don't court the press – but when you write books and present TV programmes you accept that you have to do a certain degree of publicity. It's something I'd rather not have to do – I really don't enjoy it – but I'd gone out of my way to accommodate her and it felt like a slap in the face. Funnily enough, I bumped into her again at the launch for the Range Rover Evoque. The look on her face when she saw me was a picture.

———◆◆◆———

Eventually, you have to get back on the horse. Life goes on. Suddenly, I was single again after fifteen years of sharing my life with someone, so I found that all very strange. You form relationships with people and it's all part of the healing process – it's just a very strange place to be.

The most difficult thing of all came much later. I'd reached a point where the constant reminders – Rachel's clothes in the wardrobe, her perfume, her stuff, the physical possessions that were imbued with her personality – were holding me back. What do you keep? What do you get rid of? What is a person when they're gone? Rachel existed now only inside of me, not in the physical possessions she had acquired over her lifetime. But still I found it all but impossible to do and in the end, I needed help in doing it. And do you know what? The hardest thing of all was her shoes; that almost killed me. Because for the longest time while she was ill, I'd had to put her shoes on for her – she was so weak, she couldn't do it herself.

One thing I did hold on to was a voice message from her that had been on my mobile phone from way back. It meant the world to me and I'd been careful to keep it. In fact, I would probably still have it, only someone stole my phone. It's strange, but it felt like losing her all over again.

I've always been fascinated by the history of the American West, both from the point of view of the settlers and the native peoples who were there already.

Whenever I look at these pictures of the helicopter crash in Wyoming in 2005 I ink it's extraordinary no one was killed. As you can see, it looks more like a squashed metal box han a helicopter. The wer picture is unclear because there was aviation fuel on the lens of my camera.

Gordon Hillman, archeo-botanist who knows as much about plants, their origins and their uses as anyone.

Lars Falt, one of the gre
old men of the norther
frontier and a real expe
in the ways of the nort

With Syd Kyle-Little, bush policeman, one of the last pioneers of the Australian frontier, who died in 2012.

Working and travelling in the northern wilderness is always special for me. Making snow-shoes with Pinnock Smith and building an igloo were a great part of creating the television series.

With my wife, Ruth (below, on our wedding day) and I took this picture (right) in the Arctic.

The search for Raoul Moat involved some intensive days tracking in Northumbria, during which I worked with the Metropolitan Police Fire Arms Squad.

Encounters with animals (and fish). This photo (top) may look as if it's not real, but I can assure you it is! This wolf had been specially reared to be comfortable around humans so scientists could learn more about the habit and behaviours of its wild brethren. The dog fish looks rightly pretty keen to return to its own environment, the sea.

With Her Majesty the Queen.

Working with young people is something I enjoy very much – and introducing them to the art of fire-making is always special. Empowerment is the secret of proper bushcraft instruction – it takes the fear away if you teach people simple techniques they can use themselves.

That said, I realised there was nothing I could do. The phone was gone and so was she.

Rachel was a very special person. Hardworking, full of life, full of energy, and very bright. She lit up a room when she walked in. She had a very good sense of humour and was really generous; she was always helping people out. For several years after she died, I was still receiving letters from people and I'd discover that she'd been helping or advising them and nobody had known anything about it. She was like that; she just wanted to contribute to the world and make it a better place – and she did.

26

The Light of My Life

Ihonestly did not think that I would ever find love in my life again, so I threw myself into my work to cope. I managed to function, I was still undertaking filming commitments and, on camera, I was the same as always. I was running courses for Woodlore and to all intents and purposes I had returned to the world of the living. But there was a difference and, if I am honest, I was running on auto pilot and my internal flame was very low. Thinking back, I am not even sure that I was aware of it myself until someone burst through and rekindled that flame with the warmth of her amazing personality.

That someone is my wonderful wife Ruth.

One day towards the end of 2007, I was on the final few dates of a lecture tour. It had been a packed itinerary and I found myself in a huge theatre in Newcastle. The lecture had gone well and I was finishing up, as I normally do, with a book-signing. Support staff were busy dismantling equipment, and I was just sorting myself out prior to going outside where I was going to do the book-signing. A few members of the audience were milling around and chatting in groups, as if waiting for the official instruction to form an orderly line.

Suddenly, from out of nowhere, Ruth appeared. She had a beautiful radiant smile on her face as she held her arm aloft, wielding one of my books in her hand.

'Excuse me, would you please sign my book for me?' She arrived with such energy she quite literally knocked me off my feet; I fell to the ground.

And when I got up, I felt completely different; there was just this instant connection. The chemistry was right there from the start. I've no idea how, but she broke through the fog that had been surrounding me. It was love at first sight. But of course I didn't tell her that. I said, 'The signing is outside in ten minutes and yes I'd love to sign it for you.'

Ruth was there with a group of friends who had persuaded her to come along because, as one of them had said, 'Oh, you're quite outdoorsy, aren't you Ruth?' which I later found out was true. Ruth was reading Geography, Archaeology and Social Science at Durham University as a mature student. It turned out she was into mountain biking, running and camping. So yes, she was a bit 'outdoorsy'.

She'd been given one of my books for her birthday, but she hadn't read it and when she got to the front of the queue outside, she walked up to me and said, 'There's one question nobody has asked you yet, so can I ask?' and she just came out with it: 'Are you married?'

It kind of floored me for a second, but I recovered my composure, looked at her and said, 'Actually, my wife passed away,' and as I said it, I thought, 'Brilliant Ray, nice work. That's really going to put her at ease.'

All things considered though, I thought she handled it brilliantly, even if she probably did feel like she wanted the ground to open up and swallow her whole. She touched my arm and it was like a bolt of electricity had passed between us. She looked me in the eye and said, 'Oh I'm so sorry; I feel awful. Would you like another one?' She has an excellent sense of humour. But there was magic in the air.

My heart missed a beat. She was gorgeous. I liked her – a lot. I said, 'Why, are you asking?'

She laughed, and then the people in the queue behind started getting restless, so she moved aside to join her friends. They all stayed around for ten minutes or so afterwards taking photographs and one thing and another, and I meant to ask her for an email address or phone number, but I got tied up talking to someone and when I next looked up, she'd gone. To say I was disappointed would be an understatement, but there wasn't much I could do. That was when one of the security girls came up to me.

'Oh, Mr Mears,' she said, handing me a scrap of paper, 'a man gave this to me and asked if I could pass it on to you.'

I thanked her and looked at it; it was Ruth's email address.

Apparently, she'd told one of her friends that she really liked me but was so mortified that she'd asked about me being married that she'd left. However, unbeknown to her, another friend had written her email address down and passed it on to my security team.

I didn't want to appear too keen so I'd planned to email her a few days later, but I still had a couple of dates left on the tour and it wasn't until I arrived back home three weeks later that I realised I had forgotten. So I wrote to her, saying how much I'd enjoyed meeting her and that I hoped we might meet up again. The reply I received was cool to say the least, so I assumed she was making me pay for having taken so long in getting in touch. After playing email tennis a couple of times I called her, though it didn't exactly go as planned . . .

'Hello?'

'Hi Ruth, it's Ray.'

'Oh, I'm sorry. I don't know anyone called Ray. How did you get this number?'

That was me put in my place, then!

'Ruth, it's Ray Mears.'

Then there was silence. And I could almost hear the penny drop.

'Oh, Ray! I'm so sorry!'

Well with that cleared up we talked and talked; there was no stopping us and we arranged to meet up. Ruth was to be off from university around Christmas but she wanted to spend the time in the run-up to the 25th with her young son Kristian. Christmas day was the earliest that we could meet that suited both of us.

So she drove down to meet me and we got on famously. It was as if we'd known each other for years. I knew she was the one and I asked her to marry me. She said yes. Two weeks later, she thought she had better return to see her son, who was enjoying staying with her grandmother. Eighteen months after that we married. It was a discreet affair with seventy guests at a small castle; it was just lovely. I never dreamed I would be this happy again, but Ruth has changed everything and meeting her and her son Kristian was the best thing that's ever happened to me. They both moved in with me and, with our Labrador who joined us as a puppy in 2010, we are as happy as can be.

I love Kristian very much. He was twelve when we first met and I really enjoyed getting to know him as an individual. We have a fantastic relationship, which is built upon love and trust. He is a remarkably gifted and intelligent young man and I am really excited to see what he contributes to the world.

There are so many lovely things about Ruth, we share many of the same interests. Music, taste in food, the great outdoors. We spend a lot of time out watching wildlife together and whenever she is able, she accompanies me on overseas expeditions. She is wonderful and brightens the world around her.

It was shortly after Ruth and I married that I was finally diag-
nosed and cured of a disease that had dogged me for some
sixteen years but which I didn't even know I had. My health
had suffered massively and I'd put on weight, but over time it
became like background noise. It had always been there, and
I learned to live with it and work around it.

I'd been overweight for most of my TV career but I'd always
put it down to the fact that I couldn't exercise because I suffered
from severe back trouble. Over time, it started to affect what
I could do. In my line of work, where I spend so much time
outdoors, my being unfit was making me hesitant to do things
– to go somewhere, to climb something, to cross something
– and that's not healthy.

I thought I just had a bad back but it transpired I'd had
long-term Lyme disease. Lyme disease manifests itself with
myriad symptoms – in my case, a bad back and weight gain
– and it would appear that I picked it up when I came back
from filming in Samoa for *World of Survival* in 1996. At first
I simply thought I was suffering from a trapped nerve and the
pain was intermittent. I didn't really think anything of it, but
it got worse and worse and eventually I was filming in Venezuela
one year and the pain was so bad I had to fly home. I had a
scan when I got back and it showed I had two discs that were
worn out and were pressing on the sciatic nerve, causing my
back to go into spasm. I was given morphine-based painkillers,
anti-inflammatories and muscle relaxants and told I had to
stay fit.

Talking with others who have suffered from Lyme disease
it seems that quite frequently it exploits or exacerbates an
existing physical weakness, which makes it difficult to diagnose.
Throughout this period I also made frequent trips to the tropics
and it is likely that the anti-malarial medication which I was
using had masked the symptoms. The painkillers helped to
sort it out to a degree but it was only ever a temporary fix

because they were treating the symptoms and not the cause. It was only about five years ago – shortly after Ruth and I married – that I realised it was something altogether more serious than a bad back. I went to the dentist because I thought I needed some work done but it turned out I didn't – the jaw pain I was experiencing was just another symptom of Lyme disease. I spoke to a naval doctor friend and he emailed me a list of symptoms for it and when I looked through it, I realised that I ticked almost every one. So I went to see my doctor, who treated me with anti-biotics, and I have been fine ever since. I'd had it for about sixteen years and never realised. Being pain-free and healthy again has given me a new lease of life, and it's made my life with Ruth much brighter.

I feel blessed to have been able to find such profound love. Ruth and I are inseparable. Every year since we met she has been by my side in Lapland where I teach Arctic bushcraft, we have tracked and watched African wildlife together and paddled by canoe in the Canadian wilderness. While going solo is magical, travelling in remote areas and sharing those unforgettable experiences with your wife cannot be beaten.

Ruth is the love of my life, and I can honestly say that I am the happiest I have ever been. This is a new and exciting chapter in my life.

27

Going Solo

Canoeing is one of those things that I love doing more than anything else. In fact, I'd go further and say that I think the canoe is one of humankind's greatest inventions. It became popular in Canada in its earliest days because of the relative ease with which a canoe could be built, usually requiring no more in its construction than what could be secured from cutting down one of Canada's millions of birch trees. Travel by water was one of early Canada's quickest means of transportation, particularly in its more remote regions, because there was no access by rail, car or horse.

A canoe is an amazing thing – it floats on water like a leaf, and you can travel across a continent with it, because when you can't paddle, you can lift it up and carry it. You can load it heavily if you need to. It feels as if you live on the surface tension of the water, caught between the current and the wind, and you harmonise and choreograph the process to travel in a specific direction; it's like a dance.

Canoes played a major role in the fur trade, which is an area I wanted to cover when I made the TV documentary *Northern Wilderness* in 2009. This programme focused on Samuel Hearne who, for me, was one of Britain's greatest explorers. He joined the Royal Navy and went to sea at the age of twelve as a captain's assistant, and went to war. When the Seven Years War ended, he secured a position in the

Hudson's Bay Company. He threw himself into life there and learned to snowshoe, and how to hunt. He learned to speak Inuktitut and other languages, and in 1769 he went off in search of a possible copper mine.

What set Hearne apart was his commitment. He learned to travel like a local and he did it so well that the locals respected him and treated him as an equal. He proved that the only way to travel across Canada was by travelling in the manner of the Indians, adopting their strategies, skills and equipment – particularly the use of snowshoes, toboggan and canoe for transport. He set an example that everyone who came later was influenced by. He trained David Thompson, who went on to map three-and-a-half million miles of Canada. It was his example that Dr John Rae – who discovered the Northwest Passage – followed. Going there made me realise just how stunning Hearne's achievement was. You can't ever really get to grips with just how vast Canada is, but following Hearne's route was astonishing. To go there and realise your budget will only take you so far on that route just puts it all in perspective.

There were two aspects of canoeing involved in the documentary. One was the small canoe of the *coureur des bois* (runners of the woods) – the guys who ventured into the woods to trade European items for furs – so we had one made from birch bark and I paddled that through rapids. I also told Ben Southwell, who was producing the programme, that I needed a *canot du maître*. The fur trade depended on these canoes, which were as long as 12m and carried six to twelve crew and a load of 2,300kg. I told him it had to be the real deal – not a plastic canoe *painted* to look like birch bark.

The BBC had kittens about that – there were murmurings about health and safety, insurance, the whole nine yards, but a saviour came forward in the guise of Jeremy Ward, the curator of the Canadian Canoe Museum at Peterborough, in

Ontario. He took one of their *canot du maître* canoes apart, then reconstructed it again a week before we needed it to make it river-worthy. Then we took this 36ft canoe down the river. That was important – a plastic canoe wouldn't have had the same atmosphere, the same smell, feel and sound of the boat. It's a small detail, but it's an important one. The devil, as they say, is in the detail. Always.

I was so grateful to the Canoe Museum for going that extra mile for us. Their passion for the canoe – which for me is the true symbol of Canada – their championing of it, was truly special. It was symbiotic, the way that so many things came together for *Northern Wilderness*. A TV film like that is so much bigger than any one person, because it connects so many people who are passionate about their subject and they all bring their own unique quality to it. It becomes bigger than the sum of all its parts.

For me, what's instructive is the dichotomy between what we had logistically, and what Canada's earliest explorers and settlers such as Samuel Hearne, Dr John Rae and Donald Thompson had. I'm not complaining because in every way we had it easy, but it makes you stop and think. We had cars, trucks, planes, float planes, powerboats – every means of transport conceivable to get us to where we needed to be. Those whose stories we were telling had horses and canoes, hardship and starvation. Interesting, isn't it?

As fascinating as Hearne, Rae and Thompson were, personally, one of the best aspects of making that film was that it allowed me to canoe along some of Canada's beautiful rivers. If the forest is where I'm most at home, being on the water in the vast openness of the Canadian wilderness runs a close second. Given the chance to do that solo – with no camera crew, nobody in support, completely alone – is my all-time favourite pastimes. Going solo is a large part of the appeal because the value of travelling alone in remote wilderness is how it allows you to connect both with yourself and the environment. We have so many distractions in daily life; firstly our constant stream of connections to one another and the wider world via the omnipresent Internet. Then there's the telephone and the traffic. The chance to escape all of that and get out into the wilderness is one of the things I live for.

Now please don't think that I'm proposing that we should all travel alone in the wilderness all the time. In fact nothing could be farther from the truth, for travelling with friends is one of the greatest joys life has to offer – particularly when you travel in good company with a common purpose and outlook. No, my suggestion is that just once in a while we should turn our back on our community and step into the wild to benefit from a unique set of experiences that cannot be felt in any other way – experiences that will enhance our lives and strengthen us for the journeys we make in company.

Let me paint you a picture of what it's like and just why it feels so magical.

As I begin to prepare for a solo trip, I'll think about the purpose of my journey. My intent is not 'exploration' or 'adventure travel' where mind and muscles are pitted against the wild to, in some way, demonstrate human dominion over nature; you may have worked out by now that this is something I have little time for. In the days before the world was mapped, great feats of endurance were certainly achieved during the exploration of the uncharted regions of our globe. But today I believe such genuine goals to be few and far between. The purpose of my journeys is to engage with a landscape and its wildlife, to better know and understand them. To understand nature so that it will accept me. A conceptual view of nature which, when made, seemed rather abstruse, but which in light of new discoveries in nature seems to be astonishingly insightful, was posited by chemist and zoologist Davey Rhoades in 1979. He demonstrated that in some yet poorly understood way, trees could detect damage in their neighbours and react by generating stronger chemical defences. From this I have learned that how I interact with nature can also influence how nature interacts with me.

Join me as I draw on my memories to describe a solo trip into the North Woods of Canada by canoe.

———◆———

There is an old Army saying: 'Proper Preparation Prevents Poor Performance', and so it is here. Preparation is vital and sufficient time must be allowed for it. Travelling in any remote wilderness requires a set of key skills. First of all, I must be able to navigate with map and compass (call me old-fashioned if you like, but while GPS is a wonderful tool for navigation, it will always come second in my mind to those old woodsman's friends). Secondly, I must have a high degree of first-aid training, not only because I must care for myself but also because it is the best way to develop a sober head regarding the consequences of rash decision-making. Thirdly, I shall of course need to know how to take care of myself in the wild: make fires, find shelter, get food, etc. This is one of the largest skill sets to learn and many wilderness trippers pay the least regard to these skills. Bush skills do more than dispel fear and make us safe: they greatly enhance our understanding and knowledge of local flora and fauna and show us the difference between existing poorly in a landscape and living there in comfort.

Fourthly, as I am travelling by canoe I shall of course have to know how to paddle. It is important that you learn this skill – unlike the viewers who decided to set out on their own Canadian canoe adventure with no canoeing ability whatsoever. Reading the credits at the end of my Canadian programme, they engaged the outfitters that my production team had employed and hired an Indian guide, who it turned out could hardly speak English. After a couple of days they misunderstood their guide and merrily paddled into a set of rapids that even experienced canoeists would consider walking past. The net result was a terrifying capsize, which resulted in the destruction of one canoe and a sobering near miss.

Fifthly, some investigative skills are required because mapping for the area I intend to traverse will need to be sourced and ordered well ahead of departure, which today is usually easily achieved through the Internet. Guide books, if available, will need to be consulted to establish how serious the rapids I will encounter are likely to be. They may also provide a useful reading list to improve my knowledge of the region, its flora, fauna and cultural history. I like to mark my maps with useful information. Fortunately I have made many such trips so when it comes to packing lists it is all simply a process of recital.

So, can you feel it? My journey has already begun.

But what of the dangers I might face? Well, they are all pretty apparent really: bad weather, drowning, getting lost, losing my canoe, strong winds, rapids, cold, injury, forest fire and bears, so really, without any backup, I just have to be extra careful. The truth is, there is no shortcut to gaining sufficient experience, so don't do any of this unless you have the skill sets to cope. Perhaps the one unique hazard the solo traveller faces, though, is unfamiliarity with being alone. If you are not comfortable with your own company, it's advisable to build up gradually to a long and remote journey.

Now I can contact a local outfitter, organise my transfers and hire of equipment. We will discuss make, length and material of the canoes available and water levels, and I will be able to test the feasibility of my intended route. Attention to detail is everything at this stage. A good outfitter is invaluable, but beware because they are not all good.

Fishing permits can usually be purchased ahead of time

over the Internet. One surprise may be to discover that even in remote Canada there can be rivers and lakes where there are pollutants that limit the number of any given fish species that you can consume safely in a month. Guide books in which you can look up the waterways you will be travelling on can usually be downloaded prior to departure.

Here's the outline of my journey. I am going to join a river that I have been reading about for several years. But rather than start at its source, I am going to access it from a series of lakes and rivers to its east. I shall begin by paddling up a large lake, to a river that connects via a chain of small lakes to another large lake. From its north-west corner, I shall join the river I intend to explore. This I plan to paddle down in eight days, allowing three days to lay over, fish and explore.

The joy of travelling by canoe is that it is an incredibly versatile craft that can be paddled, poled, and even sailed. Relatively light, it is capable of transporting considerable loads and, where the water is too forceful or too shallow for passage, it can be emptied and carried overland – a process that retains its name from the fur trade: portage.

In fact, my journey will begin in earnest with a long portage, but rather than carry it on my shoulders, the canoe will be strapped to the float of a bush plane – a de Havilland Canada Beaver DHC-2. It's a wonderful aircraft, a real workhorse that is so respected that its appearance has become an integral part of the North Woods aesthetic and as much of an icon in Canada as the Spitfire is here. Despite the fact that production stopped in 1967, these specialised short take-off and landing aircraft are still plying the waterways of the far North, providing a vital lifeline for remote communities, logging and mining camps.

The flight in provides a bird's-eye view of the forests, lakes and rivers that are my destination; as much as I enjoy the view, I can't wait to be on the water. Eventually the plane will circle and, with practised ease, the pilot will glide smoothly on to the lake. I'll unhitch the canoe, load it with packs and take my place inside. There's a unique sound to it – the sound of the canoe banging against the aluminium float of the plane, the water lapping against the side, the pilot walking on the float. He says, 'OK, you take good care now,' and waves. I start to paddle away; with a buzz and a splutter, the engine starts up and he flies away, back to the world of electric lighting, the Internet and 24-hour non-stop noise and consumerism. As he climbs, he looks down and I look up. Then it's just quiet until a few minutes later the wildlife starts up – they fell silent with the plane's arrival but with its departure they're in full voice again.

With the plane gone, there's just me and my inner voice. I paddle to shore and set up camp for the night on a small island where I take stock. Now my life is reduced to its simplest form. As the sun sets, I sit beside my fire drinking in the quietude but not yet becoming a part of the scene. I feel I'm being watched, being judged by suspicious eyes all around me. I feel free from the rigid strictures of preparation, and I can relax now, yet I feel a reluctance to do so. Is this what a captive-bred animal feels when released into the wild: a reluctance to leave the familiarity of the cage? A hot chocolate liberally laced with rum will help get me off to sleep.

After waking on the first morning, I allow myself some time to get properly organised. On my body I carry my knife, saw and fire-starter. In the canoe I have four packs: my clothing and equipment pack, my food pack, my day pack and my camera case. All are stowed to provide proper trim and balance. I am using a beavertail paddle and a copy of an Iroquois paddle from 1800 that I have carved especially for this journey. My compass is set with the first bearing and rests atop the canoe pack in front of me.

I pull on the paddle; the canoe resists at first, heavily laden as it is with my supplies for the journey. Two more strokes though and I am away, the compass directing me as the canoe swings on to the correct heading. In an hour my paddling has settled into a comfortable rhythm and the canoe is eating up the kilometres. The long preparations seem insignificant now and I am overwhelmed by the beauty of the lake. The first day under way is important – it is a time to settle, for muscles to adjust to the loading, for the mind to adjust to the lack of distraction from modern life and the continuous traffic from within.

It is now that the real benefit of preparation pays off. With all concerns accounted for, life is greatly simplified and with distractions removed, the mind starts to empty further with every passing hour. By an empty mind, I don't mean any loss of intelligence; with the trivia and worries of day-to-day life forgotten, there is in its place an increased awareness of the external stimuli of the environment. Consider if you will that your brain is a computer, running many applications simultaneously; now it need only run one application so all of its capacity is liberated to concentrate on the present. In short, you become more open to things – more alert, more intuitive and more observant of minutiae.

My camp site on the second night is not the best – the ground is sloping and lumpy so I'm awake and away early on the third day to allow plenty of time at day's end to choose somewhere more suitable that night. It's a frustrating day – several portages mean little distance gained and, on one occasion, time lost as I spend an hour locating the portage trail. But at the last trail there is the reward of fresh wolf tracks.

By mid-afternoon I am traversing a long lake that runs west to east. Halfway across there is a spit of land that juts out from the eastern shore. It is a perfect camp site with a well-used fire circle, nice level ground and a large pine tree with a good sturdy branch from which my food sack can be hung, out of the reach of nosey bears. The only thing in short supply is firewood, but that is easily remedied when I paddle to a fallen dead tree 200 metres or so across the channel. I take what I need using my folding saw and axe; in fact, I probably have enough to leave a small stock for the next visitor. I enjoy a wonderful evening. A calm settles over the water as the sun falls in the sky and I watch, hands clasped round my mug, as in the very last minutes of the day a loon calls across the mirror-calm water. Then, with the camp in good order, sleep draws me into my tent.

Sadly, the peace is not to last. Just after midnight I am awoken by a gale-force, howling wind. At daybreak, I find it is still blowing hard from the south but, looking at the waves in the lee of the spit, I believe I can handle the conditions and reason that, with the canoe packs lashed for buoyancy, should I capsize I will be able to get myself and my kit to shore. I decide to break the journey into small sections and take them one at a time. No heroics – if conditions prove to be unmanageable I'll head back and try to wait it out. As it happens though, my heavily laden canoe shucks the wind better than expected and my beavertail paddle provides just the right contact with the water to enable me to keep the nose into the wind. With the cheek of a pilgrim begging a life, I use the wind to ferry across to the far shore and tick along close in until I'm in the wind's shadow at the head of the lake.

I celebrate with a handful of gorp; also known as trail mix, it's an acronym of Good Old Raisins and Peanuts. It's a combination of dried fruit, grains, nuts and sometimes chocolate, and it's the ideal snack on an expedition because it's tasty, lightweight, easy to store, and nutritious – you get a quick boost from the carbohydrates in the dried fruit and granola, and sustained energy from the fats in nuts. You can buy it ready-made but I prefer to choose my own ingredients and make it myself.

Sated, I set to on a three-kilometre portage trail to the last large lake that will take me to the river. This will be the acid test – if the gale is whipping up that lake, I'll have no choice but to try and wait things out. The wind conditions on the far side are manageable but the trail is blocked by windblown trees. Well, they say that fortune favours the bold, so my axe and saw prove their worth once again, and after considerable effort I savour the moment when my canoe sits on the waters of this new lake. After all the exertion, I need sustenance again so I moor up and enjoy a well-earned lunch. Focused on the gale I find I have slipped without noticing into a new state of mind and I am now living totally in the moment. My mind enjoys the challenges. I find that decision-making and decisiveness come easily to me now. In the normal world, we support each other constantly in decision-making. Even walking into a coffee shop in company the decisions are shared – 'Where shall we sit?' or 'What'll I have?' Here though, all decisions are mine, as are the mistakes. I love it because it brings a certain clarity of vision. Perhaps all CEOs should make such a journey like this once in a while.

I sniff the wind like a veteran and feel the weather lifting. As I paddle away I feel the breeze. It is steady, with occasional gusts that I see on the water as they race towards me. I am alert but relaxed; my canoe is part of me and I settle into a steady, strong paddle rhythm. It will be hard going all the way to the head of the lake where my maps show me there are islands and the possibility of shelter, but I'm up for it. Five minutes before I find a camp site, the wind drops altogether. I feel that I have been tested and have passed. A swim before dinner and an early night.

My routine keeps the journey tidy. I fill a Thermos with hot water last thing each night so there is no need for a fire in the morning. In this way I get away early – the best paddling is always in the first half of the day. Mid-afternoon, I find a camp site, set up the tarp, swing the kettle and go fishing.

Now I am happy in my own company and I have joined the wildlife around me; we share a secret: the secret of silence. It's beautiful. As I travel, I enjoy the company of wild creatures that somehow sense that I pose them no threat. I play with a family of otters who swim just ahead of me, blowing air noisily through their nostrils in my direction. While I am fishing I watch beavers bringing back branches for the food cache beside their lodge. I thank them for their dams that have kept water in the river for me this late in the summer. I sidle up to a moose while its head is submerged in search of sedge bulbs. I could easily forget what day it is, and in truth I must admit that I have indeed done that several times already. It's only at the last minute that I realise I must paddle hard to make my rendezvous with an outfitter.

It isn't all plain sailing; it's easy to injure yourself when shifting heavy loads over slippery rocks. But what is there to do but get on with it? There is no one to complain to but yourself, and self-pity has no place here. Now one learns the true meaning of the stoic Indian. In time, and with enough experience, stoicism becomes a tool you can employ to deal with hardships. Out of this stoic persona is born the equanimity of the master bushman. Like a rock in the rapids you become a place of stability from which others can gain strength.

As I reach the final day I know that my journey will soon end as abruptly as it began. My paddle moves with the hint of reluctance but still I must follow my course. There ahead of me on the far shore is a huge black bear, the biggest I have ever seen, large enough to give a grizzly a run for his money. I paddle towards him, but with a telling glance he takes cover and I know that I will not see him again. No bear grows that large in these parts without being very wary of humans. Somehow, that thought brings me back to earth. I turn the canoe for home and overhead two bald eagles glide past. I call out a greeting to them and they break their glide in surprise as they circle, scrutinising me from above. One of them calls back to me. I smile, give a wave, and as they settle back on their original course, so too do I. In that moment I can see nature; I feel it intuitively and I understand what cannot be written. That is when I know my journey is complete.

At the rendezvous, my outfitter meets me. It is a six-hour drive back to his base – a little time to readjust to the whirligig world of today. We have covered only a few miles before the claustrophobic warmth of the pick-up sends me to sleep.

28

Manhunt

It's a perfect day for driving – warm and balmy with bright sunshine and clear blue skies. Mid-afternoon in early July and I'm heading up the M1 in my Land Rover Discovery. A heat haze rises from the tarmac ahead.

The sun's rays on the windscreen turn the Discovery into a greenhouse. Ruth sits beside me as I drive, and we're both enjoying the respite of the cold air from the air-con. With a heavy foot on the accelerator and a clear road in view, we make rapid progress but as I pilot us along the motorway, a thought occurs to me – I'm probably the only person in the country who is wishing for dark skies and heavy rain.

I have no wish to ruin this perfect summer's day for the population of England; sadly, a man called Raoul Moat has already done that in Northumbria and it's both the man and the place that are the focus of my journey. Moat is also the reason I want rain instead of sun.

Like most people, I was horrified as I became aware of the developing situation through the news reports. Thirty-seven-year-old former bouncer Raoul Moat had been released from Durham Prison on 1 July after serving a sentence for assault. Two days later he went round to the house of his ex-girlfriend Samantha Stobbart with a sawn-off shotgun. There, he shot Chris Brown, her new boyfriend, killing him instantly. Then he shot Samantha in the stomach before fleeing the scene.

He wasn't finished though – far from it. On the following day, Sunday 4 July, he walked up to police officer David Rathband's Volvo patrol car, which was parked in a lay-by. Calmly Moat levelled the sawn-off shotgun at him through the passenger-side window and blasted him twice in the face and chest, leaving him totally blind and with horrific injuries. Moat then disappeared, only to surface the following evening to rob a fish and chip shop in Seaton Delaval at gunpoint. On Tuesday 6 July, he went on the run.

At that stage, the police were using conventional methods to track Moat – triangulation of his mobile phone signal, closing off streets and specific areas to deny him possible avenues of escape. They got an early break when they received a reported sighting of the Black Lexus he'd been using. It had been found by a member of the public parked on an industrial estate and when police arrived, they arrested two men – Khuram Awan and Karl Ness – who it transpired were two of Moat's accomplices. Both were later charged with conspiracy to murder and sentenced to life imprisonment. Fortuitously for him, Moat had taken off into some nearby woods before the police arrived and that was it, he went to ground.

That's when I began to think I might be able to offer some assistance. I have unique experience in tracking. It's a perishable skill, so unless you use it constantly, you lose it. Fortuitously, I'd been uncharacteristically busy over the previous couple of years tracking leopards and bears, and all sorts of wildlife. It was a skill I'd used almost constantly and I was at a really high pitch; I knew I was at the top of my game.

Six years previously I'd been invited up to the Police National Search Centre (PNSC) to give a lecture on tracking and its capabilities as a means of search, so I put a call in to Chief Inspector Phil Thomas, a police search advisor there who I'd kept in touch with. Even as I dialled, I felt a little apprehensive. I'd tracked literally hundreds of animals over the course of my career and numerous men when training, but this would be the first time I'd ever tracked an armed and dangerous fugitive. It was within my skill set, but outside of my comfort zone. Phil answered on the first ring.

'Hi Phil, it's Ray Mears.' After the initial 'hellos' and 'how are yous' I made the proposal.

'Look, this Raoul Moat thing – there's a possibility I could help. If I come up, I think I could let you know pretty quickly whether I can or not.'

'You'll get no argument from me there, Ray. I'll put a call in to Gold Command up at Ponteland [Northumbria Police's HQ] and someone will be in touch.'

Someone did get in touch, but not for a few days. A lot happened in that time so I'll always regret not going up there and then. A few hours after we spoke the police located a camp site that Moat had established, and that would have been the perfect starting point for me to begin tracking from. If you can locate your quarry's starting point, it makes life so much easier. Sadly, in the hours and days that followed, the police trampled all over it in their search for clues, and members of the press were given access, leaving no stone unturned. So by the time I eventually got there, any signs that might have given me an advantage were lost. Was a golden opportunity missed? What might I have found at the camp site? Could the whole incident have been brought to a speedier conclusion? These questions linger to this day but I'll never know the answers. What happened is what happened.

I imagine it was difficult for the police to make a snap decision to use me. In a situation like this, I'm probably not the first person that springs to mind; tracking just doesn't fall within the normal remit of what the police do, even for search specialists. I think that, initially, it was too obscure an idea for them to live with and I can empathise because the pressure they were under to get a result was absolutely massive.

In any event, I didn't hear a thing until the morning of Thursday 8 July. I was in London for a meeting with my publisher, Rupert Lancaster, when my phone rang.

'Ray, it's Phil Thomas. It's on; can you come straight up to Newcastle?'

I signal to Rupert that I have to take this call and walk out of his office to the corridor.

'I can, Phil, but I'm in London at the moment.' My brain kicks in and I think out loud: 'Get back home, pack some kit . . . it's probably best I drive because I don't want to draw attention to myself by flying or taking the train. There's enough media attention on this as it is; I don't think my involvement being reported is going to be helpful. Call it a few hours; I'll be with you later on tonight.'

Phil was happy with that, so I made my excuses to Rupert and caught a train back to Kent. When I explained everything to Ruth, she immediately said she wanted to come with me. She's from Durham so she could spend time with her family while also being close to me. I think most people can understand that – she didn't really want me to go, given the perceived risk, but for all that she understood and was totally supportive. So we loaded the Discovery up and headed off, which is how I found myself driving up the M1 towards Northumbria, blinded by sunshine but wishing for rain.

Why rain? Quite simply, rain would give me a far greater chance of bringing Moat down. If it's dry, he can relax; the weather is one less thing for him to worry about, meaning he has more mental capacity to focus on staying one step ahead and remaining hidden. Heavy rain on the other hand would make him cold and wet. His will to carry on would be diminished so he'd be much more liable to make mistakes; he'd want shelter; it'd get inside his head and defeat him. He'd also leave more signs for me to follow. The conditions were perfect for Moat, but an absolute nightmare for me.

There were some positives, however. Moat might well be armed and dangerous, and dry, but he was thought to be in the woods and the woods are *my* world. Having taught people to live off the land for thirty years, I know what happens to them psychologically. I understand the difficulties they face; I know the signs they leave behind and I know what will break them. I was hungry to go head-to-head. This wasn't Man vs. Wild, or even Man vs. Man; this was *my* world and Moat had come crashing into it, so the balance was uneven. It was a real-life hunt; he'd crossed a line, and now it was going to end.

———◆———

It's gone 22:00hrs when I reach Newcastle. I'd called ahead to Phil Thomas who had moved up to Northumbria Police HQ at Ponteland a couple of days earlier and we meet just outside the city centre. I jump into his car with him while Ruth takes the Discovery and heads for her parents' house. As I settle down for the drive to Ponteland, Phil updates me on what's happening on the ground, and gives me some idea of the political situation I'm walking into.

I had no idea there'd been something of a storm going on behind the scenes over whether or not to engage my services. With any major incident or disaster, the police utilise a Gold / Silver / Bronze command structure to establish a hierarchical framework for command and control. Gold Command is in overall control of resources and is usually based off-site at a distant control room – in this case, at Ponteland. The Gold Command team formulates strategy and has ultimate responsibility, reporting at government level to 'Platinum Command' in the guise of the Cabinet Office Briefing Rooms (COBR – the government's crisis response committee). Silver Command manages strategic direction from Gold and formulates tactics to achieve the desired result. Bronze Command implements the tactics and directly controls resources at the scene. In this case, Gold Command comprised Northumbria Police's Chief Constable Sue Sim working with the then Deputy Chief Constables (DCC) Jim Campbell and Steve Ashman.

Silver Command had been reticent about using me from the off, based on the fact they'd be putting me, an unarmed civilian, into an environment where firearms were involved. A Chief Superintendent told Phil, 'We've carried out a full risk assessment and it ain't happening.'

'What about Prince Charles? He's surrounded by an armed police close-protection team every time he goes out. I don't see that this is any different,' countered Phil.

But there was no arguing until Phil stepped out of the room and literally bumped into DCC Campbell, who asked how things were going. Phil related the conversation he'd had with Silver Command, causing the DCC to say something along the lines of, 'This is ridiculous, I want Ray here,' so that was that.

On arrival at Ponteland, I'm introduced to the team and briefed by a Police Search Advisor (POLSA) from Northumbria Police who is part of Bronze Command. He's a real asset and I'm massively impressed by his professionalism and knowledge as he gives me some really useful background and detailed intelligence on everything they know. The night before, they'd foiled an attempt by two of Moat's accomplices to get a car and a firearm to him and I'm told about them having found his car and the tent he'd been using, both of which were in the small market town of Rothbury. Police have established a five-mile, 5,000ft air-exclusion and a two-mile ground-exclusion zone around the town.

Bronze command decides it's worth me seeing Rothbury

first-hand and I'm driven there in a squad car on 'blues and twos' by colleagues of David Rathband, the traffic officer that Moat had shot. When we get there it's dark – it's close to midnight – but still I'm stunned by what I see. It's like I've stepped out of the patrol car and straight into a war zone.

The manhunt for Moat is perhaps the largest in modern British history, and Rothbury seems to have become the physical embodiment of that. Bright lights are set up everywhere, turning night into day and giving the immediate area the look of a Hollywood film set. It's all a bit surreal. Over 160 armed officers are involved from eight of the UK's police forces, including almost fifty from the Metropolitan Police, along with eight of the Met's London-based Armed Response Vehicles (ARVs). Ten armoured Land Rovers from the PSNI have been shipped over on a ferry from Northern Ireland and an RAF Tornado GR4 jet has been made available to undertake reconnaissance sorties. Specialist police snipers are also on hand, along with helicopters and countless police dogs. The armed officers are standing around in groups, dressed in black coveralls. They all wear body armour with ceramic chest plates and Kevlar helmets, and are armed with an assortment of weapons – H&K MP5 9mm carbines and Glock 17 sidearms along with percussion grenades. As if I needed a reminder, it brings home to me the gravity of the situation.

I'm escorted into the local police station. It's a hive of activity and I acquaint myself with the latest reports and news through osmosis. I learn that Moat has reloaded his sawn-off shotgun with large-gauge ball-bearings, which do terrible damage at close range. I find out where they'd had sightings of him and the locations where they've picked up various items of his. They'd recovered several mobile phones he'd used – it shows he's not stupid and is obviously clued up on police procedures and how they might track him via conventional means. The police have done well so far, they've really closed him down and reduced the number of avenues of escape open to him, but he's now gone off the radar and it's my job to find him.

I look at a map of Rothbury and immediately see how much woodland there is in the surrounding area. It's known as the Cragside Estate and encompasses some incredibly dense forest. I pick up an envelope and start to sketch out an assessment of the situation as I know it so that I can start putting together a plan.

Point one: the weather – it's in Moat's favour. It had been dry since he'd gone on the run, which is bad for me in terms of him leaving signs, but good for him.

Point two: has he taken any hostages? It's not like it is in the movies; most people on the run end up taking hostages by accident rather than design. They'll take the easiest option, which generally means a building, but where you find buildings you normally find people and if you add a man with a gun to that scenario, those people become hostages. I want to know if he's done that – there are lots of outlying farms around the area, so I ask the police if they'd checked them. They hadn't, so they send officers round to knock on the doors.

It's becoming increasingly obvious to me that the Cragside Estate is where Moat is most likely to be. I know he's been in there already because the northern extremity is where the police recovered his mobile phone and his camp site is located at the south-west corner. It was by a river bank, which immediately suggests to me that he's been using the River Coquet as a point of communication with his accomplices. It's a dark, shadowy river at night, which rises in the surrounding mountains and runs through the town of Rothbury. It's the perfect place for someone who wants to move without being seen.

Moat's a fisherman so he'll know this river. To move around at night without a torch in an area with no natural lighting, you're going to need something to serve as a handrail to guide you. A river bank would fulfil that role, as would natural features in the landscape. There's no point my going to the point where he's discarded one of his phones; the terrain in that area has been heavily trampled by the police firearms team that found it.

The Cragside Estate bothers me; it's huge, exceptionally dense wooded forest with few natural trails, so it's perfect for someone who wants to remain hidden. There's just so much natural cover there. That suits Moat. At night, as long as he's there, he's under no pressure. I want to change that. I want to remove any sense of sanctuary from him, because then he'll make a mistake. He'll have to get up and run. And if he does that, I'll track him or flush him right into the police net.

Perhaps the biggest obstacle for me is the press. I understand that they have a job to do but there are certain members of the media who have gone too far. The police have requested that certain details be withheld as it's felt that revealing them could help Moat. At least one household news organisation hasn't honoured that request. Police have found various letters that Moat had left, and from these it's clear that he has a radio and that he's monitoring what the press are saying. Northumbria police are doing a brilliant job but they're being hampered by the media. They've asked that they hold back on reporting elements of Moat's private life as he has threatened to kill a member of the public every time there's an inaccurate report. I believe the police should have a legal power to exclude the press in situations like this. It's the curse of 24-hour rolling news coverage . . . it hates a void so you end up with reporters speculating, imagining, even inventing facts to fill the gap. This helps nobody.

An important aspect for me is that I don't want the press reporting that I'm involved. Firstly, I'm not doing it for recognition; I don't need to establish myself or build a reputation. I have the skills to assist and I feel duty-bound to use them. Secondly, I don't want Moat to know I'm there. I want the element of surprise on my side because I need every break I can get, especially as I have no starting point to track from, so I'm going to have to find one. This is the worst possible situation for a tracker and it's made worse by the fact that the area he's likely to be hiding in is big. There's no getting away from it – the odds are stacked in Moat's favour.

Ordinarily, I would have used his camp site as a starting point, but that had been compromised from a forensic point of view by Sky News having been given access to it shortly after it had been found. They'd taken in two people who'd claimed to be 'trackers' and they'd trampled all over it. Even if there was anything of use to me there (and it seems highly unlikely), I'd be seen by the press, so I make a decision to focus on Cragside. I look at the map and work out the places that would be of most interest to me if I were in Moat's place. I prioritise them and start walking through them all in my mind, area by area. I've nothing firm to go on but you need to be bold sometimes, and with the benefit of hindsight, I think what I did was right.

We drive back to Ponteland shortly after, and I present my findings to Gold Command, with the caveat that I want to leave at first light. There's a path that works its way north–south in Cragside; I want to start tracking along that. I'd start at the southern tip where it comes down to the river. That river interests me greatly, but if I begin there, I'll be showing my hand too soon. I want to get at least one day's tracking in without Moat knowing I'm there.

The Gold Command team agree with all my suggestions, so we have the makings of a plan. It's late and I think I should try to get some sleep. I'm staying in a bungalow within the police compound here at Ponteland and I literally just drop my kit and lay down on the bed as soon as I'm through the door. It's been an exceptionally long day and a very busy one. I need to be sharp for the track tomorrow morning so it's imperative I get some rest. But my mind is racing – analysing the plan I've come up with, looking for flaws and other ways of doing things. It's going to be a long night.

* * *

I'm awake as the sun comes up and a hot shower makes me feel a little more human. I dress quickly and make my way over to the canteen in the main building. It's exactly how I imagine police canteens up and down the country to be: a long, rectangular room lit with fluorescent lighting, and natural light from windows along one side of the rectangle. Along the opposite side there's a counter with an array of hot food, sandwiches and the like on offer, cooked and served up by civilian staff. Two vending machines sit along the far wall offering a range of canned drinks, plus another selling high-energy 'junk' food – Mars bars, crisps etc.

However, there's one element that sets it apart from most police canteens and that's the sheer number of weapons lying around. Sniper rifles, H&K MP5s, G3s lie on the floor and against walls. Every seat is taken by the 'Men in Black' – firearms officers from seemingly every force in the UK, all dressed in black coveralls that give them a distinctly paramilitary look. From a distance, they appear indistinguishable from the SAS team that stormed the Iranian Embassy at Princes Gate in 1980.

Phil ushers me towards a group of officers from the Metropolitan Police's specialist firearms unit SO19. I'm introduced to their tactical advisor, Mark; Derek, a team leader; and to his sergeant Paul. They've come up from London as a self-contained unit along with forty or so of their colleagues, six firearms support dogs with their handlers, and SO19's unique silver-coloured BMW 5 series ARVs. They also have all the kit and weapons they might need to cover 'the worst-case scenario'. The cars look a little out of place in Northumbria, decked out with their Met Police decals declaring 'Working Together for a Safer London'.

I'm eager to get going and implement the plan I presented before retiring the previous night, but there's a problem. There have been 'heated debates' prior to my arrival over exactly how they are going to keep me safe. They've reached the conclusion that, assuming they can get me out on the ground, I won't be able to track from the front because they can't keep me safe there. The issue is still unresolved.

'Look,' I say, 'there's no point in my even going out if I can't track from the front.'

I'm met with stony faces and the absurdity of it hits me: there's a manhunt on for a fugitive who is armed and represents a clear and present danger, and there are more armed police officers on hand than you can count. My frustration is growing.

'Look, just give me a gun if that's the issue and I'll go out and get him for you.'

It breaks the ice. They laugh. It also breaks the deadlock.

'Look, let's make this happen,' says Mark. 'If we can protect the Royal Family when they're out and about, we can protect Ray. I really don't see what the issue is here.'

'I need to be at the front,' I repeat. 'But how about if there's anywhere I can't see, your guys can check it out first?'

'I think that could work,' offers Paul. 'We've got the firearms support dogs so let's use them too. We'd normally use one for a job like this but we've got six so let's use all of them.'

They issue me with black coveralls, body armour, a Kevlar helmet and ballistic goggles so, visually, I am identical to the others except for the fact I'm not armed with a weapon. I consider taking something to defend myself, and then decide against it. The Met's SO19 firearms unit is rightly regarded as one of the best in the world. There's an innate self-belief about the guys born of the fact they don't talk about what they do, they don't brag – they just do it and their reputation goes ahead of them. I feel both safe in their care, and confident in their ability to get the job done. No, if it comes down to him or me, he's going down.

As well as affording me protection, my clothing and kit means I won't be noticed by the press, who have staked out the gate to Police HQ at Ponteland and are filming every vehicle going in and out. First off Derek conducts a briefing for everyone involved in the team that will be out on the ground with me, so we all move into an anteroom off the canteen. He goes over everything known about Moat, and 'Actions on Contact'. The objective is clear: if found, all steps are to be taken to ensure he's brought in alive so that he can be tried in court.

There are nine Met Police firearms officers in the team that will be looking after me and helping me in the hunt for Moat, and we will be travelling from Ponteland to Rothbury in the Met's ARVs. In the first car will be Derek and an officer called Nigel who will drive, with Paul and me in the back. I am quickly introduced to the six other members of the team. Finally we are joined by six of the Met's dog handlers who each have one firearms support dog.

We move to the car park and take our places in the vehicles. Once we're strapped in, Nigel edges out into the rush-hour traffic on the main road away from Ponteland. As soon as we're moving, Derek hits the blue lights followed by the Tri-Sound siren. Our car is now a moving symphony of '*son et lumière*' signalling our presence to other road users.

The traffic along the main road is a solid mass, one long snaking line of frustrated commuters. Driving on the offside of the white centre line, Nigel seeks a clear view of the road ahead. We're travelling at a fair pace and it occurs to me that the concentration required must be immense. I'm immersed in an alien environment but surrounded by the basics of familiarity. I've spent several decades driving in heavy urban traffic, but it was nothing like this. Here, the road noise is mixed with the constant stream of radio traffic, fighting for prominence with the muted sound (to those of us inside the car) of the 200dB siren focused ahead of us.

As we press on, I notice a set of traffic lights at a junction ahead of us turn red; my foot instinctively reaches for a brake pedal that isn't there. Nigel scrubs off some speed and then runs the red light – properly; not a shade after it's turned or a furtive dash for the other side, but a full ten seconds after, with cross traffic at its height. Traffic is still heavy, but we're making progress and I check our speed – 80mph in a 30mph limit.

Over a roundabout, around the wrong side of a traffic island, and we're heading towards oncoming traffic. I watch it part miraculously before us, our progress unimpeded despite the number of vehicles approaching us. My adrenaline on fast-feed, we pass through another two red-lit junctions, and onto the dual carriageway. A Gatso camera ahead of us catches us – 95mph in a 50 zone with no prospect whatsoever of a ticket being despatched. I could get used to this.

The road clears ahead and Nigel really opens it up. I watch the needle on the BMW's speedo start to climb over the ton . . . 110, 120, 130, 140mph and still it rises. There's a sense of urgency about events, made real by the strobing of the car's blue lights on road signs and the rise and fall of the siren. It is 25 miles from Ponteland to Rothbury and according to Google maps the drive should take forty-five minutes. We do it in fifteen.

We stop in a lay-by close to the outskirts of Rothbury so that we can get everyone together and kill the lights and sirens. Then we drive to our 'jumping off' point, the car park of a nearby quarry on the east of Cragside Woods. In this way, we're able to deploy together, and with the minimum of fuss – no easy task when you're in a group sixteen strong, with six German Shepherd firearms support dogs along for support.

———◆◆◆———

Tracking is almost as old as mankind itself. When humans first started to eat meat, they had to learn to track their prey. Man tracking followed shortly after – it is a natural extension of hunting both animals and people. It is physically impossible for a person (or animal) to traverse ground without leaving *some* sort of telltale sign. 'Sign' in this context is the physical evidence of any disturbance of the environment left behind by animals, humans or objects. The detection of this sign is called *sign cutting*. My job as a tracker is to identify, interpret and follow signs.

When most people think of tracking, they usually think of following footprints. But a tracker looks for far more. I'm looking for soil depressions, kicked-over rocks, clothing fibres snagged on brambles, changes in vegetation, changes in the environment, ambient noise or lack thereof. I look for the disturbance – the sign – left behind by the target being tracked. In this case, it's me against Moat. Everything else falls away.

I start as soon as we dismount the vehicles. The adrenaline's pumping, I can feel my heart racing and there's a metallic taste at the back of my throat. It's not fear so much – not fear of

Moat, anyway. It's fear of failing. There's so much riding on this; I know the police have taken a risk in using me and I don't want to let anyone down. The Northumbria Force and Sue Sim, its Chief Constable, are under intense pressure. Mine is self-imposed, but no less real. I've come into this with my eyes wide open and I want to deliver.

My plan is to cut for sign in likely areas; my intention is to take the initiative, employ the tactics of surprise and aggression. This is a hunt, and I'm determined we'll get our man. It's often said that no battle plan survives first contact with the enemy and in this case, the woods are both my ally *and* my enemy. It's clear to me immediately on surveying the environment that this will be the most difficult tracking I've ever undertaken. I have never seen forest and vegetation as dense as confronts me here. It's so thick as to appear impenetrable at first sight. The ground is dry and heathery. It holds almost no sign whatsoever. The woods are so tight, so thick, that visibility is close to zero. This is going to be like wading through treacle.

I think about the track and have a picture in my head of pushing through the forest and suddenly stumbling upon Moat, equipped with his sawn-off shotgun, and me standing directly in front of him. I turn to Paul who is immediately behind me, Derek alongside him.

'Er . . . if you see me duck out of the way, you'll know I'm close!' They laugh, and the mood lightens.

I'm sure it must be difficult for them and the rest of the guys who have to protect me but they're peerless in what they do; I feel totally at ease with them. We start off by sending the dogs ahead to check things out. Because firearms are involved, the option of using bloodhounds to sniff out Moat's location is denied to us. Firearms support dogs are trained for one purpose and one purpose only: to search for and confront armed criminals and to bark on finding them. Firearms support dogs train with the specialist firearms teams so are desensitised to gunfire.

Their handlers release the dogs, send them forward, and the dogs return quickly without signalling, so we know it is safe to move forwards. I take point, looking, searching . . . tracking.

I have the utmost respect for our police, who do a difficult, dangerous and often thankless job. They spend a lot of their time dealing with the worst excesses of society and experience things that most people fortunately never have to. Police officers can be cynical, but coppers up and down the country share a love of banter and generally cope with events thanks to a dark sense of humour. I'm impressed as soon as we get out on the ground though, because once I start tracking, they're strictly businesslike and professional. The good-natured banter and piss-taking I've observed takes a back seat and it's all about getting the job done.

I start to move. It's easy to get bogged down when you're cutting for sign and you don't find any. It's easy to think that you're walking along a dead end (metaphorically speaking) so it's important to remind yourself that what you don't find is also a form of sign. If you find nothing, it's a sign that you can discount an area, so there's a positive there.

Almost immediately, something catches my eye. I put my hand up so the guys behind me know that I'm stopping – it's a pretty universal sign, that hand signal. I crouch down for a closer look but I'm immediately sure of what I find.

'I know he was here in the last twenty-four hours. I know what way he was travelling,' I say pointing. 'He slept here.'

Paul is immediately behind me. 'What?' he says. 'There's nothing there. Nothing.'

'Look closer. Here,' I say, pointing to a rudimentarily constructed pile of brushwood. I can clearly see that somebody has spent the night on it. I teach people how to make these things on my courses so I know what they look like. I've slept on them often enough, so I know that simply by laying on one you compress it and it takes on a definable shape.

I hear Paul whistle, almost imperceptibly, like he's suddenly got it. 'Amazing,' he says. 'Amazing.'

As we're walking along, I'm reporting everything to Paul and Derek. They in turn pass it down the line – you have to remember the woods are so thick, it's impossible for us to walk in a group so we're stretched out in single file, some sixteen men and six dogs. Derek is reporting everything back to Gold Command over the radio, so there's a constant stream of verbiage backwards and forwards, one long chain of information.

I push forward a little further and after about twenty minutes I stop again, raising my hand to signal to the team. What I've found are bits of dried wood – lying on a bed of heather. They don't belong where they are. They aren't in a place you'd choose to walk but that's where the trail goes. It looks like Moat has stumbled and dropped the sticks. I can see him in my mind . . . he'd been collecting firewood for cooking but in the darkness with no way to see where he was going, with no handholds to guide him, he's stumbled in the heather and let slip these few pieces from an armful.

That one tiny detail lifts me. Picture it. He's been amassing the wood for some time, working hard to find what he wants. He's got everything he needs, he's making his way to wherever he has in mind to set up camp and he's tripped and dropped some of his cache. He wouldn't even have noticed it go. Insignificant and invisible to him. Hugely significant and noticeable to me.

I notice that there is a trail, disturbances going through the heather to my left, like he's stumbled that way and headed off in that direction after dropping the firewood. Now when I say a trail, I don't mean a trail as in a footpath as you might imagine one. To me, trail is a sign that somebody has been there. The trail leads down into some thickets, but I can't see ahead to what is there, so the handlers send the dogs forward again.

When they come back, two of the six seem to be giving an indication. I can't put my finger on it but they aren't barking as they would have had they found someone. But they are agitated, like they've seen something of interest. The guys feel it is safe for me to move forwards so I head on, and about 30ft down the trail I find some empty food tins on the forest floor: tuna, something he could have opened, eaten straight out of the tins which he'd then discarded. Small cans pack 32g of protein at a time, about 120 calories, so he'd loaded up on just what his body needed to keep him going. Every little detail adds to and colours the picture I'm building of our quarry. I take nothing away from the fact he's simply discarded the tins. It doesn't indicate carelessness on his part or anything like that. He'd been so far into the dense woods no normal person would ever have stumbled across them. He was where he felt safe – way, way off the beaten track.

I decide to walk back along the trail I've found, and a little further on I find some signs that suggest that somebody has been moving around at night in both directions. That in itself tells me a lot: in daylight you avoid bumping into things; at night, you blunder into things that otherwise would be visible. There are a couple of rocks disturbed from their original position. The way in which a rock is disturbed gives one an indication of direction. And we had sign going in both directions.

I'm left with the impression that he might have been wandering backwards and forwards in a state of confusion. He clearly would have felt safe so deep in the thicket but he doesn't seem to realise that he's leaving sign everywhere.

We get to a slight bend and the dogs give an indication that there might be someone up ahead. As they come back, they stop and their ears prick up. I can hear something too but just as I'm about to focus on the sound, a report goes out over the radio and I'm distracted by it. But I *know* I heard something move off toward the north-east. The handlers send the dogs forward to investigate again. They go far further than previously, but they come back with nothing. What I'd have given then for a live rewind button; I know I heard something, and I'm convinced the dogs sensed it too, but whoever or whatever it was has gone. It's him; it has to be. There's nobody else here; the woods have been cordoned off.

We carry on and I again notice sign in the area where I'd heard him moving. There are recent disturbances, but not through the bracken. What I'm following is a trail left by somebody who clearly didn't want to be followed. It's recent because at night it would have been impossible to walk down that trail without leaving obvious, clearly visible sign. What I'm seeing is the merest token hint of disturbance. It's very faint – like a snowy TV picture you can't tune in – just some slight areas of flattening *between* the bracken. It can only have been caused by someone carefully picking their way through it. Someone with a level of counter-tracking awareness; someone who clearly wants to remain hidden. It's yet another indication that I'm on the right track.

No matter how careful you are, there will *always* be sign to be found if you traverse ground; always. It's just a matter of knowing what to look for. And I know. I can see tiny little birch sticks, thinner than matchsticks, that have been broken. When you break birch sticks, they go grey over time, but to start with they're quite bright with a clear yellow hue to them. These are yellow so they tell me that Moat's walked through here very recently. I'm talking about the faintest sign, almost invisible to me, completely so to the untrained eye. Paul and the others, who clearly started out sceptical of my bringing anything to the party, have become almost evangelical in their conversion but, try as I might, I can't get Paul to see what I am seeing. It is there, a consistent pattern of sign passing between the bracken. This trail is the freshest of anything I've seen so far, but even so it's frustratingly non-committal. It tells me he was here very recently, but without something else to anchor it, I can't say exactly when. Following it is taking every bit of focus I have and it's immensely tiring.

Eventually I find another lying-up position – somewhere somebody has stepped off the trail into the heather and lay down. I imagine they've lain down for some time, but it doesn't indicate an overnight stay. It's in a part of the woods where the canopy lets in the sun so the ground would have been warm. It's the perfect spot for someone who was cold last night to lie down and warm themselves in the sun's rays earlier this morning.

I carry on following the sign and eventually it leads to a main track, a gravel path that runs west–east. There's a building adjacent to where the track comes out, a boathouse. It stands at the edge of what in Victorian times had been a lake, but the water has long since been drained so it looks a little bizarre standing in the middle of open land. It stands high off the ground – when the lake was there, its base would have touched the waterline but with the water gone it looks misplaced, like it's been picked up by a giant hand and moved from somewhere else.

I'm keen to go and investigate it but we are forced to hold off as a succession of frustrating incidents occurs. We hear across the radio that members of the press have been trying to get into the woods to see what is going on, so we go to ground while the police at Rothbury send a team of blues and twos to chase them off. While that's going on, the force helicopter is flying overhead taking photographs of the ground so that we'll have a better idea of the terrain ahead of us for the following day, but that has to depart at short notice because the Tornado GR4 that the RAF made available has deployed on a sortie over Cragside to search the area with its Raptor reconnaissance pod, which is so advanced it's capable of reading the time on Big Ben from the Isle of Wight. We watch as that goes screaming overhead.

Once we're cleared to move out of cover, the team organise themselves and move ahead of me to clear the building. Once again, I'm impressed by their professionalism in very testing circumstances. The dogs are sent on ahead. When they return without incident, the team move in to perform a tactical clearance. After a short time, they pronounce the building clear. Then I'm beckoned forward to investigate the boathouse interior.

It's hot and dusty inside. It's gloomy, the only light coming from some high windows that are dirty and smeared with the detritus of time. The floor is rough, consisting of heavy railway-grade gravel. There's a raised platform towards the far end of the building about four or five feet off the ground.

'He's been here,' I tell Paul, 'probably in the last couple of hours would be my best guess.'

I point to the disturbances that indicate two very definite footprints below us in the gravel. We know Moat's height, his weight, everything available about him, and it's obvious to me from the depth and clarity of the footprints that they're his. It appears that he has jumped down from the platform, landing firmly at that spot in the gravel. The frustration is palpable. I feel that we're within touching distance of him but he remains one step ahead, elusive. He's just out of reach.

By the time we leave the boathouse, we've been on the ground for over eight hours. Eight hours of moving methodically, slowly, tactically through dense forest. Eight hours of being silent, on alert, focused and aware. Tracking, at times, in close proximity to Moat. The dogs are exhausted and a snap poll reveals that all of us are in a similar state. Everyone says that they're happy to carry on, but the law of diminishing returns applies. None of us is half as effective as we were just a few hours earlier. But I tell Paul and Derek that I'm happy to continue, that if I find fresh sign I'll carry on until we find Moat and flush him out. As it turns out, the decision is made for us; Gold Command wants us to return to Ponteland for an extensive debrief.

As we walk back to the vehicles and mount up, I tell the team of my plans for the following day, Saturday 10 July. My favoured time to strike out is first light and I expect a chorus of groans to greet this news, but to a man the team is enthusiastic. I'm buoyed, there's a real sense of cohesiveness about us and I feel that every member of the team has my back and has bought into the mission.

As we drive back, I feel a sense of a job well done. When we set out this morning, I had nothing more to guide me than experience and intuition. There was no prima-facie starting position, only my informed guesses. It was like looking for a needle in a haystack, and against the odds I've pricked my finger and drawn blood. It's not just me; the others feel it too. There's an energy about the guys.

'Nice work, Ray,' says Paul. 'I'll be the first to put my hand up and admit to being sceptical, but you had me on board from the very first sign when you found his bed. Pretty amazing.'

We arrive at Ponteland and I start to put my thoughts in order, making sense of the day's events so I can relate them to Gold Command. All of the sign that I've found has been pointing towards the west and the north-west, so that gives me a pretty good indication of where he is. I ask the guys in the team what they think and without exception, they tell me that they think we bumped Moat; we disturbed him. I felt we'd got very close to him. Whether it was in one of the two areas where the dogs had given an indication or whether it was the boathouse, I can't say for certain. My money would be on him being near to the boathouse. Given that we were delayed coming out of the trail and exploring that building, there was more than enough time for him to make an escape. I'm convinced he was somewhere in that area. We all are.

I'm in the process of relating all of this to Gold Command when I become aware of a change of tempo in the room. Something's happening and then it comes over the radio:

'There's an IC1 [the police identity code for white Caucasian] male matching Moat's description, we've got him running out of the Coplish [a large culvert that leads into the drainage system under Rothbury] at the bottom of Blaeberry Hill. Standby . . .'

Over the radio, we can hear officers shouting, 'Armed police; stand still . . . STAND STILL!'

The information comes in thick and fast. It *is* Moat. He's surrounded. Armed police from the Northumberland Force are engaged in a stand-off with him and he is kneeling at the edge of a grass bank with his sawn-off gun pointed at his temple while negotiators attempt to calm him down and resolve the situation peacefully. Paul and Derek look at me, and it's clear we're all thinking the same thing. The timing is bizarre. We're convinced we got in close to him, harried him, and within minutes of us withdrawing and arriving back at Ponteland he comes out into the open and into the arms of the police.

Gold Command invite us into the control room and I watch in amazement as events unfold live from the feed on the police helicopter that is overhead, monitoring the stand-off. Eventually though, it becomes clear that nothing is going to be resolved in the short term, so I withdraw and make my way back to the accommodation. It's been an exceptionally long and exhausting day. Despite my exhaustion, I'm beyond sleep; it's been almost forty-eight hours since I had any decent rest yet I feel wired, my mind a maelstrom of thoughts.

I learn when I arise early on the following morning, Saturday 10 July, that the longest manhunt in modern British criminal history officially ended at 01:15hrs earlier that morning when Moat fired a single shot to his head. He was officially declared dead at 02:20hrs by doctors at Newcastle General Hospital, shortly after arrival.

So, in hindsight, was the operation a success? Even though Moat took his own life and would never stand trial, I'm convinced it was. Clearly Gold Command did too – one of my most treasured reminders is the thank-you letter I received from Chief Constable Sue Sim shortly after I returned home. This is what I feel we achieved: we established that Moat was still in the vicinity; we took the search to the fugitive, and more than likely disturbed him; we established an effective plan for the way forward. The SO19 team told me that they believed Moat's emergence from hiding just minutes after we left the scene was a direct result of our presence.

I've heard since that when specialist firearms officers from Northumbria Police were negotiating with Moat on the river bank, he told them that he'd been visited by a police dog while he was in hiding. The dog looked at him and then left without barking. Given our position at the time the police dogs were left off the lead, we would have been within 20ft of him and he either had to have seen some sight of us or, at the very least, been aware of our presence. He'd have been enormously disturbed by that because he'd have known the game was up. We'd found his trail, we knew where he'd been and that would have got inside his head and really upset him, because he would have known that nowhere was safe. We'd denied him sanctuary. We could follow him where he believed that nobody could. I take immense satisfaction from that.

When all's said and done though, perhaps the last word should go to Mark, Derek, Paul and every one of the Metropolitan Police team from SO19 who took such great pains to ensure my safety on the operation. Their skill and professionalism were evident throughout the time I spent with them and I came away greatly impressed by their coolness under pressure.

Of course at the end of the day they're still coppers, so I shouldn't have been surprised when I bid them all goodbye before leaving Ponteland for the last time and they shouted as one, 'Thanks for everything, Bear; it's been a pleasure!'

29

No Stone Unturned

I mentioned that when I was brought in to assist in the hunt for Raoul Moat, I felt that I was at the top of my game in terms of tracking skills, but let me give you an insight into how it works. You might recall from the beginning of this book that it was my desire to track foxes that opened the gateway to a life spent as a student of bushcraft. My confidence that I could help the police was born of my long years of learning, then honing the skills required. As I've said, it's a skill set that goes off quickly; you never forget the theory, but unless it's practised on a regular basis, you quickly become rusty in its application.

Unfortunately, because not much is known about tracking outside of those of us who practise it regularly, a little bit of ability can appear impressive to the uninitiated. There are a great many people claiming to be experienced and capable who, quite frankly, are barely beginners. Sadly, honesty in this business is severely lacking in certain quarters. You have to know and acknowledge your own shortcomings because you do nobody any good if you over-inflate your ability.

I was approached by a police force twenty-five years ago, with a request to help them with tracking. It sounded interesting so I thought I'd have a chat with them and see exactly what it was they needed. So, we met and talked, and I very quickly realised I couldn't help because, at the time, I just wasn't good enough. What they wanted was outside of my capabilities and experience so, being honest with myself, the only course of action for me was to walk away.

I've studied bushcraft for almost forty years and I've learned from the very best. In the run-up to the hunt for Raoul Moat, I'd been tracking almost constantly, so my skills were recent and fresh, which meant I was sharp. But there are still indigenous people out there, like the Kalahari bushmen, whose ability in terms of tracking makes me look strictly second-rate by comparison.

We'd made a programme on them a few years previously and we'd ended up filming in a year of drought; it was searingly hot – around 57°C in the shade, if you could find any. The Kalahari bushmen are a fascinating group of people, and their tracking ability is exceptional. I'd been back to see them again fairly recently when I was out there tracking big cats and I found some droppings that I was convinced were from a leopard. I said this to the bushmen and they said, 'Oh, they're not leopard droppings.' And of course, they were right; they're *nearly* always right. But I said, 'What are they?' and – this is one of the things about them I really like – they couldn't tell me straight away; they had to stop and think about it. So they had a good look and a poke around, they pulled the droppings apart and analysed them, and after about ten minutes, they said rather resolutely, 'Ah, these are genet droppings.'

'How do you know that?' I asked.

'Well, these are owl feathers,' one of them said pointing, 'and only a genet would eat an owl.'

It's that kind of knowledge, that eye for detail, that makes them so good.

I remember filming with two bushmen in particular and one day we came back to their village. It was a large village in terms of numbers – there were a lot of people living there. Also, it was at the end of the day, so there were a lot of footprints in the dust; there must have been thousands of them and all of a sudden, one of the bushmen said, 'Stop! Stop a moment.'

He jumped forward and I watched him study the ground ahead of us for several seconds – he was looking to see if his wife was at home. He was able to pick out her footprint from all of the others. *That's* how good they are.

━━◆◆◆━━

There's a certain type of magic you feel when you're tracking; your senses are heightened, it's almost like you exist in a different state of sensory awareness when you're focused on finding a target, and there is a definite frisson in your inter-action with the natural world. There's nothing quite like the feeling you get when you're following tracks and you get to see the personality of the animal reflected through their trail.

You have to start small though; my own tracking ability grew from me finding fox tracks in the snow. I'd go out and follow them, and then when the snow melted I'd follow them in the mud. When the mud hardened, I'd follow them in the dust and my tracking ability evolved and grew from that. Mostly it's about becoming hyper-attuned to your environ-ment. You always leave trace, even if you can't see it. It's a matter of degrees – a bloodhound can follow a few cells that have come off your body as you walk.

I also learned by working with indigenous people who have grown up with tracking and have been using the skills all of their lives. That's good because it shows you what's possible. It opens up doors in your own mind that you might otherwise have shut because if they can do it there, I used to think, then why can't I do it here? And I started to. I learned a lot just from knowing what's possible.

Usually, that means looking further afield than within our own shores and some of the best trackers I've ever come across were the Ovambo people in Namibia. During the war on the Angolan border Ovambo army trackers were so good that when they slept out in the bush, they didn't bother putting out sentries – they'd have a barbecue. Their enemies had learned the hard way very quickly because if they ever ambushed the Ovambo and didn't kill every single one of them, they were never able to get far enough away that the Ovambo trackers couldn't catch up with them. When the Ovambo tracked, they *ran* and they would shout, 'We're coming to get you!'

Terrain makes a difference. Some terrain lends itself to tracking, as in Namibia and much of the rest of Africa. Cities and major conurbations, such as you find in England, are much harder. The terrain varies massively and there are other variables: more vegetation; more disturbances; other people coming along; the weather. It all makes life more difficult. On the plus side, however, it's all good training for when you go to other places. Hardest first – that's the way to do things. The conventional wisdom says that when you launch a business, the time to do it is in a recession – if you can make a success of it in the tough times then you'll find things much easier in the boom times. If you learn to track here in the UK, you can track just about anywhere.

Sometimes I see sign when I go out normally, in much the same way that some people hear background noise all the time – the traffic sounds, the sirens, the soundtrack to living in a city. I have a visual version of that where I see sign everywhere. Ruth and I were out walking our dog one day just before last Christmas, and Ruth went one way with the dog while I went the other. She tried to sneak ahead but she'd left sign without realising it. As soon as I saw her footprint, that was it – I found her.

Tracking animals is different to tracking people. Tracking people is, in some ways, more interesting but when you're tracking an animal, you generally have more options simply because what you can do is very much determined by the nature of the ground. In urban areas, which is where most people live, there aren't as many clues. Take Africa, for example: depending on where you are, the ground can be very sandy so it can hold a lot of detail – all the more so if there has been recent light rainfall, or there's moisture in the ground. In other places, the ground might be more granular, consisting of coarse gravel, so it will hold sign, but not the fine detail that makes life easier.

When you begin tracking for a specific animal, the first thing you're looking for is fresh sign. That will allow you to establish details such as the size of the animal, any distinguishing marks in its tracks. Next, you want to establish the direction that it's moving towards, and look at the landscape. You do this to visualise how the animal – let's say a leopard – saw that landscape; was he moving at night, for example, and if so, what did he see? You need to work out the age of the tracks, identify when they were laid down; you can make a mark beside them to see how a fresh mark looks in comparison. The size of the track may give an indication of the size of the animal and its age – that information will allow you to assess whether he's the dominant male or not. Knowing that, you can then predict his likely behaviour.

When I was tracking Houdini the leopard in Namibia, in 2007, I also found tracks of another male who was visiting the area and we managed to put up a trail camera to catch it on film. When we reviewed the footage, he'd behaved and moved exactly as I had described and that felt great because it's so rare that you get to see the leopard that you're tracking. Moments like that make it so rewarding. It's a form of validation; as I say, it's all well and good knowing the theory, but it's nice to get confirmation that you're on target every now and again.

The whole point of tracking is to locate the animal you're

hoping to find, or to ascertain what the animal has been doing, where it's come from, its nature, how it behaves. These are all things that you can discern from its tracks.

Animals can be quite predictable in that they will generally follow game trails; they are interested in food; they are interested in sex; they want to drive out territory invaders; so in a way, it can be a little predictable. Don't get me wrong, it's still really exciting to follow and the reward is the same when you finally locate the animal, or have your suspicions on a certain aspect of its behaviour confirmed. In 2012 I ran a tracking course in Erindi and I gave my students the task of establishing which female leopard was the mother of some cubs. To do that, they had to find the cubs' track, see if they could find a leopard associated with them and, if so, establish which one was the mother. That was quite a challenge, but they accomplished it successfully, so they felt an enormous sense of achievement.

I find following people much more interesting though. People do crazy things; they're a lot less predictable than many animals, so it's much more of a challenge. That said, they are the animals that we understand the best so they're predictable to a degree; you could argue that people are also interested in food, sex, etc. just as big cats or game animals are, but we do a great many other things as well. It's bizarre what you can discern sometimes. But the principles of tracking humans are, of course, exactly the same: the way you use the light, identify the sign, establish direction, and so on. The same basic principles apply – it's the same process.

What many people don't realise is how effective a technique tracking is – it can be used in many, many environments and it works very well in Britain. I think there is a general belief here, especially in the search and rescue community, that tracking has limited uses. That's actually not true at all. The problem is, those people who work with genuine trackers very often impose some sort of limitation; the tracker should always be the one determining what is and what isn't possible, with regards to the capability of tracking.

So, tracking in a rural environment is great but when it comes to people and an urban environment, although it's nigh on impossible to track them through the heart of a city and over a long distance, you can discern a lot of other information. You might find, for example, where somebody has been moving on waste ground around a lockup, which might lead you to the garage where they're storing stolen goods. You might be able to identify when a potential thief has been checking out a place, or determine where he's entered and exited places – there are opportunities, and many of them can be linked to forensic evidence.

I've found that those who are best at tracking are those who are constantly immersed in the natural environment. There are, as I've said, numerous people purporting to be 'experts' and while they may be experts in theory, having read lots of books, and formulated lots of ideas about the subject, that is a million miles away from actually being able to find that crucial, usually really tiny, piece of evidence. And I'm not talking about footprints here – I'm talking about the tiniest disturbances in leaf litter, or a bent or bruised piece of vegetation, which might be invisible to the unpractised eye. Being able to do this is hugely significant as it is generally the linking piece of evidence that solves the tracking problem. It takes *years* to learn and I get very irritated when I hear some of the nonsense that's being spouted forth by these various 'experts' who do more harm than good.

So how do you grade tracking ability?

There's a whole list of qualities that all trackers must have, but to my mind the key thing is that they must be honest with themselves so that if they can't see something they say so; that is the single most important skill. They must be patient and have perseverance, determination and tenacity. So, if you have a person with the right traits, and you teach them a proven system that they then practise, they will successfully find and follow sign. Expertise comes through long-term application of the skills in circumstances that range from straightforward to complex.

I have experimented and honed different methods of teaching tracking over the last thirty years and I've largely settled on a system akin to the method used by the military. We use their terminology so the two systems are comparative across the board – things like 'last definite sign', 'trail axis' and so on – but we do things slightly differently, in that we put an emphasis on different areas. When you do something for a very long while, you are able to assess the importance of certain aspects because you have a better understanding of what's important.

Tracking Raoul Moat was the most difficult tracking I've ever done. The sign was very vague and there was one point on the trail where he had deliberately hidden his sign, stepping carefully over the bracken, so it was extremely difficult to spot. But even the most cautious quarry leaves a trail – if you know what to look for.

I think Moat was massively spooked by the fact that we'd followed his trail and all of a sudden he was having to hide from armed cops and dogs. He knew we were hunting him and he knew he was prey. We'd denied him the freedom of the woods and forced him out into the open.

This man had murdered; he had attempted other murders and he had told the world he was going to murder again. He was in the woods, effectively saying, 'Come and get me.' There was only one thing to do at that point and that was to get him before he was able to kill again. There is no question in my mind that whatever the reasons for his murderous spree, once he'd crossed the Rubicon there was only one possible response and that was to find him. What he did was a game changer for me. I have a persona when I teach that is distinct from what the world sees when I'm on TV, but I'm a different person in other circumstances too, such as the hunt for Raoul Moat. He'd stepped into my world, and he'd committed violence. There was only ever going to be one of two outcomes: he'd have been found and sent to trial, or he'd be cornered and he would die. It was his choice to evade justice by ending his life.

I debated long and hard about whether to talk about the role I played in tracking Raoul Moat in this book. I know there was speculation as to my involvement in the media around the time of the events but that was only because there was an information vacuum, so there were all sorts of rumours flying around. I could have lived with that, but what I don't like are wannabe 'trackers' going around the circuit claiming they were there, that they were involved, in an effort to bolster their credibility. I've even been told of one particular individual who opens his 'lectures' by throwing down a plaster cast that he claims is an imprint of one of Moat's boots. I'd love to know how he could possibly have come by that, given that the only cast that was ever taken was made by the police forensic team in the aftermath – and they still have it.

What happened was tragic for everyone concerned and I think it's immoral to try and claim some involvement in bringing Moat down for reasons of personal gain, or from some misguided and perverse idea that it'd bring some sort of 'glamour' by association.

As I say, I felt honour- and duty-bound to offer my services to the agencies involved in the hunt for Moat because I believe that if you have the tracking skill and something like that occurs, you can't stand by and do nothing. Maybe I couldn't join the Forces, but it's still nice to be able to contribute to my country in some way. At the end of the day, this is what I'd trained for and anybody who trains for many years wants to put the skills they've acquired to use.

I'd be lying if I said I didn't feel a great sense of achievement tracking Raoul Moat but what I find infinitely more satisfying is the fact that from my earliest days, I've wanted to introduce people to bushcraft – the proper subject, not shorthand survival – and I've done that. I've no problem with survival training – it's very important and has its place, but it's only a part of bushcraft. I wanted to introduce people to this much larger subject and take it away from people who want to wield big knives, the Rambo-types, and make it healthy and wholesome, which it is. I really do believe that I've done what I set out to do. I think it's a very good way to introduce people to nature because it's not just about remembering the proper names for flora and fauna. Nature has practical values and when plants and animals become your friends and allies you want to cherish them, you want to take care of these things, and I've spent a lifetime learning how to do that.

30

Thirty Years On

It's hard to believe that this year marks Woodlore's thirtieth year in business. It's also my fiftieth year on this planet, and 2013 also marks the twentieth anniversary of my running courses in the Arctic, so there's a nice symmetry in those figures. Yet in many respects I feel as if I'm only just beginning.

Never in the furthest reaches of my imagination did I ever dream my life would follow the path it has. I never set out to make bushcraft my career, and neither did I have any great desire or plan to have a twenty-year career in television, but that's just the way things have panned out. It has felt at times like I am a passenger on a train; I'm loving the journey but I'm not at the controls, so I just go where the engines take me. It's never felt like work; how can it when I've spent my life doing something I love? It's been a lifelong exploration of a subject that fascinated and inspired me, even as a child, and the best part of all is that I've been able to share some of the knowledge I've acquired with a wide audience through my books, courses, lectures and television documentaries.

It's been an enormous privilege to travel the world as widely as I have, spending time learning about and from the numerous indigenous people that are dotted across the planet. And I've felt humbled to be invited to train members of our armed forces and equip them with tracking skills that are saving lives in Afghanistan by enabling soldiers to find and identify IEDs. I spent nearly a decade training the members of 22 SAS Regiment in survival techniques, and have delivered lectures to our police on a number of areas of interest. I've been trusted to do that, and listened to, which truly is an honour. Ultimately, I didn't learn any of what I teach on a course, or at university. Despite searching there was no school for me to attend that could teach me what I wanted to know and, aside from a few small pieces of the puzzle, it wasn't written down in manuals or books. What I've learned, I have learned from the forests, the mountains and the deserts of our planet. I guess I'm fortunate in that I don't remember the hardships, just the high notes.

———◆———

I was immensely lucky to find a friend and mentor in Kingsley Hopkins, a man with the patience and desire to teach me what he knew. For the first twenty years of my life, he shaped, informed and coloured my interest in the outdoors and brought to bear sage advice and wisdom acquired in one of the most testing environments in recent history – on the front lines during World War II. I still miss him and the influence and counsel he provided me with, but his legacy is something that lives on within me.

In the way that Kingsley was there in the first twenty years of my life, Lars Fält has been there for the past thirty. I feel fortunate and privileged to count him as a friend and he has played a major role in shaping one aspect of Woodlore with me. Lars Fält is a household name in Sweden, the founder of the Swedish Army Survival School and in reality the father of Swedish Survival. He is a former Parachute Ranger who, throughout his long military career, had a reputation for being a 'hard soldier', cut from the cloth that only airborne troops really understand. His thoroughness in training reflected his heartfelt dedication to the welfare of his students. Lars cared deeply that, when tested, his troops would survive against the odds and return with honour. Knowing that he would not be at their side, he drilled them hard in the lessons of survival.

But there is another side to Lars; behind his craggy exterior is a warm-hearted family man with a sense of humour that's even sharper than his axe. The Lars I know is a passionate woodsman and a consummate professional. He retired from the military in 2001 and, since passing on the baton of responsibility for military survival, he has been able to express the quieter, more philosophical side of his nature. While he is always up to date with the latest technological advances, it is his passion for older knowledge and native tradition that inspires his own bushcraft.

For twenty years now Lars and I have worked together in Swedish Lapland teaching Arctic survival and bushcraft. We have shared good times and bad, weathered extreme cold and dried our socks at the same fire in years of abnormal warmth. I trust him implicitly, and his judgement is totally reliable. With a telepathy built on shared hardships, I can predict with 100 per cent accuracy his response to a crisis, as he can mine. Lars would say that we drink from the same cup. We have both travelled to remote areas of the Arctic and had the privilege of living for a time with various bands of First Nations. But what unites us most strongly is the belief that traditional knowledge and skills are only validated by testing them on the trail, on real journeys.

Lars has been a very important person in both my own history and that of Woodlore. We first met in the early 80s when he attended a lecture that I was giving about survival at the Royal Geographical Society. There were a lot of people in the audience but Lars stood out from the crowd. After the lecture, a delegate came up to me, saying I hadn't made fire by friction correctly in my demonstration; of course, he was talking out of his bottom. So I asked him to demonstrate what he was talking about and he replied rather arrogantly, 'No, I am only here to observe,' and made a quick getaway before his bluff was any further exposed. The subject of survival and now bushcraft have sadly always attracted Walter Mitty characters such as this, that have read much and done little. Overly willing to impress the gullible with their self-professed 'expertise' they can cause no end of confusion. Fortunately for me, his departure provided the opportunity for Lars to introduce himself and we talked for a few minutes, and when he left he gave me a copy of a book he'd written, together with his business card, and we went our different ways.

At that point he was a captain in the Swedish Army, running its survival school. At the beginning of the 1980s, the Swedish Army realised that none of its conscripts had the rural skills of twenty years earlier; society had become more urban and people had lost the traditional knowledge of how to take care of themselves. The army wanted to redress this situation and their solution was survival training. The search was on for someone with the skills to run the course and somebody suggested Lars, saying, 'He's a pain because he never stops talking about survival, but he's your man.'

And he was – he was just perfect for the job. Lars was passionate about survival as a subject. The bulk of his military career was spent at the height of the Cold War when the threat of invasion or war with the Soviet Union was very real, so survival training was an absolute priority. After appointing Lars to write and run the course, he was sent around the world to spend time with allied armies on their own survival courses. He came to the UK and did the SAS course in 1982 and then went back to Sweden to establish the Swedish Army Survival School. I'd heard about the school but it was only after I came back from the Africa walk that I made the connection and realised it was Lars who was running it, so I dug out his business card and made contact. When I went over to see him, I noticed that his house was just like mine inside – chock-full of knives and survival gadgets with a great library on survival. He was definitely a kindred spirit and we hit it off straight away.

Eventually I set up a Woodlore course with Lars and we ran our first one together in Lapland in 1993. We've been collaborating ever since, making Lars Woodlore's longest-standing instructor aside from myself. We run two courses each year at the height of Swedish Lapland's winter, and through all those experiences we've come to know each other very well. That's a very special thing because it's so rare in an industry where anyone can set themselves up as an 'expert' without necessarily having the judgement that can only come from walking the path. He's walked that path and back again, so I know that in a crisis we can depend upon each other absolutely. It's people like Lars that make the world tick for me.

———◆◆———

Closer to home, Gordon Hillman is another man I feel privileged to know. Gordon is Honorary Visiting Professor in Archaeobotany at the Institute of Archaeology, University College London, and someone who has shaped and informed another aspect of bushcraft for me. Archaeobotany is the study of how people used plants in the past and there is nobody more knowledgeable than Gordon on this immensely wide-ranging topic. From the moment that we first met it was obvious that we had the same passion for plants and were asking similar questions about their edibility. It was inevitable that we would collaborate in the pursuit of our shared interest. That said, it's his personality that makes him shine; he's one of the nicest fellows I've ever had the good fortune of knowing and a pretty remarkable human being.

Gordon's greatest work as an archaeobotanist was at a site called Abu Hureyra on the Euphrates, which is widely accepted as the place where mankind made the transition from hunting and gathering to farming. He did a massive amount of work there, although most of my dealings with him were much more parochial, and we spent a great deal of time in Scotland, where Woodlore runs advanced courses that teach students to live off the land. Having Gordon there with me helped to share the pressure of teaching, and it gave the students a different perspective. If I had to head off somewhere, I'd say to him, 'Gordon, remember, they'll only really remember ten plants,' yet I knew that when I got back there would be a hundred or more plants laid out, which was his way. His love for his subject is infectious and the students can't get enough of him. He's quite the most wonderful man, a real Gandalfian character in appearance with his white hair and trademark chinstrap beard, and whatever the weather, he'd always take a skinny dip in the loch.

Sadly, now in his later years, Gordon suffers from Parkinson's disease. It's such a hideous disease, so cruel. I could see that the outdoor life was becoming more and more difficult for him to cope with, so it was no surprise when he eventually told me one night that he wouldn't be able to join me in Scotland any more. We sat by the fire afterwards and it was one of the saddest moments of my life. It felt very strange knowing we'd never be able to share the experiences we had again.

As well as running courses with me over the years, Gordon and I also worked together on the BBC TV programme *Wild Food*. This series rode on the back of ten years' research we had made, investigating the wild foods that Britain's last pre-farming hunter gatherers may have eaten at the end of the British Mesolithic. Many of the plants we needed to experiment with are now considered as arable weeds and consequently in very short supply. At Enoch Dhu near Glenlivet in Scotland we came across a field choked with Hemp Nettle, a plant whose seed we needed in quantity for an experiment. To collect these seeds Gordon had improvised a rather Heath Robinson collecting apparatus that involved the frame and handle of a carp fishing net attached to a hand-stitched canvas bag and a child's purple and pink tennis racket. He did look a sight as he went into this field beating the heads of the plants to knock the seeds into his bag. It's one of the funniest things I think I've ever seen.

We had a lot of laughs like that. I remember on another occasion we were trying to cook some roots. My contribution was my knowledge of the Aboriginal approach to cooking. Gordon's contribution was his incredible understanding of the genetic relationships between species – for example, you might have one plant species that is genetically similar to another, and perhaps some of the edible qualities will be inherited because of their similarity. Anyway, we were sitting there cooking a particular root that he'd theorised would probably be safe to eat, although I was a little more sceptical than him. When they were cooked and we'd started to eat them, I looked at him and said: 'Gordon, are you sure this is edible?'

'Oh yes. Theoretically it should be fine.'

'So why is my mouth swelling up?'

Bang goes the theory then. That was the nearest I've ever come to poisoning myself and it was a good reminder that even specialists sometimes get things wrong. I miss working with him even now, although whenever I walk across those same landscapes, they evoke wonderful memories and I'm enormously thankful for them. Some things you don't forget.

Both Lars and Gordon have added immeasurably to the success of Woodlore. It's vital to me that everything and everyone connected with the operation reflects the same high standards that they have set. This is not easy as we search for specialists who are not just authorities in their fields but also people with a humble demeanour who gain their reward from seeing their students acquire new skills, confidence and aspirations.

At the end of the day it all comes down to people – having the right people in the team. I am proud to say I work with the most amazingly dedicated and talented team at Woodlore it is a tight knit-team. There is a 'can do, will do' expedition ethic that drives the business. As a business we believe that we can help make the world a better place and strive to do so. It is hard to believe how it all started when I see the professional and energetic team carrying on the work I began thirty years ago. Through the last thirty years I have had the privilege to lead courses and expeditions to many of the most remote and fascinating environments on the planet. The ultimate goal, to inspire respect and appreciation of our natural world. The best part though, is hearing our clients tell of their successes, the challenges they have overcome and what they are planning to do with their newly acquired skills.

In terms of bushcraft, I'm still learning new skills and there remain things I want to develop. As you learn more, you ask more questions and those questions lead to more learning, and I still have a long list of questions for which I need answers. A long time ago, I came to the realisation that one lifetime is simply not enough.

Also, there are a great many places I haven't visited yet, so there is work still to do. I have maps on the walls on which I plot where I've been and I've marked places I've been to many times such as Africa, Australia, Canada and the globe's various rainforests. I've never been to Japan though, and that remains a long-held ambition. With the influence that judo has had throughout my life, I'm very interested in the culture, the traditions and crafts – and also the wildlife. Japan is a very wooded country with bears and a host of other interesting creatures, all of which intrigues me.

My life to date has been pretty varied and fantastic but I've never become complacent and never rested on my laurels. Nothing should ever be taken for granted; I've never done that and I don't intend to start now. I'm grateful for every opportunity presented to me, for all the wonderful people I've had the privilege to meet and for the truly special experiences I've had along the way. But there's so much more to learn and do, so many tracks to be discovered and places in which to immerse oneself. I just hope Father Time is kind to me because I have a long road ahead of me still to travel, and a wonderful wife with whom to share those experiences.

Acknowledgements

No book is ever the work of a single person; my name may be on the cover, but it stands as testament to the industriousness and efforts of a whole team of people, each of whom has been essential to the project's existence.

First and foremost, I'd like to thank my wife Ruth, and son Kristian, for their steadfast love and support, endless patience and belief in me. You make my world complete, thank you.

Also to Jackie Gill, my long-standing friend and agent. Jackie – I couldn't have done this without you.

Also, my heartfelt thanks go to Steve Gurney, my right hand man who over the years has become a friend as well as a very important part of Woodlore. Also Jane Mitchell, Steven Bullen, Diana Taylor, Daniel Hume, Keith Whitehead, Rebecca Brewster, Harvey Taylor-Meek and the rest of the outdoors team at Woodlore; you are the bedrock on which our success is built. As much a family as a team it is a continuing privilege to skipper such a brilliant crew.

I would like to pay tribute to the calm professionalism and efficiency of Rupert Lancaster and his team at Hodder & Stoughton who have worked so hard in recent years on all of my books. To Rupert must go my foremost editorial thanks – he has lived with this book, and many others, for as long as I have. His delightful assistant Kate Miles has been wonderful throughout. I'd like to thank all at Hodder for their support over the years. Thanks too, to Tara Gladden for polishing the manuscript, and to Rose Alexander for casting a watchful eye over it – you both did a really sterling job.

To Ben Southwell, Barrie Foster, Paul Watson, Alan Duxbury, Andy Morton, Sam Cox and Tim Green – thanks for making the journey so much fun. And to Collette Foster who first saw something in me and encouraged me on my first steps into the world of television.

I'm indebted to all of the elders and the many indigenous people who have given up their time over the years to so generously share their wisdom and experience with me and who remind us all what it means to be part of the human family.

To Lars Fält, friend of the northern trail; thank you.

Lord and Lady Selborne who first provided me with access to land to experiment with the techniques of my profession and to establish the courses which still set the standard for Bushcraft education within the UK today.

The many students who have attended the Woodlore courses, without your patronage none of this would have been possible. Teaching is a two way street you have taught me so much and greatly broadened my outlook, thank you.

Thank you also to the Seventh Purley Scout Troop and my friends in the British Deer Society.

Sally – thank you for being there when I needed you.

Edward Cadogan for being the truest friend. Dr David Campbell for providing astute advice regarding the medical hazards of my more exotic expeditions. The Grey Family for their continuing inspiration and support.

Peter Fincham, Alison Sharman, Diana Howie, Puiey, Phil Coles and everyone at ITV for giving me such a warm welcome.

Finally thanks to my many friends, in all branches of the armed forces, for whom survival skills are a necessity. I have the deepest respect for the selfless service you provide. Your, very often appalling, sense of humor in the face of adversity continues to be the most powerful lesson in survival.

Picture Acknowledgements

Most of the photographs are from the author's personal collection.

Additional photographs: © Mary Albion: 9 (top & middle). © Ed Bagnall: 16 (bottom). © BBC: 4 (bottom), 12 (top right). © The Bowen Collection, University of Bath Archives: 3 (middle left and right). © Phil Coles: 15 (top). By kind permission of Joe Hill: 11 (top). © ITV: 15 (bottom). © victoria-kaye.co.uk: 13 (bottom left). By kind permission of the Metropolitan Police/ photo author collection: 14 (bottom). © Martin Pailthorpe: 8 (bottom). © Rex Features: 3 (top left), 14 (top), 16 (top). © Ben Southwell: 12 (top left and bottom).

Every reasonable effort has been made to contact the copyright holders but if there are any errors or omissions, Hodder & Stoughton will be pleased to insert the appropriate acknowledgement in any subsequent printing of this publication.

Index

NORTHERN WILDERNESS

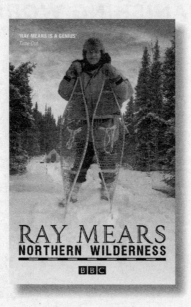

'Amazing scenery, fascinating history and
oodles of good old-fashioned scouting skills'
Daily Telegraph

'NORTHERN WILDERNESS is different, grown-up,
wider ranging, a trip through the Canadian tundra
in the snow show tracks of the early explorers . . .
effortlessly beguiling'
Sunday Times

This book is rich in bushcraft, as Ray explains the
unique survival techniques of the Native Canadians
and the Inuit, as well as how the prospectors in the
gold rush used bushcraft skills to survive in this
inhospitable but awesome landscape.

HODDER

RAY MEARS
VANISHING WORLD

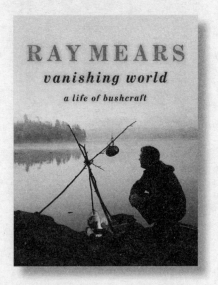

Ray Mears reflects on his experiences in some of the most remote and beautiful places on Earth along with his own stunning photographs of the landscapes and people he's encountered.

Fascinated by photography from an early age, each of Ray's pictures captures an instant of life, a powerful experience he has compared to releasing the trigger on a rifle when hunting.

This book reveals our dramatically changing planet and inspires us to look more closely at the changes around us. See our vanishing world through the eyes, ears and camera lens of Ray Mears.

HODDER

WILD FOOD

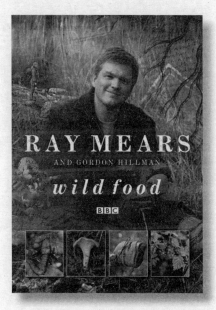

Ray Mears has travelled the world discovering how native people manage to live on just what nature provides. What has always frustrated him is not knowing how our own ancestors fed themselves and what we could learn about our own diet.

We know they were hunter-gatherers, but no-one has been able to tell what they ate day-to-day. How did they find their calories, week in week out throughout the year? What were their staple foods? Where did they get their vitamins? How did they ensure their bodies received enough variety?

In this book he travels back ten thousand years to a time before farming to learn how our ancestors found, prepared and cooked their food.

HODDER

BUSHCRAFT SURVIVAL

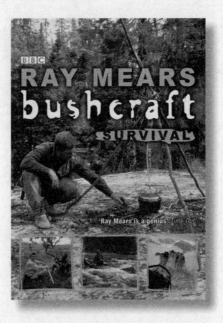

In BUSHCRAFT SURVIVAL Ray Mears travels to some of the most remote and beautiful wildernesses in the world, and experiences first hand the survival techniques of different indigenous cultures.

From the Hudson Bay in Canada, via Tanzania and the jungles of Venezuela, to the moors and highlands of Britain, BUSHCRAFT SURVIVAL explores a range of locations and techniques from indigenous peoples. Drawing on centuries of knowledge as well as his own experience, Ray demonstrates how our enjoyment of the wilderness comes through respect for our surroundings and the people, plants and animals that live there.

HODDER

ESSENTIAL BUSHCRAFT

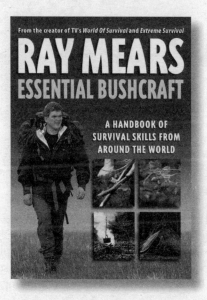

Ray Mears is well known to millions of television viewers through his acclaimed series *Tracks*, *Ray Mears World of Survival* and *Ray Mears Extreme Survival*. Now, based on the bestselling BUSHCRAFT, he has created a handy portable compendium of vital survival skills and wisdom from around the world. Packed with essential wilderness techniques, this book is an invaluable companion on any expedition.

HODDER

An invitation from the publisher

Join us at www.hodder.co.uk, or follow us
on Twitter @hodderbooks to be a part of
our community of people who love the very
best in books and reading.

Whether you want to discover more about a book
or an author, watch trailers and interviews, have the
chance to win early limited editions, or simply browse
our expert readers' selection of the very best books,
we think you'll find what you're looking for.

And if you don't, that's the place to tell us what's missing.

We love what we do, and we'd love you to be a part of it.

www.hodder.co.uk

@hodderbooks

HodderBooks

HodderBooks